MY BLUE NOTEBOOKS

LIANE DE POUGY

My Blue Notebooks

PREFACE BY R. P. RZEWUSKI

TRANSLATED FROM THE FRENCH BY DIANA ATHILL

HARPER & ROW, PUBLISHERS

NEW YORK

Cambridge London
Hagerstown Mexico City
Philadelphia São Paulo
San Francisco Sydney

1817

This work was originally published in France under the title *Mes cahiers bleus*. © 1977 by Librairie Plon.

FIRST U.S. EDITION

Library of Congress Cataloging in Publication Data

Ghika, Marie Chassaigne, princesse, 1869–1950.
  My blue notebooks.
  Translation of Mes cahiers bleus.
  Includes index.
  1. Ghika, Marie Chassaigne, princesse, 1869–
1950. 2. France—Princes and princesses—
Biography. I. Title.
CT1018.G48A3513   1979   944.08'092'4   [B]
ISBN 0-06-011083-X   79-1659

79 80 81 82 83 84 10 9 8 7 6 5 4 3 2 1

PUBLISHER'S NOTE

When Princess Georges Ghika (Liane de Pougy) began to keep this journal, she thought that it might one day be published. Twenty-two years later, when she signed the last page, she thought the same, although in a very different spirit. It is apparent, however, that during the intervening years she often wrote in her blue notebooks simply because the habit of keeping a diary had grown on her. Often this increases the value of what she has to say, but sometimes it results in triviality. For this reason cuts have been made in this translation.

Material cut consists of comments on the weather or on minor ailments; passing reference to the news of the day (on this Liane is almost always more dutiful than enlightening); references to people who do not figure importantly in the events recorded and who are not described fully enough to become interesting for their own sakes; mention of books read, if not enlarged with comment; a few accounts of events, such as a purchase made, the receipt of a letter or a visit by an acquaintance which cannot seem as important to other people, now, as they did to the writer at that time; and the few entries which are dull and perfunctory because nothing had happened to interest, amuse, annoy or otherwise animate the writer.

When a cut occurs within an entry it is indicated thus: ....

When a whole entry has been omitted (in a few cases more than one), it is indicated thus:

. . . .

We have followed the French edition in using Liane de Pougy's spelling of names, e.g. Nathalie for Natalie (Barney).

ILLUSTRATIONS

PREFACE

by R. P. Rzewuski

My personal memories of Liane de Pougy, Princess Ghika, belong to two periods: the first about 1924 or 1925 when I was living in Paris, the second during the Second World War, when I often had occasion to meet her in Lausanne, in Switzerland, between 1939 and 1946.

I met her for the first time at a big luncheon given by Madame Ganna Walska, the wife of Mr Mac Cormick, a rich American manufacturer of agricultural machinery.

The luncheon took place in the big winter-garden of our hostess's house in the VIIIth arrondissement, where she had collected a considerable number of guests round a large oval table: a rather odd party, to tell the truth, though very smart. To begin with I looked in vain for a face I could recognize, and felt rather out of place; but the singularity of some of the guests and my own always lively curiosity soon dissipated this feeling.

I was sitting on our hostess's left, while the place of honour on her right was occupied by a rather strange-looking man. He was small and swarthy and at first I took him for a Latin American, although his elegance – in spite of having something slightly disquieting about it – was not undistinguished.

The lady on my left was ravishing. Very elegant, she was wearing a classic, very English-looking tailor-made of pearl grey. One could well have taken her for a visitor from across the channel had it not been for her pretty hat, the same colour as her coat and skirt, which contributed a wholly Parisian refinement to her appearance.

What was her age? Difficult to say. But in spite of her supple figure and the perfect beauty of her features I concluded that she was not in her first youth. Perhaps, I thought, she is between fifty-five and sixty. If so, she carries her years very lightly and well. Her perfect profile like that on an antique cameo, her radiant eyes and the charm of her smile had not yet suffered any of time's outrages. That smile – yes. It was certainly very pretty; yet – without preventing her personality as a whole from appearing restrained and genuinely distinguished – it did just verge on the raffish.

Our conversation during lunch gradually revealed that my charming neighbour was none other than Liane de Pougy, that courtesan so celebrated at the end of the nineteenth century and the beginning of the twentieth; and that the mysterious gentleman for whom protocol had reserved the place of honour at the table was the Roumanian prince whom she had married several years earlier, Georges Ghika.

The luncheon party went by very pleasantly, thanks to Princess Ghika's gift for agreeable conversation. She had a pleasing voice which still sounded young. She spoke with a slight drawl and expressed herself elegantly and always with precision. She touched lightly on subjects connected with the arts: music, painting, and especially poetry – without forgetting politics; and evoked in passing memories of Saint Petersburg to which she had made several visits in the past.

I exchanged a few words with her husband after lunch; and that was the last I saw of Liane de Pougy and her princely spouse during the remaining years spent by me in Paris.

It was in Lausanne during the Second World War that I met the couple again, in circumstances very different from the first occasion.

It was just after the start of the war in 1939, or perhaps it was already 1940. I had left Paris in 1926 to become a Dominican. I was the spiritual director of our international seminary in Fribourg, and used to visit Lausanne from time to time in order to see an exquisite old cousin of mine who was paralysed and had taken refuge for the duration of the war in the nursing-home at Bois-Cerf, headquarters of the French Trinitarian Sisters of Valence.

Coming down their big staircase one day, I saw in the hall a rather surprising couple. One's usual encounters in that place consisted of clerics who happened to be passing through Switzerland, old ladies learning to walk again with the aid of sticks, or children who had recently been operated on by the celebrated orthopedist Nicaud.

This couple was entirely surrounded by great quantities of very expensive luggage of every kind and gave the impression of having got there by accident and coming from who knows where – perhaps from another planet. He was fussing with the luggage while she, slender, tall, distinguished and very elegant in her mink coat and her little hat with its long, face-framing veil, appeared to be no less irritated than exhausted. She sank languidly onto a bench and let her head rest against the wall, with the look of one who is determined to suppress her impatience and accept bravely whatever happens next, come what may.

Days – perhaps weeks – then went by before I returned to Bois-Cerf. When I did, I was greeted just as I was about to enter the lift by the gentleman of this couple, who reminded me most amiably of that distant lunch in Paris at Ganna Walska's house.

'Liane,' he said, referring to his wife without ceremony – 'Liane thought she recognized you on our arrival the other day, in spite of your habit. To make sure, she asked the directress of the clinic. Since that distant lunch,' he went on, 'we have heard no news of you, and Liane was amazed to rediscover her young neighbour at table in a Dominican.' Prince Ghika told me that his wife had not been well and was much confined to her room at present. She would like to see me, however, and hoped that I would pay her a little visit.

So during the next six or seven years I often saw Liane and Georges. Sometimes, when Liane was feeling up to it, we lunched together in the big dining-room at Bois-Cerf. When she was feeling less well I would find her reclining on a bed covered with pale blue sheets, blankets and cushions: pale blue, she explained, in honour of the Virgin to whom her mother had consecrated her at birth.

In spite of the years which had passed since our first meeting she was still beautiful and time had not diminished her charm. Perhaps her face was slightly thinner and longer-looking, which gave it a touch of serenity, even of severity. Even in bed she was as elegant as ever. When she was well enough to come down to the dining-room she walked just as gracefully, though perhaps a little more slowly, leaning on Georges's arm.

The couple, knowing no one in Lausanne, were lonely and soon made it clear that they welcomed my company in spite of the irreligiosity of which Georges liked to make a display. He took the same pleasure in demonstrating his advanced and often exaggerated taste in literature, particularly in modern poetry, and he himself wrote poems which were not to Liane's classic taste. I should add that in spite of Georges's agnosticism he was always friendly to me and showed respect for my calling. Liane, on her side, took me very quickly into her confidence. I saw her every time I came to Lausanne and it did not take me long to understand the double role I was to assume: that of a friend who brought a bit of interest into both their lives, and – for Liane – that of a confidant from whom she hoped to get help for the advancement of her religious and spiritual life. For so long as I remained in Switzerland (before being recalled to France at the end of the war to become Master of Novices at the Dominicans of Toulouse) I played this part in her life.

It will be obvious, therefore, that I am not always able to make use of my personal memories when speaking of Liane de Pougy and her personality; which remained, in spite of her reputation, simple and often touching. There was also something in her, very deeply rooted, which made her reserved when talking about herself and particularly about what she used to be.

Reading these notebooks today, I think I see that under this appearance of control and discretion was concealed a wish to reveal fully what this ex-courtesan had always known to be her true self. It is to that, I believe, that we owe these journals, quite as much as to the encouragement of enthusiastic admirers among whom Salomon Reinach was not least.

The self-portraits which Liane likes to draw of herself throughout these notebooks are striking in their sincerity and sometimes even cruelty. She has a lucid view of her own deficiencies and faults. By nature changeable, she is almost unhealthily sensitive and susceptible. Quick to fall into enthusiasms and friendships, she is no less impetuous when it comes to breaking them off for no good reason; but she doesn't bear grudges and when the eclipse is over she is delighted to rediscover the friendship which one had supposed to be over for good and all.

The most typical example of these fluctuating relationships is her friendship with Max Jacob, which plays a large part in her notebooks. She liked him and admired his curious gifts, she often wrote to him and received many very good letters from him. She had him to stay in Brittany or Saint-Germain, and spoilt him tremendously. When he was ill she looked after him as though he were a child. Then Max would start to get on her nerves, she would start to run him down and soon she would be longing for him to cut his visit short. He would do so – but was it a final break? Far from it. A few months later Max was back and was again being cherished and admired. It goes on all through the journals!

There were, however, a few exceptions: she was, for instance, consistent in her dislike of Colette. Nevertheless, when the latter opened a shop selling aids to beauty, Liane lost no time – perhaps it was merely feminine curiosity? – in going to see it and buying some of its products.

And there is the odd and mysterious business with Nathalie Barney, friend of her early youth in Paris: her beloved and matchless Flossie. They were united by forty years of mutual affection. They were often apart, but whenever they met again the bond between them would seem to have become stronger, unbreakable. Well, it was not. One day – it was important to her, because she records it – Liane was in Toulon and unexpectedly met Nathalie – almost bumped into her – in a narrow alley. She thought she discerned a mocking smile on the Amazon's lips, turned her head away and went by without saying a word. She never saw her again.

How did little Anne-Marie Chassaigne, later the young Madame Pourpe, become first Liane de Pougy, then a Roumanian princess, and end her days aspiring to nothing less than sanctity?

Concerning the Pourpe-Pougy metamorphosis I shall quote Boni de Castellane, who told me about it before I ever met Liane. She married a ship's officer and left him and their child very soon afterwards. In Paris she stayed with a friend whose morals were light and was soon swept away into the city's turbulent life where her beauty earned her a high place among the pleasure-seekers. She met a gentleman who bore the name of Comte – or Vicomte – de Pougy and became his mistress. The affair did not last and when Anne-Marie left him she simply kept his name and tacked onto it that of Liane, which had been bestowed on her by the dissolute set in which she moved.

As I have said, Princess Ghika disliked talking about her past in the demi-monde; it lasted, however, for almost twenty years. I do remember one story she told me about receiving a contract to play quite a big part in a play at the Théâtre Michel, then the Théâtre Français, in Saint Petersburg. All she had done hitherto was appear on the stage at the Folies-Bergère to exhibit her beauty in a few dance-steps or by appearing in mimed sketches. She freely admitted that she never had any real talent. But Russia offered tempting prospects, so she decided to ask the great Sarah Bernhardt to be good enough to give her a little coaching before she undertook this adventure. Sarah agreed, but was not encouraging. Her lessons –

exceedingly expensive – always consisted of the repetition of the same verse by Sully Prudhomme, a then-fashionable poet: one beginning '*Le vase ou meurt cette verveine* . . .' (The vase in which this verbena is dying . . .). Sarah hoped that as she learnt different ways of saying these lines, Liane would show herself capable of an intelligent interpretation of the parts she was to play in Saint Petersburg. Alas! After five or six lessons she told her: 'My dear, there's not much I can do with you. Display your beauty, but once you are on the stage you had better keep your pretty mouth shut.' Occasionally, with a characteristic little smile, Liane would dispense a drop or two of memory of this kind.

When she got to Saint Petersburg she still wanted, nevertheless, to act at the Théâtre Michel. It was a fiasco. She resigned herself to the fact but stayed on in the capital of the tsars, where she soon found a café willing to engage her to give the turns she had already perfected for the Folies-Bergère.

In Paris Liane was famous for the splendour of her jewellery, her luxurious town house, the 'secondary residences' she owned in Brittany and Saint-Germain, and her luxurious carriages. The press was always publishing articles about her and pictures of her, and spoke of her as the greatest beauty of the day. The three great courtesans of the Belle Epoque, Otero, Cavalieri and Cléo de Mérode, were foreigners, respectively Spanish, Italian and Belgian. Liane, proud of being French, boasts in the journal of having become 'the nation's Liane', a sort of national monument universally known and admired. When her immensely valuable five-row pearl necklace was stolen in mysterious circumstances, she was not unduly afflicted. A few days later one of her admirers gave her another one – only two rows, admittedly, but each pearl was worth four of the stolen ones.

To everyone's amazement the career of 'the most beautiful courtesan of the century' came to an abrupt end while still at its most brilliant. Her marriage to Prince Georges Ghika (who was younger than herself) was announced.

Once she was a princess Liane had the good taste never to parade the fact. Besides which, her relations with her husband's family would hardly have allowed it, because they never fully accepted her. By the same token she was never able to create an authentic place for herself in society. Her past always weighed on her. Nevertheless her notebooks contain a whole string of names of people she describes as her friends.

This medley contains a good many personalities from the theatre: writers of the day such as Bernstein and Henry Bataille; actors and actresses such as the Guitrys, father and son, Balthy, Yvonne de Bray, Yvonne Printemps, Cécile Sorel and others. There is Reynaldo Hahn, and – later – Poulenc and Auric. And Jean Cocteau, of course, who was much admired by her husband. Great figures from the world of *haute couture* are often mentioned: Paul Poiret, the classical Doucet, Madeleine Vionnet and Coco Chanel – whose generosity as it appears in these pages contradicts her legend, because she became the leading benefactress of the Asylum of Saint Agnes which was so dear to Liane's heart from 1928 on. We also find the names of the main priestesses of Sappho, because Liane de Pougy does not try to conceal the nature of her amorous leanings.

We see her at those great Parisian social occasions provided by theatrical first nights, where people come over to her in order to congratulate her on her elegance and on the beauty which seems to be immune to time – and there it ends. Liane continued to be alone. Not wholly so, it is true, because after her marriage and up until a certain moment in her life, Georges Ghika was always there.

Liane states repeatedly that for the first sixteen years her marriage with Georges was a happy one. The couple lived in mutual fidelity. Can that really be possible with a husband about whom she writes later that he was always a degenerate, even abnormal, and hysterical?

But Liane had the will, in this case the good will, to make herself believe that her past had gone away, that her household was stable and that the two of them were faithful. And even after all the difficulties she was to have with Georges, she still showed him gratitude for having rescued her from 'the morass'.

Liane sincerely wanted to consign the years of her worldly success to oblivion, and even to forget them herself. Forget the princes, the grand-dukes, the politicians, the financiers who had heaped their crowns, fortunes, celebrity and talent at her feet. That world, however, continued on its way and was neither able nor willing to forget her; and – cruel as it can sometimes be – it did not do so.

By the time I met the couple in Lausanne it was possible to guess that their relationship had been less than good for some years, and that the happiness to which Liane had lent herself with so much good will had received some painful shocks.

The ostentation of Georges's attention to his wife's comfort gave a pretty clear hint of hidden guilt. Liane on her side treated him with a visibly forced maternal benevolence, and received his allegiance with a grace in which traces of pity and boredom were discernible. It was very obvious that this ill-assorted couple's existence was overshadowed.

As I was to learn later, what had darkened the horizon was Georges's flight, on which he carried off a cherished young friend of Liane's. I will not dwell on this sad event. Liane's notebooks tell about it at length, as they also do about the unfortunate consequences which this event had for a time on the moral equilibrium which she believed she had regained with marriage.

Then came the return of the repentant fugitive and the forgiveness which – I like to believe – his wife sincerely granted him. But the wound Liane's heart had received left a scar on their relationship which resulted in a reversal of their roles. It was no longer she who felt guilty opposite her princely spouse; it had become *his* task to earn complete pardon. There were times when it seemed to me as though this reversal did not displease the princess.

What more can I say about her? Some two or three years after we met in Lausanne, on the death of her husband, she confided in me her desire to be received under the name of Sister Anne-Marie into our Order of Saint Dominic, as a tertiary lay sister. I readily agreed, because everything I had seen of her during this time convinced me that the renewal within her made her worthy of our black and white habit. She received it at a little ceremony in the clinic's chapel. Having become a tertiary she was faithful in carrying out the obligations laid on her by her new condition: daily recitation of the order's little office, the rosary and the gospel. She was also greatly attached to the *Imitation of Jesus Christ*, of which she read one or more chapters every day. And it should be said that at Bois-Cerf, and later elsewhere, she was loved and respected by all who had to do with her: the Mother Superior, the sisters of the Trinitarian congregation, and the doctors and clerics who met her. A saintly bishop, Monseigneur Herzog, who was formerly charged with promoting the canonization of Saint Theresa of Lisieux, became very fond of her. He often came to see her and the new tertiary's reserve and other qualities earned his esteem. She in return felt the deepest respect for him.

Did Liane become perfect? Her husband was sometimes ironical about her little faults: pious Liane might be, he said, but she was still capricious and changeable in her feelings. But does not God allow some apparent imperfections even in His saints? It is hardly surprising that someone who had once been probably the most adulated woman of the century should still show traces of something which was so much a part of her temperament.

One afternoon when I went to see Liane in Lausanne I found her, as usual, lying on a bed draped with pale blue silk and lace, but very much upset. She told me that she had just that moment had a telephone call from Aunt Jeanne telling her that Georges had been taken ill at his aunt's hotel and that a doctor had been called.

I was wrong when I said the couple knew no one in Lausanne. Georges's aunt, Jeanne Ghika, was also a refugee there and Georges used to go to take four-o'clock tea with her every afternoon, returning to Liane in time for dinner. Aunt and nephew were very fond of each other, and since the difficulty in transferring Liane's income from England had made the couple's financial situation precarious, the aunt generously allowed Georges enough to supply their needs.

Liane asked me to go round to the Hotel Mirabeau and find out what had happened, which I did without delay. Princess Jeanne took me into her bedroom where I found Georges stretched on her bed, the death-rattle in his throat. He was in a coma after a stroke, and the gravity of the situation was obvious. The aunt told me, in great distress, that the doctor had just left after telling her there could be no hope. Georges was unconscious. Princess Jeanne, like her nephew, was a member of the Greek Orthodox church, but unlike him she was a believer. I asked her if she had any objection to my administering absolution according to the Catholic rite. She was very willing, so I administered it. A few moments later, while I was praying beside the bed with his aunt, Georges rendered up his soul.

I hurried back to Liane. She had apparently guessed how serious it was and had foreseen Georges's death, because when I came in she was sitting on her bed and she said simply, in an expressionless voice: 'He is dead.'

I must say here in Liane's favour that I could only admire her attitude and behaviour in these sad circumstances. There was no false note, nothing exaggerated or theatrical. Her commonsense emerged, with considerable dignity. In spite of what had happened between her and her husband, Liane had undoubtedly preserved a sort of maternal fondness for Georges. His death left her on her own – very much on her own – deprived of someone to whom she was bound by thirty years of conjugal life, and who had not been able completely to destroy the truth at the heart of their mutual affection even by the 'trick' he played on her – which was how she used to refer to his flight.

The practical woman surfaced, and she occupied herself gravely with the immediate material considerations which the death involved: the funeral, the question of what service to have and so on. She telephoned to Aunt Jeanne to discuss matters with her. As for me, I spent the rest of that sad day at Liane's side.

By the time I knew her in Switzerland Liane was far advanced in her terrestrial career – or perhaps I should say 'careers', because she had certainly had several and they had varied greatly, both in a worldly and material sense, and morally. This variety did not mean that she had ever lost her nature's basic sense of reality. So she fostered no illusions about the proximity of her end. Everything else seemed to her to be buried in the past. She wanted to end her life as a good Christian, and even more, aiming for the highest as she had done all her life, in evil as well as in good. By now it could only be a question of good.

She told me that she had rediscovered her faith some years ago. But had she ever really lost it? Even during the 'great years' of her disorderly life, when she was the most notorious and spoilt courtesan of the fabulous Belle Epoque, I doubt whether she had truly lost it.

But what had occurred in the life of Liane de Pougy to bring about the consistent serenity and patience which I witnessed when I visited her room in the Bois-Cerf clinic, and later – when their money troubles had become more severe – in an even more modest religious establishment?

It was because life had given her – and this more than a quarter of a century earlier – a beneficent shock which had transformed her existence.

Liane had always believed, from childhood. She had had faith from the day she was born into a pious family. As she grew older the good sisters at her boarding school trained her in the pious exercises of that time and place; they taught her her catechism, her rosary, and devotion to the Breton saint Anne of Auray. They also took care of her education, gave her her pretty manners and the good handwriting which still revealed the care taken in those days in the upbringing of a young lady. According to what she herself said, even in her stormiest years she never failed to go in and light a candle if she went past a church. When she came to be married to Georges Ghika in 1910 she wanted to be married in a Catholic church. There happened to be nothing to prevent it, because although she had been divorced by her first husband, the ship's officer Pourpe, he had been dead for over twenty years by then. But it was the death of her son Marco, the airman who fell on the field of battle in 1916, which dealt her the cruel blow which gave new life to her religious instinct.

One can conclude from the notebooks that Liane had never stopped trying to find and love God. But she did it in her own way, just as she liked to have recourse in her own way to the bounty of her beloved Saint Anne of Auray, mother of the Virgin Mary. Beyond that her faith came up against what seemed to her an obstacle: how could she bridge the gap between the demands and the purity of the Son of God, His teaching and His example, and what she knew to be the truth about her own life, her past and even her present? And besides – this, perhaps, was the crux of the matter – Jesus was a man. . . .

And yet. . . ! It happened to her in the most unexpected way, in 1928.

When the couple was out driving one day, in Savoy, they came to a long wall belonging to a convent. When they reached the door, Liane had the whim of telling Georges to ring and find out what went on in this withdrawn place. It was the Asylum of Saint Agnes, where nuns devoted themselves to the service of abnormal – sometimes monstrously so – children, struggling to give these afflicted ones a chance to open up and reveal what remained of the human within them.

The spectacle revealed to Liane was appalling, the work was impoverished, the nuns who did it were heroic. In spite of the crumbling walls the building was as clean and well-kept as was possible. The children's appearance was sometimes frightful. Liane was horrified to see these little beings in whom it was often difficult to discern anything human. There were dwarfs and hunchbacks; others with enormous deformed heads on tiny bodies; others with rudimentary, hardly visible limbs. Their eyes, usually staring, seemed neither to see nor to understand. And this sight was accompanied by gurglings and squeals and moans. What did life hold for beings such as this except the utmost misery? It suffocated Liane, but it also – extraordinary event! – won her over. Paradoxical though it may seem, it was here, faced by this image of degraded humanity, by the horror of this poverty, that Liane suddenly understood the depth of her own degradation – more than that, her own monstrosity, what she had been and what she still was. She, Liane de Pougy, Princess Ghika – was she not, in spite of her charm and beauty, the very essence of that human degradation which had made necessary the presence here on earth of our supreme saviour, Jesus Christ?

So it was there, in that poor Savoyard asylum, that the existence – better still, the presence – of Jesus came into her life, and the demands made by His worship became not only acceptable to her, but necessary.

In the notebooks for 1927 Liane laments over her existence: 'I don't even want to think much about myself, I want to keep busy, devote myself to something .... My aspirations are always lofty. Will they ever be crowned in keeping with their elevation?'

Five years later, after finding the Asylum of Saint Agnes, she wrote: 'What a long way I am now from Paris and its dissipations! Here is my wealth: the friendship of this saint and a little part in this work of abnegation and sacrifice. That is my road to Damascus! Oh! that my return to Paris does not make me forget this little corner! Please, God, do not let that happen! .... It seems to me that You put the Asylum of Saint Agnes and its inmates in my way on purpose, as though to tell me: "Help them, and I will help you".'

And Liane really did find in that place that which she had been seeking for so long.

I no longer remember the exact year of Georges Ghika's death: 1943? 1944? Whenever it was, I often saw Liane after it. In 1946 I had to return to France. Correspondence became difficult, on her side because she was now very old, on mine because an absorbing occupation left me with little time. I knew her, anyway, to be in the excellent hands of the Mother Superior of the Asylum of Saint Agnes, and as it were stabilized in her holy life as a Dominican tertiary.

After the war ended her material life became easier. She was able once again to enjoy the income from what had formerly been a considerable fortune. Her age and her health, however, did not allow her to end her life, as she wished to do, near the inmates of the Asylum to whom she had devoted her heart for over a quarter of a century. She became resigned to spending the last years of her life installed quite comfortably in the Hotel Carlton at Lausanne, and it was there that she departed this life on the day after Christmas, December 26, 1950. She was laid out, as she desired, in her Dominican habit. She was taken to Savoy and buried in the little cemetery beside the buildings which shelter the unhappy children who had been so dear to her.

My relationship with Liane did not, however, end with her death. In 1954 I stopped at the Hotel Terminus in Lausanne on my way through Switzerland. It must have been about a dozen years since I last set foot in that hotel, but on my arrival the porter handed me a letter. It bore a date in 1950. It had been written by Liane just before she died. She said that she could no longer find my address in France but remembered that I often used to stay in this hotel. She wanted me to know that she was faithful to the memory of our friendship, and above all to her vocation as a Dominican tertiary. It was moving to receive this posthumous message from Liane de Pougy, Princess Ghika.

It has certainly not been my intention in writing these lines to make a saint of Liane de Pougy, or to canonize her; but who can claim to discern the thoughts and ways of the Most High?

Did not the great theologian Saint Thomas Aquinas believe that when a human being foregoes by reason of his sins the grace which binds him to God, and then regains it by means of fervent repentance and authentic confession, that grace regained, bestowing love renewed, may be superior to what it was before?

An ancient talmudic Midrach expresses the same thought in a more picturesque way: 'Man is attached to Eloïm by a thread. If his sins break the thread, Eloïm then takes the two ends and ties them together in a big knot. This shortens the thread so that the man is brought still closer to Eloïm.'

1919

∾∿∾∿∾∿∾∿∾∿∾∿∾∿∾∿∾∿∾∿∾∿∾∿∾∿∾∿∾

Saint-Germain-en-Laye – July 1 to September 10

July 1. I have been reading Marie Bashkirtseff's life, or rather her journal. It touched me to the heart and here I am, carried away to the point of longing to write my own. My husband is delighted. Our friend Salomon Reinach* is also urging me on.

Marie Bashkirtseff, that little girl who died long ago and who throbbed with such a feverish passion for life in all its forms and above all for fame – she haunts and inspires me. But my journal could never be like hers. She was an innocent girl . . . and who am I? Princess Georges Ghika, born Anne-Marie Olympe Chassaigne and then put together from Madame Armand Pourpe and the notorious Liane de Pougy. She had a thorough, well-planned education; I had six years in a convent and heaven knows how many of experience picked up at random.

July 2. It is my birthday. I was born on July the 2nd, 18—. Look it up in the parish register of La Flèche (Sarthe).†

Maman was on a visit to some military friends. She was not expecting me to arrive before August 15th. Why? Simply because the Holy Virgin had appeared to her in a dream, sitting in a beautiful white cherry tree, and told her: 'You will have a little daughter on my feast day. She will be called Marie. I will protect her. After an eventful life she will end up in Paradise as a great saint.' Maman said later: 'July 2nd is the Visitation. It's the most important of the Virgin's feasts so the dream came true.'

Maman was very pious, half Spanish on her father's side. At the time of my birth she was forty-three and a half years old. She had

---

* Philologist, archaeologist and art historian who was custodian of the National Museum of Saint-Germain-en-Laye. He died in 1932, at the age of seventy-four.

† Liane de Pougy was born in 1869.

gone to see my brother Emmanuel who was a pupil at the Military School of La Flèche, and had dropped in on her good friends the Chapelains. What a visit! A baby popping into their arms without warning – and into the arms of a most delicious neighbour about whom I will have more to say! Madame Navarre, née Atala de Monpeyssin, a creole from Martinique who became a sort of second mother to me during my early childhood. Because I couldn't pronounce the name Atala I called her Maman Lala.........

Maman Lala has been dead for some time now; she became the friend of the timid little girl I was, taking me for walks on Sundays, stuffing me with coconut, guava jelly and sugar candy dipped in the rum of her beautiful homeland, about which she told me such fabulous and amazing stories. Maman Lala always took me to her house on public holidays and when my brothers and their friends were home from school, to rescue me from their rough games. She did the most exquisite embroidery on linen, making dresses of it for her spoilt little 'Poupette'. I remember, too, that she used to say her prayers aloud, very loud, and that she would scold the saints and perhaps even God Himself if they weren't answered. I adored her. How bitterly I cried, the night when my parents thought I was asleep and I overheard them saying that she was going blind.

I left her when I was eight years old. Floods of tears, cruel grief. Then, when I was sixteen, I took my husband Armand Pourpe to introduce him to her. Seeing me again after such a long time, she said: 'My little darling, do you still have yo' teet' of pearl and yo' coral nail?' Then, in a whisper: 'Yo' husban' look too husbandish!'

I saw her twice more after that. I showed her a fiancé – who only half pleased her and pleased me even less – a stiff, narrow Englishman with whom I broke once I had thought it over properly. And then I went to embrace her a week before she died. She made me swear that I would never go on the metro – there had just been a fearful accident on it – and I have kept my word.

July 3. Young heart, young face, but the years are here, the aches and pains, the sorrows, the empty spaces . . . Oh, my dear departed ones! My brother Emmanuel died in 1886 (Lieutenant in the marine infantry, killed at Tonkin); my father (retired Captain in the Lancers, Pierre Blaise Eugène Chassaigne) dead in 1892 at the age of eighty-one. Dear old Papa, all white-haired and upright, who had me when he was sixty, so gentle and indulgent like a kind grandfather. Maman Lala dead in 1905 and Maman in 1912.

My most piercing grief, the one which came near to killing me and which threatened my reason (I spent fifteen months in cruel nursing-homes) was the death of my son, my only child, the aviator Marc Pourpe, a volunteer who fell on the field of honour near Villers-Bretonneux on December 2nd 1914. Time has passed, I have made myself accept the inevitable. And so many others have fallen since then. And anyway it is true that great sorrows are dumb. There is no consolation; it is a matter of regaining one's balance.

July 4. Friday, market day. I love to go shopping with my little Fatoum*. The noise, the bustle, the hurly-burly – all of it delights me. I love buying and choosing. I love carrying my booty back to the house. I am greedy; I try to be a good housewife. Things which might well bore me, which I have to do whether I like it or not – those things I really concentrate on enjoying. I got this from Reynaldo Hahn. One evening, when we were having dinner together, I hardly deigned to look at the menu. Reynaldo took it gravely, consulted it with much care, ordered some substantial and delicious food, then said to me: 'Look, Liane, the way to live is to bring all the enthusiasm you can muster to everything: studying, talking, eating, everything.' I understood him so well that I made it a rule of conduct. And that is how the prosaic Saint-Germain market has led me to the poetic Reynaldo.

We were devoted to each other. For several years he was certainly the sweetness in my life. Then I told him that I was getting married and he replied: 'Goodbye Lianon. I hate married people.' No doubt he disapproved of my stormy and disturbing entry into a family of such great distinction, which had reigned in its time. Nowadays I think too bad for Reynaldo, losing a friend like me. I have become a creaky old granny, a little fatter and a lot more stubborn and combative, turned by my sorrows towards thoughts of religion. I dare not say towards God, I still feel so far from Him. But I need to believe that we will all meet again, that I will see them again. I need God. I seek Him, and I feel that He has tested me so severely in order to bring me back to Him.

July 5. A day of migraine. It happens to me once a month – still! I stayed in bed till after lunch.

Read *le Jardin classique* – a collection of lectures at the Conserva-

* Her favourite little Negro maid.

toire by famous actors and actresses. I summoned my husband; I gave my imitation of Sarah (I do her very well. I also do perfect imitations of Berthe Bady, Lavallière and . . . Albert Brasseur!!! And beautiful Otero as well). Dinner was served. I made quite an effort. It was a mistake, the pain became atrocious. Georges crept quietly into a little bed placed at the foot of mine. Darkness. I went into a semi-coma, was flattened by it. But I wanted to say my prayers and in the middle of my invocation to my darling patron Saint Anne of Auray I got a clear vision of Georges lying in bed in Professor Hartmann's clinic. I took his hand and it was already ice-cold. I was alone; they made me understand that he had to be buried. I lit the lamp and jumped out of bed. There he was asleep, his beautiful brown wavy hair on the pillow – I felt completely changed. Had it been a warning? I was terrified, pouring with sweat, feverish, trembling. In September Georges is going to have an operation for a big stone in the bladder. I promise that if it's successful I'll go to Lourdes and to Saint Anne of Auray as well, and then I'll give a thousand francs* to the poor in one lump. That will not be easy for me, because since the war our income is much reduced.

I told that to Georges. The pilgrimages made him pull a face; the thousand francs made him furious!

July 6. My migraine has flown away! I can almost laugh at my terrors. I say 'almost' because I take my husband's operations very hard. He's had six already, three of them since we have been together. . . . .

July 9. No journal yesterday, not for lack of enthusiasm but because my migraine came back. I wrapped myself in God, because He is everywhere. It did no good. So I prayed to my two patrons, the Virgin Mary and Saint Anne. I offered them my pain and my resignation.

I once rejected the Church to such a point that she had no choice but to reject me. But still when I remarried I wanted it to be in my Church. I was obscurely attached to it by a thousand little threads. Having been divorced, it wasn't possible, but I had been a widow since 1892. So on June 8th, 1910, the civil ceremony was performed uniting Madame Marie Chassaigne (who had attained her majority – I paid them fifty francs not to say my age out loud) and Georges

* In January 1919 the franc was 26 to the £ sterling, 5.47 to the dollar.

Grégoire Ghika (also a major). On the same day, in the little chapel of the catechism in Saint-Philippe-du-Roule, the union between Madame Pourpe, widow of Armand Pourpe, and Georges Ghika was also blessed. I had been to confession the day before . . . For Liane de Pougy to make her confession must have been quite awkward, don't you think? She polished it off like this: 'Father, except for murder and robbery I've done everything.'

July 10. Jean Cocteau has sent us a copy of his *le Potomak* with a lovely dedication. Ever since *le Coq et l'Arlequin,* and particularly since *le Cap de Bonne-Espérance,* Georges has been very keen on Cocteau. He says that Cocteau ranks among the leaders of the modern movement; Gide and Cendrars are ahead of him, perhaps, then Apollinaire who died in the nick of time. He says in addition that Cocteau has risen superbly above his early work, and that now he's redolent of craftsmanship, originality and, in fact, real talent. . . . .

On the 23rd it will be thirty-five years since my mother-in-law brought Georges into the world for me. I teased her once, saying that. She answered impertinently 'That was not my intention.' I stretched my neck and replied with insolent disdain: 'Too bad, Madame. It is an accepted fact.'

We have had our skirmishes, Mariette and I. In 1912 she came to Algeria to make my acquaintance. She had been told such horrors (with thirteen rs!) about me that she found me charming. She invited me to visit her in Roumania. We spent two months with her – one of those things you do only once! She visits us in France almost every year. She doesn't like me for my own sake (how wrong of her!). Nor me neither, because I can't love anyone who doesn't love me. She appreciates my elegance and beauty, she blows hot and cold. She is a bizarre woman, a true boyar by descent, decisive, authoritarian, great-ladyish and impulsive. She can be perfectly maddening. She is pretty, subtle, coquettish, extreme, unexpected, changeable, reads a lot – but can be very comic in her interpretations of what she has read. She is sensitive about outward appearances and adores her children, when they are there. Georges was certainly just the right husband for me, and I think that Mariette suits me no less well as a mother-in-law. She makes no secret of believing in neither God nor the Devil. She is quite without hypocrisy, and knows how to give way gracefully when she has to.

In Venice, when we were on our way to stay with her, we bought some pipes. I said to her on arrival: 'Madame –' (she calls me Liane and I call her Madame, because I can hardly in decency say 'mother' to a woman scarcely ten years older than I am) – 'Madame, I must confess to a vice: I smoke a pipe.' I wanted to test her a little. She looked at me with raised eyebrows and pursed lips, then said: 'So much the better. I much prefer the smell of a pipe to that of cigarettes.' The pipe stayed in my suitcase.

July 11. I've just finished Cocteau's *le Potomak*. It is fascinating. It disdains orderliness and classicism. It is modern with passion, and with control. So that slender Jean with his great eyes is a real artist! His book is full of beautiful things.

Yesterday an aeroplane flew over Saint-Germain and dropped leaflets. Georges picked one up in our little park: it was announcing the aerial victory parade. One of my friends said: 'But you are the mother of that young eagle, Marc Pourpe – they should have given you a seat.' – 'Ah no! To take advantage of something so terrible . . .' The idea made me shudder. Grief, and nothing but grief. I did not love my son enough when he was alive. I was all woman – woman, not mother. My love was not able – didn't really want – to make a place for itself in his gloriously beautiful, excessively independent life. Oh how I have regretted it, how I have wept and been punished!

July 12. We have talked about the war so much that now we really need to shut up! It was a toxic experience, and going back over it stirs up all the poisons. My son's death, my illness, my husband's devotion, a few former friends who revealed such a vile and cowardly spirit that we had to let them drop, money losses, a hard and simplified way of life, six weeks when my house was turned into a dressing-station, and the victory of France! From my point of view, that is how I sum up those five horrible years. And then there is the disappointment – where is the purification through war which we were promised? 'There is no such thing,' says Georges. 'The war lasted too long, and the further we advance into peace, the more obvious that becomes.'

July 13. Sunday, eve of the victory parade. Oh, my country! My first country, because now I have become a Roumanian.

Georges is deeply hurt if anyone says, by way of a compliment, that he has a tiny (!) trace of a charming foreign accent. He thinks they must be deaf or trying to insult him, draws himself up and replies with a barrage of 'I have a horrrrror of everrrrrything Rrrrroumanian!' Georges is an angel, a love, an exquisite little boy, an ancient sage, a boring philosopher, an erudite scholar, etc etc. He is sometimes accused of being – too handsome. People are rather beastly to him. After we were married, the first time we went to a first night, which is my way of going out and about, I caught glances, spiteful smiles in our direction, whispers. So in front of those three powerful, widely distributed news-sheets known as Henry Bernstein, Pierre Mortier and Pierre Frondaie, when one of them asked me how I was: 'I am happy and enviable, my dear. I live with the two bravest men in the world.'

'???'

'Yes, my son who is a famous aviator, and my husband who had the courage to marry me.'

It was at the Théâtre-Français, a performance of *Primerose*: it went the rounds in a flash, and I had won the mockers over to our side.

July 14. The literary supplement of *Figaro* has published interviews with some of our intellectuals about the benefits of peace. Henry Bataille's answer was short and good: 'Freedom of thought.'

I have known Bataille for twenty-five years. It was Lorrain who introduced us. I was still a flighty girl, he was living with Bady and was on the verge of becoming famous. We still feel a certain tenderness for each other. The memory of our youth, of all those years gone by. We have not gone down, we have survived: we meet from time to time, exchange a kiss and a smile, tell each other how well we are looking! There was never anything serious between us.

July 15. . . . . Dreamt about Blanche d'Arvilly, a friend of my theatre days who went all over the place with me. She used to pick up the crumbs of my frivolous glory, was often very useful to me and more often treacherous and disagreeable. When I had my serious motor-car accident and was immobilized in the hospital at Beaujon, I saw her approaching my bed. Instinctively I shut my eyes. She came right up to the bed and bent over me – I could feel her breath on my face – and then she turned to the nurse and said in a tone of voice quite impossible to describe: 'So she is not disfigured?'

How can I hold it against her when we shared so much laughter? We had met one summer in Ostend, working in pantomime. She filled the role of a gnome, I of a pretty columbine, seductive and seduced. She also filled a costume made of virulent green wool. It was a hot night, her dance was energetic – and she was found unconscious in her dressing-room, her tongue black, half-poisoned by the arsenic in all that green, mixed with her sweat. Her pals were moving on the next day. She was ill. I took her on and nursed her and she stayed round me for years.

July 16. One of Cocteau's jokes – thanks to *Potomak* we are all completely encoctocated at the moment. Talking of a chameleon, he said: 'Its master put it down on a tartan rug and it died of over-exertion.'

Let's come back to Georges. He has a very ironical turn. Because he is also rather heavy-handed, it can make him seem ill-natured. When he's got hold of some nice, spiky little tease against someone, he fairly lets fly with it! When I pointed this out in a reproachful way, this was his clever defence: 'I have noticed that whenever I put someone down, the opposite opinion instantly prevails. So when I'm nasty to my friends I do it out of niceness, for the pleasure of hearing people sing their praises.'

I have just finished *Clarissa Harlowe*. It's very good; I like this book better than *Liaisons dangereuses*. Lovelace has charm. I once knew one of those: Henry Bernstein, an Israelite sub-Lovelace, full of talent. From writing all those plays about love with their last acts full of melodrama, he'd started introducing it into his own life, and into that of others. In the course of one year I took from him just enough to amount to a charming memory. Oh the splendours and the miseries he invented for me! 'I shall kill you!' – or 'If you won't say you'll marry me I'll throw you down and grind my heel into your pretty face!' or again: 'Think! Soon you'll be forty, my girl. You'll be *forty years old* – ' leaning on the words. 'No one will want you any more and what tears of blood you'll weep when you remember your Henry, and how much he would have loved you.' I had just turned thirty-five at the time!

When I drove him out and hid in a little back-room, he disguised himself as a postman bringing a registered letter I would have to sign for. When my friend Valtesse gave me sanctuary in her manor house in darkest Ville-d'Avray, he broke his way through doors and footmen and came bursting into her drawing-room. He had em-ployed detectives to find out where I was! At Cap d'Ail, where I'd left him flat and taken a train for Paris, he went so far as to report me to the police: 'Liane has made off with a necklace of thirty-one pearls, which she will be wearing. A case of morphine-addiction: she is a sick woman so on no account should she be alarmed, but her whereabouts must be discovered and I must be told where she is hiding. I will deal with the trouble. I will look after her.'

After that he went to see Clemenceau. His police spies had failed to find me and he was in a terrible state. 'Maître,' he said, panting and gasping (Clemenceau lived on the fourth floor and there was no lift), 'just look at how pale and ill I am. That woman has left with the deliberate intention of breaking my heart, and her spite is such that she has carried off the manuscript of *Samson*, a play on which I have been working for a year and which I have to deliver to Lucien Guitry almost at once, it really is a matter of life or death to me . . .' In fact he had written about four or five pages of this famous *Samson*. But he was very plausible and touching. They set off in pursuit of me and brought me back. Whereupon he fell at my feet, full of repentance and love. He wasn't one to abuse his victories: for two – sometimes three – marvellous days he would treat me like a queen. The rest of the time it was blows, threats, insults, sneers, brandished revolvers. One Christmas night, in front of his trembling and paralysed brother, he dragged me by the hair half-naked from the top to the bottom of my staircase.

I was often able to escape while he was in his bath. One day, I remember, he hauled me off to London with him. He would reverse our roles, so that he became the victim – almost believing it sometimes. 'If I kill you, people will say that hussy drove poor Bernstein mad. Yes, my girl, I shall have the star part. I'll get myself consigned to a nursing home for six weeks, and afterwards – the women will be madder about me than ever!' I loved his flashy, insincere smile. He was my last fling: Georges turned up, as Fate had ordained – that boy soon had everything in its right place, helped by Marie Murat who was quite determined to adore Henry. He was the storm necessary to carry me out of the unhealthy stagnant morass in which I was miserably stuck, back into life and under the eyes of Georges. Now when I hear from time to time about his adventures, I smile. His marriage made one rather anxious for that pretty little girl, but he knows so well how to make us happy, sometimes. . . . .

Did I mention my 'morass'? Ugh – the memory of it still sickens me. No hubbub and grand gestures there, nothing but whispers, sly looks, devious scheming, nasty little crimes. Perhaps I'll write about it, simply to get it out of my mind once and for all.

July 17. My house is big and well-run, polished so that it reflects itself, without a speck of dust, light and airy. It is a beautiful old wing of the château which the Duc de Noailles built for himself when he was governor of Saint-Germain at the time of Louis XIV. I have about three acres of well-designed grounds – traces of Le Nôtre's taste; the building is by Hardouin-Mansart. I have two historic and listed trees: a cedar and a Japanese copper beech. Their waist measurements are more than five metres! I have dungeons, old floors, old panelling; my reception rooms are six and a quarter metres high and on the little landing between them there is my Marco's dear little room, empty for ever but so full of memories. I can see him now in his sky blue pyjamas, with his smooth skin, his hair which grew so beautifully, his complete lack of mustache. He looked like a fifteen-year-old girl. I was always scolding him for not loving me enough.

I've got to talk about the 'morass'. It will be less easy.

I had an intimate friend, as intimate as one can possibly be, a girl of twenty-seven. I was thirty. She was Yvonne de Buffon, a descendant of the famous Buffon. She was with me always, ran my house, everything around me and within me. She was pretty, intelligent, cultivated, a liar, a schemer – vicious. She loved wine, women, disorder, deceit, dubious relationships . . . and she sniffed! All this often came between us. Whatever has happened, I have always remained simple and straightforward. I was often quite hard on her because of her faults, but I couldn't do without her. She slept in the room next to mine, our doors stayed open. She came into my big bed; there was something protective and masculine about her friendship and her charming face was adorned with a pretty little mustache which would have been the envy of any sixth-former. And above all, a limitless devotion.

I used – I abused – her tenderness, I even tyrannized her, and I loved her. I loved her for what she was, so hard that I truly believe I still love her today. She lied from habit, to everyone. She brought bad luck. No sooner did she arrive in my house and my life than a fabulously rich friend whose whole life was devoted to me dropped dead; and another, a millionaire who had delighted in obeying my slightest whim, told me he was getting married. My servants? Absolute apaches, stealing everything, breaking everything. My beautiful five-row pearl necklace disappeared (May 13, 1903, 13 rue de la Néva; I'd been in Paris thirteen years . . . oh that thirteen!) It was worth five or six hundred thousand francs in those days, so *what* would it be worth now? My son went into open revolt against me. My health, my nerves let me down; I became a mere rag. I wanted to be alone, far away from a world in which everything wounded me. Yvonne came after me relentlessly, I only loved her the more for it. I found myself a little rustic house between the fields and the sea, at Roscoff. I became a creature of nature, a recluse. The lies, the fantastic stories she told me! The purses she lost! . . . Never mind. That winter I had an engagement to fulfil at the Moulin Rouge, where they used to put on revues and operetta. We returned to Paris. I felt rather than saw the evil which engulfed me more and more, day by day. I was depressed, discontented, weary; my heart was empty of delight and full of disgust.

One day, backstage, I met a little Israelite with fine eyes and a high forehead, who seemed very shy. Lorrain introduced him to me, overwhelming him with praise: 'Max Maurey, subtle and cultivated, intelligent and clever – my friend. He admires you . . .' and he left us. We looked into each others eyes, disturbed and smiling, and on that day at least I think that both of us had the same thought: let's make happiness together. He daren't woo me, I led him on; he daren't visit me, I called him; he daren't love me, I set about adoring him and managed to communicate some of my fire to him. His success made him bold. He loved my love, that was all, and began to bully me, lie to me, deceive me. When I tried to escape he came running after me, sobbing, haunting the street where I lived night and day. I was touched, asking – alas! – for nothing better. Yvonne and he loathed each other. There were floods of tears, flouncings out, threats, appalling things were said. One fine day, however, light dawned in me; I felt that I could no longer endure their treachery, their lies, their baseness. I left. I went to Cairo, then to Alexandria, Athens, Constantinople (leaving instructions with my solicitor to pay Yvonne de Buffon an allowance of 150 francs a month, against receipts. I include this detail because after my marriage, and perhaps after her own, she wrote an open letter to a newspaper declaring that she had never had anything to do with me!). I saw nothing, or very little. I gained a few vague impressions of landscape, home-sickness undid me, and the Orient Express soon carried me back to Paris.

In my front hall I found Max, a rose in his hand, and a smug smile on his face. Yvonne had vanished. He said he had seen nothing of her. Liar! They had met to cry on each other's shoulders over my brave departure. Then she had led him on to confidences; she was gentle and maternal to him and their attitudes towards each other changed. Their feelings for me, too. Soon they were tearing me apart tooth and nail, and the hour struck! The hour of love following on hate. Yvonne was pregnant and he was stuck with her.

They are said to be married; it was never announced. They had two, three, then four children. Max, I know, has become Yvonne's punishment, her grief. She is the maid of all work, prisoner of her duties. They live like convicts chained together, miserable and discontented. Yvonne, cheated in her turn, has wept useless tears.

July 18. Received a circular letter from Germaine Bailly, Poiret's head *vendeuse*, letting me know that the house of Poiret, shut when the war started, half-open during, is opening again properly this month with a marvellous collection. We have always greatly appreciated Poiret's taste. He was an innovator, very much discussed.

I considered him an extraordinary being. I invited him to my wedding. He came, presented his wife to me and they became friends of ours. Yes – except that it's not really possible to stay friends with people who sell you things. I still like his taste, I often buy his clothes and I'll continue to do so . . . and that way everything is for the best in the best of all possible worlds!

They have installed a dance-floor in the garden surrounding the couture house, and asked us to the opening. We didn't go. At present we are going nowhere.

Speaking of Poiret and his parties. He has quite sumptuous ideas but the execution falls short. One day, when the pre-war kings were still around, the Poirets called on us to invite us to a dinner dance. It was to be a big party and everyone was to come dressed as a 'royal'. Poiret himself was to appear as the King of Dress-Design. We accepted, and because there was a lot of talk at the time about the Albanian throne, the 'cradle of the Ghikas', we decided to appear thus: the King and Queen of Albania, with their Favourite. The favourite was to be the Italian greyhound wearing a collar of gold and lying on a velvet cushion carried by Halima Larbi (my little white Moroccan, who was given to me by General Bailloud), who would lead the procession in sumptuous raiment. We would pace majestically behind her. I had dug out my rich Roumanian embroideries, royal blue and apricot cloaks trimmed with beautiful fur. Our heads were crowned with heavy toques of fur, to which aigrettes were fastened with huge diamonds. Our costumes came off perfectly. As soon as we arrived I saw that they were far too good.

The others were the kind of thing you see in the streets at Mardi Gras. My two black Africans, Zorah and Fatoum, dazzling and covered with jewels, walked behind us holding up our trains. I wore all my pearls. I really can't bear to describe the chaos and squalor of that evening. It was after ten before we sat down to dinner. Everything was badly done, ill-prepared, disgusting. The wines as well as all the rest – the guests became drunk on the hubbub. Obscenity soon took over from unseemliness. It was sordid and deafening.

On our way home, in the darkness of the carriage, I bewailed the time we had wasted there, scolded Georges for having agreed to escort us. I begged my little ones to forgive me for taking them there, and my dog too – I even asked my dear pearls to forgive me for having worn them!

From that day we began gradually to withdraw from intimacy with the Poirets. . . . .

July 19. Max Jacob* has sent a message that he is ill and has been taken by cab to some friends in Montparnasse who will look after him until he is better, and that they are letting me know because they found my invitation for the 23rd in his pocket diary. I am sorry, because he amuses Georges. He appeals to my compassion because he's so feeble. In other words, I don't like him at all. He's a poor creature, very gifted but doomed to come to nothing much. There is something grubby (in every sense) and demoralizing about him. Beautiful, ravaged face . . . He has changed his religion, which is something I can never approve of. Why want to deny his race? Ridiculous! And anyway he hasn't been able to change his nose! In 1917 he lived with us at Roscoff for two whole months. It was pretty difficult. I did everything I could to show it as little as possible. I am not very sociable. I attribute all kinds of qualities to people, then pouf! Everything changes into its opposite as though by magic just because of a word said or not said, a gesture, a look, a giggle. I'm wrong, obviously. But my nerves are so poor and I get more and more worked up until I explode.

July 22. A postcard this morning from Vivières (Aisne). It is Henry Bataille's portrait of Yvonne de Bray. Yvonne has been Bataille's besotted mistress for ages, and it never ceases to amaze those in the

---

* Max Jacob had a considerable reputation as a 'cubist', or *avant-garde*, poet. He was born at Quimper in Brittany and died in a German concentration camp at Drancy in 1944, at the age of sixty-eight.

know. She drove off Berthe Bady, then took her place. Bataille always loves the one who is there! When Bataille finally left Bady after twenty-five years of close intimacy, I wrote to him: 'Your separation scorches my heart. To me it seems like an amputation and the woman you are taking on will always be, for me, your wooden leg.' Bady stirred up a scandal, mobilizing all the men of letters; Henry had to promise her a fat pension; 'Which', she cried, 'he never paid during the war, taking cowardly advantage of the moratorium.' We met her about a year after the split, and when I enquired affectionately how she was, she gave me this nice answer: 'Better, thank you Liane, much better, I'm crying no more than once a day.'

July 25. .... Today we acknowledged that Paul (Poiret) deserved his nickname, the Magnificent. He arrived by car, at midday, surrounded by boxes, suitcases, his most elegant and favourite mannequin, Germaine his faithful ambassadress (her diplomacy earns her the title), and my *vendeuse*. Nearly twenty models, each more ravishing than the last . . . I chose three dresses: 'Tangier', in thick black wool with touches of white embroidery and fringed with the same. It's ravishing. 'Saint-Cyr', in black silk, rather full pannier-style skirt, black bodice with little short sleeves, and three over-lapping flounces of white organdy making a cape fastened with two silver tassels and a bow of violet velvet. 'Agrigento', two splendid lengths of glitter knotted on the shoulders and at the waist – that's all, but such a ravishing all! He had some superb coats, one of them Venetian, black and gold with a collar and cuffs of sable! 7,500 francs, a mere trifle! But a dream of beauty.

He was charming, allowed me a discount of 800 francs on the three dresses, which made them 3,000 net. Georges was pleased. Poiret had returned to being our dressmaker friend, so nice, with no pretentions except being very good at what he does. We hugged, celebrated, paid compliments, made plans. Poiret promised me he'd look after the sale of my house; he could strike a rich vein, with his clientele. At my first hint he said: 'It's dresses I sell' – 'Yes, but there'll be a commission of 50,000 francs.' – 'Oh well that's different, that's interesting'; and then we talked about it seriously.

July 26. I feel sickened, exhausted, even fed up at having ordered three dresses! I said to myself: yesterday we babbled, we didn't talk; we told lies; we schemed. I allowed myself to appear inferior to myself! I am angry with myself, and with others, for spending a whole day so far from what is true, upright, sincere, beautiful, real – from God. We were spiteful, we behaved with a Parisian kind of flightiness, like theatre people. Any why? Poiret is scared of the future. He wants to sell up, realize the assets he acquired before the war and live in the country with fresh eggs, chickens, his family. Goodness, how bored he would be! He's a townee to the marrow of his bones, and a business man too. He has made it up with Cocteau – another encoctocated one! He prophesied ruin and disaster. He is anxious, lacks confidence. I foresee trouble for him. The impression made on me is really bad. He told me: 'In Paris Denise spends all her time dancing, she adores it. For the opening of our dance-floor I made her a full-skirted, short dress of silver lamé. She was lovely. She looked like an epergne!' Puppets! I am no longer up to date and don't want to be. I wear nothing but black, white and grey. My soul, too, is dressed in gravity, gentleness and nobility. In fact I have been quite unable to digest that frivolous, demoralizing day.

Ah, my darling Flossie*, with your high-necked black dress, your fur and your unpretentious little hat, how different you are, how comforting, and beautiful. I detest letting my thoughts dwell on nastiness. . . . .

July 27. Georges wanted to celebrate my half-name-day, because I'm called Anne-Marie. He has ordered my favourite dishes for to-morrow, Sunday. He has written me a beautiful letter, a bit literary, but so much 'him'.

This morning I went for a long walk with Steinilber and we talked about gestures. Each period, each fashion, gives rise to its own. That of the snuff-box, mittens and curved arms over crinolines, handker-chiefs held by the middle. What a charming gesture it was to lift the skirt to show just enough to excite desire by suggesting the rest . . . Now we wear low-cut dresses. Is it cold? There's a pretty, shrinking way of spreading your fingers over a fur crossed at the throat. Skirts are short, no more need to lift them. One stretches an arm, lifts the wrist to eye-level: how else read the time from one's wrist-watch? There have been the charming movements of the lips against the mesh of a veil; the lipstick gesture, so frequent that one no longer notices it, and the powder-puff, which has become so

* Natalie Barney, an American whose salon in Paris was a centre of lesbian society. In their young days she and Liane had a famous affaire.

～ 37 ～

natural; the sharp little tap of the walking stick, or the way of tucking it very high under one's arm-pit when not using it. I like taking a stick when I go out. It gives my spirit a touch of virility! I feel protected, and truth to tell, when I'm a little tired – well, I'm quite glad to lean on it a little; not much, not so that you would notice.

Walking stick, spectacles! Last April my mother-in-law took me to her oculist to get my first pair of spectacles. I use them when I read or write by artificial light. Walking stick . . . spectacles . . .

Poiret's little mannequin has a pretty enough face, lifeless, and beautiful auburn hair. I said kindly: 'Your hair is ravishing, so young and such a colour! One can tell at once that its natural.' My civility earned me this answer: 'Well, I'm young. I've got years before I need dye.' – 'Listen, you pretty fool, I do not dye and it wouldn't take you long to count my grey hairs. May you have as few when you're my age, or earlier for that matter. And let me tell you that when I was twenty-four I'd have thought myself an old has-been if I hadn't already clocked up a husband, a divorce and a seven-year-old son!' Poiret looked quite embarrassed.

Mannequins have always struck me as pathetic. Poverty of spirit, of flesh and of digestion. Oh! That bad breath from eating too little, too fast, and that obligatory smile degenerating into a painful grimace. What a miserable fate: poor relations summoned from afar to the sumptuous banquet, just to be useful!

. . . .

July 31. Benjy [Alfred Benjamin, London stockbroker] arrived yesterday at eight o'clock in a superb car. The dear old thing is just the same; he seems to have shrunk a little, that's all. Same clever, long-nosed face, same bald head covered with down like a duckling, same good humour, same fondness for us. He is easy-going. He told me: 'I've brought you a little piece of nonsense that I'm sure you won't have,' and out of his golf bag he wrestled an umbrella with an aluminium handle which opens out into a camp-stool. The umbrella's pointed end sticks into the ground: it's too comic – Briggs's latest invention. He said: 'If it rains, there you are, an umbrella. If you are tired, you sit down.' – 'And what if it rains when I'm tired?' Hoots of laughter. He's brought me a big bottle of my beloved English scent, Penhaligon's 'Hammam Bouquet'. You can get it in Paris at Carnaval de Venise, but it's no longer so fresh.

August 1. Migraine on the left side. Very painful, particularly, with a deaf English guest, full of energy and refusing to speak a word of French! As charming as can be, all the same. I'm going to put myself on a diet and send him off to play golf.........

....

August 4. Have seen the new honours list in the papers. Henry Bernstein has been made a *chevalier* of the Legion of Honour. At last! Yes, but Pierre Wolf has been made a *commandeur*. Oh dear!

Pierre Wolf was once brought to see me, Liane of the Folies-Bergère, at lunch time. I invited him to stay to lunch. Wolf was in bicycling clothes, britches and leggings, which put me off to start with. My mother was lunching with me that day, and four or five close friends. The witty Wolf elected to show off his gift of the gab on dirty stories, sparing us no obscene detail or word. I was seething. I controlled myself as best I could, and he noticed nothing. As we waited in the hall for coffee after the meal, convinced of his success, he suddenly remembered that as well as being the star of the Folies, I was his hostess. So he came over to me all smiling and gracious, still quite tipsy on his own talk and my wine: 'Liane, my lovely Liane, what an exquisite lunch! How delighted I am to have met you. Tell me, tell me – what can I do in my turn to give you pleasure?'

At these words I jumped: 'Give me pleasure? You would like to do that, really?'

'Yes,' he said, surprised.

'But really?'

'Of course,' – already a bit nervous.

'Well, that's simple. You can give me enormous pleasure this very minute.'

'How?' and he leant towards me, his lips pursed.

'You can get to hell out of here!' And I called to the footman who happened to be passing: 'Get M. Wolf's hat and stick. He's in a hurry. Goodbye, Monsieur.' And I left him standing there. Flabbergasted, he grabbed his stick and made off. That evening I received a magnificent potted palm wrapped in rich Japanese embroideries, with an apologetic note. We became the best of friends. He remembers that little incident and often tells the story.

August 5. Just back from Paris. We were met at the station by a fine car and were driven to Professor Hartmann's nursing-home in Neuilly [Georges Ghika was to have his operation there on September 15]. I went over it and chose our rooms. Afterwards we buzzed off to the Ritz and to Martine's and to Poiret's and to Linker's and to Rebattet's and to Panizou's. The car was loaded with cakes, scent, hats and coats for Georges and for Benjy's wife........ At nine o'clock in the evening the bell rang. It was André Germain on his way back from Etretat, wanting dinner. We were just going to bed. He had a friend with him: it was a bit bad-mannered, not to say impertinent. I made up my face, shook out my hair, put on a silk wrapper trimmed with valencienne lace, got into bed – then thought to myself: 'Dammit, no! I don't want to see them. André Germain never answered the friendly note I wrote him a month ago, he takes the liberty of turning up so late, without notice. He's not one of our close friends, after all, he thinks he can get away with anything because he's the son of Henri Germain, the founder of the Crédit Lyonnais.' But you can't refuse someone a dinner. Georges wore himself out making excuses and had them served some soup, noodles and bacon, cold veal, coulommiers cheese, cakes and fruit. They expected to see me afterwards but I held firm. They left rather embarrassed, and disappointed. How ill-mannered people have become!

August 7. Joncières announces that he's coming on Saturday, so we'll hear all the latest about everything and everyone. Joncières is not well-bred but he's a close friend. He is horrid but he answers letters. He takes liberties but he will be anxious for news of us if we are ill, etc. They are doing one of his plays at the Comédie-Française, *le Fil d'Ariane*, starring Piérat of course. He's on his way back from Bataille's, they are passing him on. He's the homeless one who is at home everywhere.

The Roumanians have entered Budapest as conquerors and the Americans are telling them to get out of it again. The poor Roumanians, betrayed, beaten, rent apart, ruined: they make a last effort and vanquish their enemy, only to be told to renounce the victory. It's a bit much! That new nation is abusing its youthful strength.

Salomon told me some charming lines which he has written in English about Flossie, who is grieving us all by leaving for America on the 9th:

Analyse her
You'll be wiser
Steel and gold
All is told
. . . .

August 9. A thought from Alexander Dumas the Younger, picked up in the literary supplement of *Figaro*: 'Begin by marvelling at what God reveals to you and you will have no time left in which to seek what He hides from you.'

When I was at Roscoff this year I read the *Mémoires* of Alexander Dumas the father. The volumes came to me from the library of my grandmother Olympe. She was very cultivated and composed songs, both the music and the words. Among her papers when she died my mother found quite a correspondence with Victor Hugo . . . My mother told us this openly, but when we asked to see it she put on a prim and disapproving look and said: 'Out of respect for my mother's memory I have burnt them.' She had, too. Towards the end of her life I drew her into my own existence more tenderly and intimately than before, here and there, in London, Paris, Monte Carlo . . . She saw me being celebrated and sought after, admired the luxury and order of my household, was dazzled by my clothes and jewels. One day I heard her say: 'Oh daughter, if I'd only known! I think I'd have really loved to be an actress.' Perhaps at that moment she would not have burnt the letters of my grandmother and Hugo!

You can see clearly that Dumas exaggerated and played games in his *Mémoires*. In several places my grandmother has corrected him in the margin. For example, he's talking about a session of the Palais de Justice, something about Hugo and a trial. Madame Olympe has written at the bottom of the page: 'You are lying, Alexander. They didn't say that. I was there.' It's amusing and made me feel fond of my beautiful, clever, formidable grandmother who ruined us all by her luxurious way of life. She had herself carried off by the man who loved her because her parents wouldn't give her to him. Carried off and put into a convent, in order to drag the longed-for 'yes' out of them. Later, when her love faded, they separated. There was no such thing as divorce. She was capricious, managing, independent. And I can see myself in all this. No doubt she loved her three children, but she loved herself more! Oh Grandmother, why did you bequeath me that, too? I'm said to resemble her physically, which flatters me – but she died of a dropsy and that horrible illness, so ugly and deforming, really frightens me.

Grandmother, does everything have to be paid for? Or is life on earth sufficient punishment for everything?

Joncières is here. He's been staying with Bataille who, he says, is still tired and ill. Yvonne de Bray nurses him, adores him, and he can no longer do without her. Everyone is a bit puzzled by this: their house is a mess, their servants are untrained and their cook is unspeakable . . . .

August 10. Léonce tells us all kinds of tittle-tattle: a witticism of Bovy's, a clever Comédie-Française actress, about Robinne, also of the Comédie-Française. Robinne is superb, classical, voluptuous, magnificent, but everything about her is a bit overdone – her hands, her cheeks, everything. 'She looks like an enlargement.' We couldn't help laughing because that's exactly it.

For Joncières, when it comes to looks, intelligence and talent there is no one but Piérat. He loves her madly and follows her everywhere, wants to see her four times a day, telephones her every morning, goes shopping for her, sings her praises, does his best to push her reputation, leaps into bed with her at night, gives her good advice, makes jealous scenes, swears by her alone, talks of her alone, lives for her alone. It makes him exceedingly boring and puts one off her. She wears her clothes well but no one ever wants to copy her dresses. There's nothing ugly about her but she is ordinary-looking, stringy, a bit meagre – the look of a housemaid in a good house. She doesn't act too badly, her technique is correct . . . .

So that's *my* Piérat. She is not at all like Jonce's. She's married to Guirant, known as de Scevola, and they live their separate lives together in a perfectly friendly way. A well-established modern marriage. They each contribute what they can to the common stock, horrors, money, merits. They have a country house in Provence, a corner in Versailles, a good flat in the avenue Villiers. They live handsomely and keep good company. Apart from Joncières they know only rich people. Their close friends change often, according to the . . . shall I say heart's? . . . barometer. But Léonce is always there. He is closely and deeply attached to them. When there is a crisis – it can happen – he packs his bags and takes himself off to us, either here or at Roscoff. Whereupon he suffers, and his suffering exudes in the form of bad temper, complaints and grumbles. Then – it doesn't last long, it can't – back to the nest and we are more or less dropped. I don't mind. It's funny, if only because from listening to Joncière's talk I am able infallibly to pin-point Piérat's lovers, and I entertain myself with this as though it were a game. Last time it was a rich carpet merchant. At present there's a military man on the horizon. Lightly, he let fall the name of Marshal Pétain. Too good to be true!

August 11. Joncières plays the piano well. He says ingenuously: 'I play by ear, I never had a lesson.' I have heard *that* before! Lucie Delarue-Mardrus woke up one fine morning speaking perfect Hebrew: she had never had a lesson. Neither had Colette Willy when she played Schumann's 'Nut-tree' right through without one mistake. Vincent d'Indy's daughter, the pretty Marguerite de Bec-de-Lièvre, said almost the same thing when she played 'something of Papa's' at a party of mine, in my studio. Although 'something of Papa's' is very difficult!

That one knew how beautiful she was and delighted in shedding her clothes so that people could say it to her . . . so that they could prove it to her! What a delicious scatterbrain! An exquisite nymphomaniac, childlike face, golden skin, brilliant black eyes full of mischief, fair hair, haughty mouth, perfect teeth. It was impossible to love her deeply – the thought didn't occur. She was easy and vivid like a passing breeze, a whiff of scent, a fruit which one picks casually, a flower one smells almost without thought . . . .

. . . Georges is made of stone. Everything breaks against him. It looks as though I lead him by the nose, but not at all! He does what suits him, what falls in with his own ideas, what he condescends to approve of, but as for anything else – useless to go on about it. No use crying, raging, threatening, loving, joking, reasoning. His stubbornness is impossible to budge.

August 13. Our friends are sometimes astonished at our living so much on our own. For us peace and happiness lie in shutting our doors of an evening and finding each other again, alone with the beloved Italian greyhound who seems to enjoy the moment with all the voluptuous tenderness at her disposal.

I have had a letter from Marguerite Roquet, née Godard. Her mother was the daughter of my friend Valtesse de La Bigne, the Tesse of the *Idylle saphique**.

* Liane published this fictional account of her affaire with Natalie Barney in 1901.

That charming woman's death has left a hole in my life which no one else has yet filled. She would have suffered from what is called progress, that's to say from the tendency to accept and excuse shoddiness. She would have suffered but she would not have let it show. She was controlled, self-contained, reserved. Very lovely, sensual and intelligent, making a distinct separation in her life between the pleasures of the body and those of the mind. She never told me she had a daughter, yet we were friends to the limit – both permissible and forbidden. I was unforgiveable. One day I took Flossie to her house, went into a bedroom with Valtesse, locked the door and refused her nothing, highly amused at the thought of Flossie speculating and suffering on the other side of the door. How remote I feel today from the part of me which used to foment such stupid little nastinesses. Valtesse, so haughty and proud, whose motto was a superb 'Ego' and who once said to me: 'I am a courtesan, and how I do enjoy my work!'

August 15. Mary, Holy Virgin, I offer you this day. I hail you and I ask your forgiveness for everything within me which might offend you. I shall be tolerant, kind and gentle. I offer you Max Jacob and André Germain whom I do not like, but whom I shall try to like in your name, with all my compassion.

August 16. I have been given a pot of white marguerites. I have put it in Marco's room.

Yesterday I reread the letter he wrote me for my birthday in 1914. His fame, courage, luck and success had enlarged his spirit. He no longer resented the things about me which had wounded him. We loved each other tenderly: I was proud of him and he was glad about my marriage. Everything had become loving and sweet between us . . . my darling, how glad I am that you left me this memory of our sweetest understanding following after our savage times, and quite effacing them.

Max Jacob, nervous to begin with, was soon reassured. I told him that I meant to make the day go smoothly, having offered it to the Holy Virgin. He was witty and full of friendliness. This evening he leaves for Brittany, to Concarneau after stopping to see his mother and sister in Quimper.

Madame Jacob, his mother, has an antique shop on the quay at Quimper. She is a charming period piece herself, in the midst of her antiques, with her rustling high-necked silk dresses, her white wavy hair, her caustic look and her subtle, ironic mouth. Her conversation is a delight – old house, old papers, spirit of the past. She becomes quite forceful and funny, one feels her to be formidable and trenchant, very amusing anyway, knowing how to turn everything to account. She would have been at home anywhere where there was a government to lead, people to direct. Max has modelled himself on her. One can see him in her along with something settled, calm and established. Her voice is dry but she ends her sentences with a smile which turns up the corners of her mouth and sounds the tinkle of mockery. She's quite small but she looks tall because of all that she emanates. She has a superior mind. She doesn't choose to believe in anything . . . a majestic bearing in spite of being tiny and a gracious manner in spite of being in business. I like her enormously for her natural easiness and gracefulness and for her tart quality, blend of great lady and old woman who in her declining years has acquired the philosophy to control and illuminate emotion. . . . .

Mademoiselle Jacob, Max's sister, has a beautiful and gigantic head. Hair like Absalom's to catch in the chandeliers, huge dazzling black eyes, full plump lips, a nose out of which you could make three . . . she's the shopkeeper who buttonholes passers-by in the street. That was how she accosted us. She wears antique ear-rings of gold and coral which suit her. She's a handsome queen of the fair ground who looks as though she spends her life on a roundabout. She stands there knitting rapidly and ceaselessly with enormous needles, trailing fat balls of dust-coloured wool wherever she goes. . . . .

August 17. I've ordered a mauve shift. And another of grey crêpe de chine. I've been thinking a lot about clothes for some time, since Poiret's visit I believe. It stirred up the dregs of my old frivolity.

August 19. Salomon has declared that he would have loved Pauline* more, and after her Flossie, and from a great distance me, if we had led lives of perfect purity! I gave him a violent and eloquent lecture to prove that dung is necessary to the blooming of lilies and that perhaps Pauline's genius was so admirable and special precisely because she had given free rein to the materiality of her earthly envelope. That Nathalie remained the Exquisite, the Incomparable in spite of having allowed every kind of touch; and that as for me,

* Pauline Tarn, an English poet with whom Natalie Barney had a famous love affaire, better known under her pen-name, Renée Vivien.

I kept myself pure in spite of all the filth, kept my soul above it all though my body was given over to desires, remained ME in spite of everything, always and for ever.

After a declamatory speech in the style of Tonia Navar, I amused and rather surprised Salomon by reciting him a scene from *Femmes savantes* with a great deal of poise. Reichenberg gave me lessons for six months when I was eighteen. I could recite simply, clearly, with intelligence, but my voice didn't carry. It was all breath, and anyway I hated learning by heart. Reichenberg exclaimed: 'What a pity! I'd have to teach you nothing but technique. If you weren't so lazy you could be making your debut at the Vaudeville in six months time, and not in a supporting part, either.' Dear little teacher, how she scared me. Tiny and blonde, with her candid little face, her soft blue eyes, she simply terrified me. I remember begging her to turn her back so that I could let myself go a little in my speeches. She was proud of me. One day she invited Ignace Ephrussi and Prince Sagan to come and hear me. I couldn't open my mouth. So she laughed and hid them behind a big velvet curtain, and her 'little pet' was able to show her paces.

I met her one day at Virot's, just after my debut at the Folies-Bergère in – a conjuring act! She came up to me and said gently: 'Little pet, what a shame! What you are doing is so silly. I shall never come and see you down there, you know.' Emboldened, I replied: 'Yes, you will, you must promise me to come. The king of England (Edward VII who was then Prince of Wales) came to my première. You must come too.' Then she said: 'You are a silly, and the people who go to see you are even sillier, and I am the silliest of the lot, you know, because I was there on the first day! Goodbye!' Such kindness. People nowadays don't have the time or the inclination to be kind.

August 20. Been reading some Marie Bashkirtseff. It has disturbed me. That child had the whole of life ahead of her, was full of desire and ambition. She wanted the Duke of Hamilton to fall in love with her, then she wanted fame. As for me, my active life is over. I contemplate my past, I ponder Good and Evil. Georges has given me a relaxed, intelligent and harmonious present. I shall never again create anything. It is a matter of enjoying what has been acquired; it is the beginning of the end.

August 21. I am furious! Ever since April I've been longing for a beautiful rabbit-skin rug in big squares of black and white, edged with bands of black and white and lined with black velvet. Lewis is selling it on commission and we have not been able to strike a bargain. A month ago Laxton, the furrier, wanted 1,250 for it. I hesitated, then wrote again on August 18, and now he wants 1,400! I'm afraid of setting my heart on it. Something in me recoils from it and another part of me wants it more and more. Is it really reasonable, just before an operation? Yes, but is it reasonable to be nothing but reasonable? I shall end by tossing for it. That's the way I have made all the most serious decisions in my life: my marriage, buying the property, etc. There, I've just tossed. It's tails. I have to renounce the rug.

I have had four pages from my Salomon. He will have two of mine, on the subject of the nine painful months which followed my legitimate initiation. That makes me feel embarrassed, I don't like talking about it. My poor mother adored describing her pregnancies which were the most important and treasured events in her life. She said: 'I would have liked to have a glass stomach so that I could follow my child's development inside me day by day.' What a beautiful thing for a mother to say! But what a frightful image, all the same! . . . .

August 22. I have to admit that I'm up to my neck in frivolity, buried in dresses to the point of ruin! Fifteen different garments! My wardrobe jam-packed! My girl, this is not the way for an old woman to behave – particularly since you never wear anything but black and white, or a little grey, so that you always look as though you were in the same dress. Why fritter away your money so absurdly?

August 23. Am I vain? At bottom, yes. Not outwardly. I am aware of my beauty, naturally enough – the nation's Liane could hardly have remained unaware of it – but age is here. I often say 'Every age has its happiness and its beauty'. So my vanity finds words to console itself. I know that I am not a fool. I am prouder of my friendship with Salomon than of my husband's love. I am immensely and painfully proud of being Marco's mother. But I have a persistently naïve side which makes my first reaction to anything one of delighted amazement, whether it's a dress, a painting, a house, a piece of furniture, a book, a poem, a gesture, a face. On second thoughts I return to reality. So I seem very changeable and in fact I *am* changeable, oh dear yes, tremendously so. I'm always turning coats completely, and doing it with the utmost sincerity. So I have intelligence, but it has holes in it! And I never get to the bottom of anything, I have neither the time nor the inclination. I learn nothing. It's like wearing a watch, which I've never dreamt of doing. If I want to know the time I ask whoever happens to be at hand. In the same way, if I want to know something – all right, I'll ask the encyclopedia, or Georges, or above all Salomon. The Gascon's prayer would be the prayer for me: 'Give me not wealth, oh Lord, but the company of those who possess it.'

Wit? I am quite quick-witted. It still comes spontaneously when I write but it is slower when I'm speaking. My attention is drawn and held by exterior objects and I don't even think about what I am going to say. As soon as I start thinking, there's the repartee, easy and clever – and biting, too.

I am kind, really instinctively kind. I can be devoted but only to special people. Then I am infinitely so. I'm generous too. I like doing without in order to give – the old Catholic side of me, says Georges. I can't refuse anything if I'm asked for it, yet I'm afraid of being deprived. I keep accounts. Like an American, I want to get value for my money. I'm careful over five francs and spend five thousand without a thought. I'm never wasteful in little everyday matters – the good order of a household depends on that. I haven't always been rich so I take money seriously as a means to an end and to liberation. I save it when I can. I can seem miserly even to myself, and that disgusts me! I pause to question myself, I examine the facts in detail, I calculate. No, I am not miserly, I am prudent. I have profited from some hard lessons and from the example of other people's experience. But it's just as well to examine oneself from time to time, because it's a slippery slope: method leads to economy, economy leads to avarice – and that is really dreadful!

That and laziness. I abominate idleness. I like to have plenty to do, to organize and to look after. On days when I've trailed lazily hither and thither and nothing special has happened, I feel uncomfortable when I examine my conscience in the evening, as though I had done wrong. There are heaps of little daily duties to be performed, that's where one should turn for occupation. How can one ask everything from those around one if one gives nothing oneself? Before the war everything was so easy and abundant. In this big house where now I have two little maids and a cleaning woman, I used to have four Arab servants, a cook, a lady's maid, a scrubber and a housekeeper! I never put my hand to a thing. It was one long party! Everyone talked at the top of his voice, swore, frittered, guzzled, had a good time. Sometimes I used to pull myself up and tell myself: 'Life is too good, it can't last! It's against nature. Georges loves me, our health is more or less all right, my son is famous, I have charming friends, almost enough money . . . any change would ruin it.' The war came . . . catastrophes, sorrows.

August 24. Shall I draw my physical portrait? Tall, and looking even more so: 1.66 metres, 56 kilos in my clothes. I run to length – long neck, face a full oval but elongated, pretty well perfect; long arms, long legs. Complexion pale and matt, skin very fine. I use the merest touch of rouge, it suits me. Rather small mouth, well shaped, superb teeth. My nose? They say it's the marvel of marvels. Pretty little ears like shells, almost no eyebrows – hence a little pencil-line wherever I want it. Eyes a green hazel, prettily shaped, not very large – but my look is large. Hair thick and very fine, incredibly fine, a pretty shiny chestnut brown. Hardly any grey hairs. One or two, to prove that I don't dye. Bernstein once gave me the pretty nickname, Sable. 'Fine hair, the colour of a sable.' Marco had my hair, same colour, quality, quantity, growing into seven little peaks all round the head. When he brushed it back he was a real beauty . . . .

August 25. . . . . Giorgio has had a telegram from my brother-in-law: 'Can I visit you on Wednesday afternoon?' Giorgio doesn't want to answer. Henri has twice made appointments with us and then not turned up. We are affectionately cross with him and can do without his condescending presence. He has married a woman who doesn't wish to meet me. She is ugly, red-headed and – no doubt – virtuous. Her mother was a Drosso, which doesn't amount to much. The Drosso grandparents were, I believe, grocers. That kind of person will never forgive a dancer for bearing the same name as they do.

August 26. A ray of light in my sky! Laxton has written to say that he will let me have the beautiful black and white rug which I covet so badly for 1,250 francs. I thank him; I shall try to get it for 1,200, I order it at last. I tossed for it and got 'no', but my mysterious guardians have decided that I've had enough troubles to deserve this fugitive pleasure. I will not order any more dresses for a whole year.

M. Simon, our neighbour who owns the Duc de Noailles' former orangery with 22,000 metres surrounding it, asks if he can visit us. Oh, if only he can buy our wing of the château, what a relief that would be! His gardener has been round our grounds – he admired the trees and the design of the paths and lawns, and he showed me heaps of little details overlooked by my own gardener. Ignorance and ill-will combined.

The other day someone asked me how old Emilienne d'Alençon is. Fifteen years ago I heard people saying she must be fifty, and she is not that even now. There is just a year between us. How pretty she used to be! Enormous golden eyes, the finest and most brilliant complexion! A proud little mouth, a tip-tilted nose you could eat, an oval face rather in the style of my own.

We were friends, she was my leading light in the ways of the theatre and of our pleasures. She could be beastly, but was really so pretty that one couldn't hold it against her. For instance, she said to me: 'I know you are going to be at this big dinner tonight. Don't dress, I shall be wearing just a coat and skirt and a blouse and one row of pearls. You do the same, so that we'll be alike – and send your carriage away, I'll take you home.' So at eight o'clock there I am in my simple little suit and one row of pearls – and at nine o'clock in sweeps my Emilienne resplendent in sumptuous white and gold brocade, dripping with diamonds, pearls and rubies, no hat, her curls full of sparkling jewels. 'Oh dear – am I late?', with a delicious little pretence at absent-mindedness! One careless, hardly even teasing, glance at me, and she doesn't speak to me for the rest of the evening. But as she leaves she says goodbye and offers me her lips with the choicest nonchalance. And I go home in a cab, confused and cross, brooding bitterly on these lines which I found in a notebook belonging to my grandmother Olympe:

> In each young girl with gentle eyes you see
> A sister, not a rival . . .

Two days later and it might never have been, on my side as well as hers. With an impudence as great as her beauty she had moved in on me, had installed herself in my bed, at my table, in my carriages, in my theatre boxes – and all, I must confess, to my great pleasure. I couldn't be strict with her. But fore-warned is fore-armed, and I no longer believed what she said.

~ 5⁰ ~

We went to Nice together, to the casino and to fancy-dress balls. We gambled together at Monte Carlo. Everyone admired us and ran after us; we were fêted, we were spoilt. Darling little Mimi! Last year, at the Majestic, she came to spend an afternoon with me. It was very moving to see each other again after twelve or thirteen years, and we were pleased to find each other still so beautiful. Her face is still ravishing, mine too. We cheered each other up. Our lives have gone completely different ways. She laughs, she dances, she stays up all night, she smokes (opium), she enjoys everything just as she used to do. She is rich, she has lots of friends. Bad friends – but that doesn't worry her. Her expression is still childlike and amused. When you tell her a joke she chuckles like a delightful chicken. She has become a woman of letters and has published a collection of sensitive and well-turned verse. She never stops falling in love, following her whim for better or for worse. She is adored, she's always changing lovers. They weep for her a little – too little – and console themselves rather too soon, but they are proud that she was there. How often have I heard someone drop her name into a conversation with a smug little look! She used to be my favourite model, vicious and ravishing, not like the others. Nothing about her was banal or vulgar, not her face, nor her gestures, nor the things she dared to do. It was she who made me cut my hair. She turned up with a pair of scissors and 'snip', it was done. Then she said: 'Come along, we'll try some henna.' Three months later, we were corn-coloured. Then in a flash we became brunette. We did have such fun with ourselves – and how we laughed at others, both men and women. And then, little Mimi, your lips were so soft, your gestures were so coaxing and . . . but here we are, my dear, a pair of nice little old ladies.

I received Salomon like the Queen of Sheba, reclining in a mass of mauve and blue chiffon, lace, scent, cushions and silk with the Italian greyhound lying at my side. We sipped beverages from China, nibbled sweetmeats from the South and pastries from the Ile de France. I read him some poems by Vehaeren. We talked about Renée Vivien and Flossie.

Poiret is angry and doesn't want to take back the badly made dress. I'm sulking and trying to gain time. Georges telephoned him and came up to my room quite green from having had to listen to the Magnificent as he fulminated. It's impossible, I'm always letting myself be taken in. Poiret's models are lovely but there is always something wrong with the workmanship.

Lewis has sent me a beautiful box of chocolates. He is burying the lost rug under sweetness; it costs less, appears to be gallant and can't be answered. Let him continue! In the ranks of the unbearable, Lewis comes lower than Poiret – *he* really is the king of them all!

One day in Monte Carlo, when I was competing with Otero in the display of jewels and dresses, an old Austrian Jew suddenly asked me, without ceremony, to have dinner with him. 'Oh no,' I said. – 'And why not?' – 'I don't care for your manner. That is not the way kings get accepted.' – 'Kings? What kings?' – 'Yes, kings, I love no one but kings.' – 'But the other day you had dinner with M. Goudstikker. He's not a king.' – 'Yes he is, he's the king of jewellers.' – 'And I've seen you dining with M. Battard . . .' – 'He's the king of cooks.' – 'And M. Lewis?' – 'He's the king of milliners.' He went off baffled, but the night brought council. Next day he sent me marvellous flowers, kilos of chocolates, a beautiful doll and this note: 'Have dinner with me. I am the king of fools.'

August 27. . . . . I am devouring Rabelais. He has one chapter which exactly fits Georges: 'How Pantagruel meets a man from Limousin who counterfeits the French language.' Georges constantly employs odd, little-used words, which make his speech sound silly, pedantic and boring. And he believes that he speaks so purely!
. . . .

August 29. Poiret has sent me two letters in the same envelope, one business, one friendly. Taken together they are impertinent and mean: whether or not your dress is all right, you will keep it and you will pay, or watch out! I shall pay. That is what princesses are for. . . . .
. . . .

August 31. Madame Calmette wanted to do table-turning last night. Louise Balthy* is a great believer: she says that her sister Justine is a good medium and that the whole of her glorious and lucky theatrical career was foretold when she was only fourteen years old and working for a haberdasher who specialized in mourning. To think of comic Louise, immersed in funeral crêpe!

Louise has a rare elegance and chic, wears enormous hats no one

* Louise Balthy was known as Polaire.

else could get away with, dresses in black and white, wonderful shoes, the latest thing in jewellery whether real or sham, and knows antiques as well as the sharpest dealer. She strokes a glaze or a soft paste like a connoisseur – a gourmet – and has furnished herself a little house fit for a queen with the finest of fine things. She had a tremendously successful sale. The little Basque peasant has come a long way and could stand as a symbol and example. She laughs, sings, dances, loves, recites, lies, groans, jokes – what vitality! Everyone likes her because gaiety is the quality that lasts best. Her voice – grave, sonorous, well-modulated – has extraordinary charm.

One day I heard some pretty idiot tell someone, in front of Louise: 'Louise is ugly.' The person addressed replied: 'Louise is ugly only in the eyes of imbeciles.'

September 1. The Queen of Roumania has given the *Revue des deux-mondes* an article on 'Tsar Nicolas II: a Martyr of the Great Tragedy'.

I saw Nicolas in Petersburg in the winter of 1891 when he was still the Crown Prince. An officer of the horse guards was getting married and giving his last party as a bachelor, and I was invited. The Crown Prince made his appearance at the beginning of supper and hurried off ten minutes later because he had to get back to Tsarsko Selo, where he lived with his parents, by a certain time. He seemed to me timid, embarrassed, gentle, good-natured and very mediocre. A few months later he lost his father. I was back in Russia that winter, for an engagement at the little Marie theatre. My engagement fell through because of the public mourning – and because I didn't want to stay on for it. I was at the Tsar's funeral. I saw the Crown Prince in the distance, transformed into the great Emperor of All the Russias, more pitiable than ever under his heavy burden.

How well I remember the wonderful ceremony, full of legendary symbols: the 'Old Reign' personified by a man in iron armour, all black, and so heavy that the man condemned to fill the role died on arrival at the fortress of St Peter and St Paul – if not on the way there. The 'Old Reign' led a black horse caparisoned in funeral draperies. He was followed by the 'New Reign'. He was a knight dressed in gold, riding a magnificent white horse adorned with white and gold.

I wrote a long letter to Meilhac describing this famous funeral in detail. My letter was so vivid and well-written that he read it out to some friends. Arthur Meyer was among them. He asked if he could have it for *le Gaulois*, and my letter was published word for word . . .

Dear Arthur's readership was pious and aristocratic; and he was as brave as a rabbit and as sly as – an Arthur Meyer. He published my letter without putting my name at the end, describing the author as 'One of our friends, an elegant Parisienne who is at present in St Petersburg and was able to attend the funeral of the Tsar' – and that's how little Liane had the honour of filling several columns in *le Gaulois*, certainly a respectable newspaper if ever there was one. The following New Year's Day, Arthur sent me a box of Pihan's chocolates. Pihan let him have them at a discount . . .

September 4. This morning I found a ravishing pair of adorable little Louis-Philippe vases for 4.75 francs. I note the fact here because it's so unusual for me to do good business with an antique dealer.

Tomorrow I am going to confession. I have begun to examine my conscience: no big sins. I was talking about it to Georges in front of Steinilber, who said 'Those are primary school sins.'

. . . .

Neuilly – September 11 to October 5

September 11. Intense and suffocating heat for the journey. Arrived in the light, airy house. Our three little rooms – Georges's bedroom, my bedroom and a dressing-room between them – seemed like a palace. A dreary little nursing-home dinner at seven o'clock. Hartmann welcomed us very affectionately.

September 12. Agitated night, almost no sleep. A bad beginning, as far as I am concerned. Jeanne de Pallady came this morning with two sheaves of pink carnations. She had been to the station to meet Mariette. Poor Mariette – her train had missed the connection at Trieste and she won't be here until tomorrow. She must be hot and enraged!

Georges swigged castor-oil at five in the morning, then two big cups of some herbal brew.

Bernstein heralded his arrival with an enormous bunch of enormous roses. He brought us the dressmaker Gabrielle Chanel – the taste of a fairy, the eyes and voice of a woman, the hair-cut and figure of an urchin.

September 13. Hartmann has thoroughly examined yesterday's X-ray photo. My God, there is only You! Georges and I are one and it is You who made us so. Surely You will not separate us? Endure everything! Suffer everything! Accept everything: people's cruelty, unkind judgments, illnesses, grief, ruin – but let us be together, for always.

September 14. Tomorrow's the day. The operation will be more delicate – they have got to get past the peritoneum – and longer. I went to church, I tried to pray, but it wouldn't come. I entrust myself to God and His will with a beautiful resignation.

Giorgio is admirable in his serenity.

September 15. Last night Giorgio and I bade each other farewell, love's sweet, sad farewell. Dear Giorgio, all childlike profundity and wisdom even in your follies; fatalistic, resigned, loyal, generous, attached and devoted even unto death – tonight I see none of your faults!

It is morning. The nurse is here, the hour is approaching. Georges is calm. So am I. I feel cold and distant, almost like a nun.

It's over, the operation has been a success. Georges is beautiful, pale, his magnificent features so rested. Hartmann is radiant. He hit on the stone at once, the whole thing lasted no more than forty-five minutes.

Sacha Guitry sent me a *pneu* which arrived during the operation: 'We are thinking of you', with his signature and his wife's. It brought tears to my eyes. Balthy telephoned. Salomon was standing by his telephone waiting for my call and asks for further news during the evening. Jeanne de Pallady, kind as ever, came early and took me out for a walk at the actual moment.

Flowers, telegrams, telephone calls, visits. I'm at the end of my strength.

September 17. A bad night. I'm depressed. Georges who was very ready to sleep after his morphine injection, was kept cruelly and stupidly awake by an appalling din, an atrocious and endless cacophony. Motor traffic, and then towards ten o'clock, the time when ill people get their deepest sleep, the Richer company going by with all its paraphernalia: the clip-clop of heavy horses, the rumbling of heavy caravans, the yells and oaths of heavy drivers, whinnying, braying, bellowing, etc.

I have been beastly, I have failed to practise Christian charity today. Georges wanted the door between our rooms to be shut during the night so that if I had the luck to fall asleep I wouldn't be woken. I shouted: 'You know that I can't sleep, you know that I'm alone and I'm frightened.' He persisted – ponderously, as he does everything. So then I slammed his door and locked the second door. I refused to go in to see him, and I can tell from the hundred thousand devils inside me that nothing and no one will be able to make me set foot in there this evening, and perhaps not tomorrow either, for the whole day. Not a nice character, Liane.

I really do adore Georges, but I never give way to him. At the beginning of our relationship I gave way all the time and he started using me as his pin-cushion. So I treat him rather more toughly and our household is the happier. I have been suffering dreadfully for him during these past few days, I was ready to die for him, I feel all his mother's cruelty towards him and my love is increased by pity and becomes even more tender and maternal, and then he opposes me stupidly without a thought for the terrible trials my poor nerves have been through. As I write this my throat constricts. I'm almost in tears. I feel quite shattered by these nights without sleep, I no longer know where I am.

By Mariette's 'cruelty' I mean the destitution in which she leaves Georges. She has had plenty of money since the war, but she lets months go by without sending him any under the pretext that the exchange is unfavourable. Rich as she is, she keeps her sons in the most complete dependence; they have nothing of their own. She makes them an allowance of barely thirty thousand francs a year, by dribs and drabs. And she brought them up on the footing, and with the tastes, of three hundred thousand francs a year. They can count on nothing; she promises and doesn't send, she announces and nothing comes because she has changed her mind. It is shameful and sordid. Hartmann took out Georges's appendix in 1916; we couldn't pay the bill. Very kindly, he consented to wait. So now Georges asks his mother to pay for both operations and give Hartmann a present for his obligingness. This is the answer he got: 'What nonsense! The exchange is terrible. I'll pay for one of the operations, perhaps. As for a present, certainly not!' There's nothing sublime about *that* mother! A French family might have cut off a son for marrying Liane de Pougy, but since she seemed to want to preserve some dignity for her son and herself and didn't do that, why doesn't she behave better? She has the tight, thin-lipped mouth of a miser.

September 18. I can't go on staying here, it's impossible. It will kill me, and my presence is useless to Georges because he insists on keeping the door shut. I'm going to try to move across the street, to Cautru's place. We stayed there in 1916; it is possible to sleep. My devotion and my discomfort are serving no purpose, and it's really stupid to ruin my health when I have had years of trouble re-establishing my nerves. I shall visit Georges during the day, and at night he has an excellent nurse, there is nothing I can do for him. This morning I can hardly stand, I'm on the verge of tears, seven nights without sleep have left me shaken, trembling and distraught.

So that's done! Here I am installed at Cautru's in a dreary little room with a bathroom, overlooking the back garden. It has been quite hard. Except for Marco's funeral, we have never been apart. With the tragi-comic stubborness of a true Breton, I tell myself over and over again: 'I have done right to retire to this quiet little hole rather than die of sleeplessness outside his locked door.' I'm terribly stubborn, and he, who knows me, is incurably given to putting his foot in it. He never thought I'd do this, and neither did I for that matter! I'm a little scared. Darling little Giorgio, now we are apart I love you; in the next room I'd be bad-tempered and boring.

Heaps of visitors: Max Jacob, Lambert, Noblet the actor, René de La Jaille, Hélène Miropolsky, Duret. This evening I daren't talk to God, or pray to Him, and yet . . .

. . . .

September 26. . . . . I talked to Georges about his mother. I said to him 'She has a sad, anxious face, closed to every kind of pleasure, rather aggressive. We should be sorry for her, she has no pleasures, she has nothing but functions.' He answered: 'Not at all. She loves everything that affirms her personality. She has chosen her destiny. The only thing she loves is increasing the value of her Roumanian estates, and she gets her happiness from that.' Poor little widow, far away from her sons, struggling on in her oceans of corn, vines and forests. She lives almost alone at Mascatene, an hour's train journey from Jassy, under the thumb of her German maid who is the only being who has mastered her and whom she loves, confides in and always treats with much consideration.

September 27. .... A most touching surprise: Maître P. A. Huillier (eighty-four years old) has forwarded me a communication from Indochina in which he is asked to tell me that the town of Tourane (Annam), where my son made some magnificent flights in 1913, has just given one of its streets the name of Marc Pourpe! I am so happy and quite overwhelmed. Maître Huillier will send them my thanks and a copy of a codicil added to my will this very morning, bequeathing twenty-five thousand francs to the town of Tourane.

September 28. I have just written Mariette a letter full of good and soothing news. I can see her from here, pulling a face when she sees my handwriting, not because she hates me but simply because she isn't used to it. Oh, these Balkan types! When I first knew Georges I adored him. He was twenty-three years old and I was thirty-five. I analysed the situation, I still had enough sense left for that, and the conclusions I drew were hardly cheerful because the gentleman was giving me a lot of trouble: he affected vices which he hadn't got, he told me about his past and future conquests with just enough reticence to be tormenting, and finally he thought up this: he would say he'd be with me at two o'clock and would not turn up until six. When he did me the favour of arriving at last, I daren't even complain. Once I said gently: 'Georges, you told me you would be here at two o'clock.' I brought this answer down on myself: 'I know, but I couldn't manage it. I was lunching with Madame Paul Reboux and afterwards we went for a long drive. And Madame Paul Reboux is uncommonly pretty . . .' My blood froze. I restrained myself, however, and made an appointment for the next day. Two o'clock came – no Georges, naturally. Jeanne de Bellune was there, so I said to her: 'Janot, you've a motor-car. Take me for a drive.' Good fellow that she was, Janot whirled me off to Saint-Germain for a spin in the woods, then to Versailles for tea at the Reservoirs; and then she said 'You are coming to have dinner with me.' I accepted, and it was midnight before I got home. There was my young Ghika in a Japanese kimono, pale, bilious, anxious, looking really unhappy. When he hadn't found me at home he'd been unable to believe his eyes, he'd eaten no dinner, he was completely shattered. He threw himself on me: 'What have you been doing? Where have you been?' Calmly I replied: 'I've been following your example, darling.' Silence, speaking looks, raptures; and never another lapse. He told me: 'That day's upset taught me that I can't exist without you.' I understood his character, I based my own on it, and as a result you

don't find many couples as deliciously harmonious as we
are.........

September 29. A photo of myself as a dancer: the ballet was directed
by Mariquita, terrible little old woman, as talented as she was
horrid.

Dear Madame Mariquita! How she could fray my nerves and
reduce me to tears, but she did drag something out of me – out of
the wooden creature whose first steps on the stage she produced – I
have to admit it – in the Folies-Bergère of 1894. You could hate
her but you couldn't despise her. She knew and loved her job; she
was its master, a genius, a pro. In the midst of my independent and
disorderly life she represented authority, duty, order, restraint,
education. She gave me my calling, self-confidence and grace.
Posture by Mariquita, hair by Marcel, dresses by Callot, hats by
Lewis, it really was quite a show! ....

....

October 2. Mademoiselle Mermillod, the ex-nun from the Companions
of Jesus who had special charge of my soul (she taught me literature,
history and geography and was my tutor at table and for games) and
who has been wrestling with life as a laywoman since the closing of
the convents, has written to say that she will be in Paris early this
month and ask when and where she can meet us. I answered at once
to tell her that we'd be back at Saint-Germain on the 7th. Dear
Amélie, she operated on charm: beautiful, dark-haired, white-
skinned, with pretty features and a most persuasive and eloquent
tongue, she could get us to do anything she wanted. We made up
fantastic stories about her – love stories, of course. We piously
preserved scraps of her writing, stubs of pencils, threads from the
fringes of her nun's shawl. What a fierce need to love children have!

Amélie was one of my first loves (she, and a bareback rider in the
Bazola circus called Annette Secchi, whom I rediscovered some
twenty years later training horses at the Olympia while I was miming
the part of Madame Paralière in *Watteau*, a pantomime ballet by Jean
Lorrain). I have seen her since and at first it touched my heart: poor
bird, thrown so brutally out of the nest. She didn't know how to
pay for a taxi; she was unable to believe that people could tell lies.

Amélie knew my father, my mother, Marco when he was a baby,
and me in all my first candour and purity. The first time I met her
again was after my car accident. She was rather stiff and embarrassed,

and said to me: 'My dear little Marie, when you were under the motor-car, did you think to make an act of contrition?' I answered with a laugh: 'Oh no, Mother Gasperine! I was in too much of a rage at dying.'

I met her again after my marriage. In the course of a conversation I said to her: 'Amélie, you are still beautiful, you could perfectly well get married.' Startled, and rather indignant, she replied 'I may be out in the world, Marie, but I am still the servant and spouse of Our Lord, and so I will remain.' Six months later something happened . . . she had her hair waved, she began to go to the theatre and to make up her face, she was looking for a husband!

Dear Amélie, I have to dismiss thirty years of thoughts about you in order to get used to what you have now become.

October 3. A photo of me taken in St Petersburg in 1892. Hat by Lewis. It was a whim and not the theatre which took me there. I was nineteen and a half years old. When I arrived in the melancholy of that wintery Russia I felt so sad that I cried. Even though I had held quite a court on the train. One old count whose name I forget, one of the Emperor's chamberlains, had started to cry thief in the middle of the night. Panic, hubbub, explanations: 'My watch has been stolen,' he yelled. 'It's been stolen while I was asleep. I wound it before I went to bed and it's of immense value to me. It was a present from the Emperor. A thousand roubles to anyone who finds it!' Everyone started to look for it, people were searched, every smallest corner was examined and the watch was found . . . under the old count's pillow! He had been suffering from a copious dinner and a great many glasses of champagne.

That country frightened me. I returned there three or four times and I could have married a Russian or two – a handsome officer in the horse guards, a hussar: a great name, a fortune, but no security.

I have belonged to the Society of Authors since the day when Félix Faure died, I have forgotten the date. On that evening (when I was starting typhoid) they played a little one-acter of mine at the Funambules, directed by the mime Séverin. I even had the honour of being interpreted by Séverin Mars and Henriette Roggers, who have been accepted by many important writers since then. Bouchor made me write a letter to René Fauchois, president of the play-wrights' union, saying that I wanted to join them. I was all for it. I am always on the side of the weak, the oppressed, the rebellious! And also for whatever will work . . .

October 4. .... In the old days at the Folies-Bergère I was great friends with a pretty little English dancer, another shooting star, Mimi Saint-Cyr. She drank enormously. Once I saw her in Maxim's, waiting for twelve o'clock to strike. She had twelve glasses of kummel ready on the table. At the twelfth stroke the table was clear! What dexterity and what a capacity! I watched her with my mouth agape. Everyone crowded round to congratulate her. She wasn't very drunk, just as gay as can be, and believe it or not she danced with her usual skill. It was that evening that she made a long-lasting conquest of the little Prince of Annam.

My Georges has been for a walk in the garden and in the afternoon he went out of the grounds as far as the Boulevard Bineau. Great progress. I've written to Robert Goldschmidt, asking him to lend us his Rolls Royce for when Georges goes home. It's the smoothest car in the world. Goldschmidt is a flirt of mine but not at all a restful one. He can be shameless and rude, with the most discouraging candour. He is in Brussels at the moment and has both written and telegraphed that he's delighted to put the car at our disposal for Thursday. So I shall be rather less worried about the bumpiness and length of the journey.

My Roscoff friend Madame Garat, or Camille .... is a natural child recognized by her mother who gave birth to her in a charitable institution at the age of sixteen. Mother Besnier's amorous career took place in Mans, which she never wanted to leave. She became quite the thing and ended by owning almost all of the rue Verte, the most ill-famed street in the town. In her old age she went into antiques and acquired a name, even fame, as a dealer, and a fat fortune. She wanted her little Camille to be well brought up, left her for a long time with a foster-mother and then sent her to a very expensive boarding school in Neuilly. Later, when Camille's schooling was finished, she made her take courses at the Conservatoire, gave her Mademoiselle Dumesnil of the Théâtre-Français as a teacher, and entrusted her to the care of the Countess de Buffon, mother of my friend Yvonne. It was through Yvonne that I got to know Camille. Imagine what might have happened to my Camille in that setting! No punctuality, no order, no duties! As soon as her mother paid them her monthly rent, off they went to the theatre and to restaurants. After that they were flat broke and lived from hand to mouth. They planted radishes on the drawing-room balcony, and Camille, heiress and rich paying-guest, used to hear the Countess call: 'Camille darling, a horse has just plopped in the street. Here's a tray – run quickly and collect it, it makes marvellous manure.' And Camille would rush out into the street to collect this precious treasure. They would buy salad and my Camille would be sent round to the grocer with a little jar to buy two-sous worth of ready-made dressing. Three times they sold the same ancestral portrait by Philippe de Champaigne. Each time they sold it, it was on condition that a copy should be made for them to keep, for sentimental reasons. Then a handy man called Garnet would antique it with much care and skill . . . But on January 21, the anniversary of the death of Louis XVI, they all wore black and windows and piano were kept shut.

When she got back to Mans Camille started to take lovers because she liked them, and quarrelled with her mother. Then she got to know Jules Garat, a romantic writer and friend of Peladan, who was not without talent and possessed two hundred thousand francs. He had read Tolstoy and decided to rescue this lost soul. Eventually, when the first love and excitement had passed, he made her the most wretched woman on earth. He ate the hearts of the artichokes, Camille nibbled the leaves. He gobbled the plums, Camille sucked the stones. He picked out the perfect pears, Camille made do with the rotten ones. And so on. He beat her, bullied her, insulted her. Even worse, he read her all his outpourings – and that was, indeed, an appalling fate. He started roaming the countryside dressed in flowing red robes, with crowns of ivy or vineleaves entwined in his hair. At last he left her, came to Paris, took up with the aesthetes, second-rate poets and their women, and went right out of his mind. He committed suicide.

Poor Camille, abandoned by everyone, turned to God. She has become very pious.

October 5. Salomon came to pick me up most punctually at 9.45. The car was an open one and we glided off to the cemetery at Passy. Dear, brilliant Marie Bashkirtseff; dear, rather brilliant Pauline – you must lend me your beautiful voices for the celebration of this, my first visit to your tombs. I was so much moved when I saw the chapel where my little muse reposes! There are epitaphs in verse round the walls, beautiful poems, sad, desolate, definitive. At the far end, one of her paintings: a desolate woman in a fierce pose, seated, gazing despairingly into the distance. Nearby stands the misty figure of another woman, weeping into her hands. It seems that they put the furniture from her studio into her tomb. There is her bust in white marble, wilful and proud, and a little reading chair covered in bronze plush with a flowered strip down the middle, all buttoned. It was the period for buttoned upholstery. Her chapel is large and was designed by Bastien-Lepage, the ultimate offering of a loving and broken heart. She lies under a little dome, rather Russian: 1860 – 1884.

Pauline's chapel is long and narrow like a little bed. Yes, like her: long and narrow. A photograph of her, after Levy Dhurmer, is placed in the middle, under the altar; in front of it, an incense burner. The windows are yellow, with figures, bordered with violet; two ivory virgins, one Christ, two old Delft pharmacist's pots containing thistles dyed mauve, church embroideries flung here and there, little bunches of dried violets hung on the grill with lilac ribbons, a selection of her lovely poems carved all around . . . On the exterior wall two verses which went straight to my heart:

> See, I have passed through this door
> Oh my thorn-bedizened roses.
> Gone is what used to be. For ever more
> My dreaming soul with God reposes
>
> Calmly asleep, forgetting strife,
> Having with its last breath,
> For love of death,
> Forgiven that crime, life.

Dear Pauline, have you forgiven me? We were tender rivals for Flossie, then friends. When I was in hospital having been crushed by my car on the public highway, you sent me flowers and copies of your books with beautiful inscriptions. And then one day your intimate friend, that little gnome Janot de Bellune, told me something very tart which you had said about me. I was ruffled and wrote you a letter – also very tart. Later I learnt of your illness and your death. Bitterness vanished from my heart. This morning's little pilgrimage was my symbol of repentance. Pauline died an edifying death. She suffered; she suffered in many ways. The dead are on the road between God and ourselves. . . . .

Georges has given Hartmann's nursing-home a name: 'The Cancervatory'.

October 7 and 8. Here we are, back home . . . . I have had a fire lit in my big bedroom with its Louis XIV panelling painted royal blue. It's nice, warming and cheering. Georges is in an armchair with his feet on a stool. He is progressing very well. I am tired, good-tempered, happy. The grounds have a distressingly forlorn look, we must find gardeners.

Georges's operation has cost us 10,930 francs. Fourteen tips had to be given, fourteen thank-yous and mementoes.

October 9. I can't help laughing when I think of the things we buy, of the way we satisfy our expensive whims, and of the expression Mariette's face would wear if she knew about it! In front of her we bewail our poverty better than any beggar at a church door. 'That's a pretty dress, Liane!' – 'I've been wearing it four years, Madame.' – 'That hat really suits you.' – 'This is its third winter.' – 'What a ravishing rug.' – 'I got it in exchange for my old moleskin coat which needed altering, but I really couldn't afford to have it done.' – 'Where will you be going this summer?' – 'To Roscoff, the cost of living is lower there and one doesn't have to dress up.' – 'How cold your house is!' – 'Oh dear, I know, but coal . . . but wood . . . It's all so expensive.' – 'Georges, I've never seen you looking so shabby.' – 'But, Maman, I haven't a penny to spend on clothes.' And so the litany continues – it's odious but essential. When we are honest we get nothing, all because of that famous exchange and also because of Mariette's . . . well, her *careful* temperament.

Joncières has telephoned twice. He must have had a tiff with his Piérat and need a little suburban repose.

October 12. I've been to mass, or rather, dear Lord, I crept into the basement of Your house, into Your sanctuary while Your faithful were at prayer. I did it out of obedience, and humility, and to prove my gratitude. Accept, o my God, all that part of me that reaches towards you.

October 14. Squalls of rain, an icy house. I walk about our rooms wearing a coat, a pretty coat, light and warm, which is two years old. It's not fashionable – it never was – but it has a period look: it's the coat Madame Hanska would have worn as she got into a berlin on the way to visit Balzac!

Salomon came. Such delight, walk in the grounds, tea and cigarettes, and the conversation which is one of the pleasures of our life, these days. He is re-cataloguing the museum and has to look at all the showcases: an enormous and exhausting task.

October 15. The Great Mademoiselle has made her appearance, on the arm of Goldschmidt, The Great Mademoiselle is Sorel [Cécile Sorel, the actress], who has well and truly made it. She's looking for a house in the country, near Paris, and she loves whatever is old and has a beautiful shady garden – in other words Goldschmidt thinks of doing us a good turn, and her too. She came lilting in on winged feet, her smile flowery, her face framed in ringlets blond *for ever* [in English]. She was wearing a lovely black velvet coat trimmed with skunk and a Louis XVI hat which shaded her face. She bestowed honeyed words on the invalid reclining among his multi-coloured cushions, on our discreet and exemplary love, on the happiness of marriage, on my childlike complexion, on Giorgio's curls, on the negress, on the staircase, on the white-veiled nurse, on my pearls, my trees, my bits and pieces. She admired everything most conscientiously, murmured a tactful word about Salomon – glad of a chance to let me know that she, too, has a Reinach who comes to visit her. She sipped an old plum brandy, was kind enough to nibble a biscuit, said nothing foolish, made Goldschmidt swear that he would bring us to see her one day, etc. Could hardly have been pleasanter. A second-rate creature at bottom, always tense, artificial, on her guard, with no intimate, inward life.

About twelve years ago, in my Liane de Pougy days, I wrote an article on her and Henry Bataille read it and said 'You catty thing!' Sorel didn't catch on, at first. She ordered fifty copies. Then someone enlightened her, and I was told 'I think she's got it in for you, you made such fun of her.' But did I really make such fun of her? I admire her without question, for a lot of things. She has made a magnificent success of her life, without a hitch. She is absolutely tiny, it's the fashion. She told me: 'It's terrible, I live the life of a jockey in order to keep my weight down, and it's no joke because I'm horribly greedy.'

Goldschmidt was all bustle and bliss, letting us tease him and giving us such fatuous looks that we almost giggled. Happily I was wearing a pretty Poiret dress, two years old, but Poiret is always *up to date* [in English] so it didn't show: a long dress of off-white bouclé wool – in the style of Peau d'Ane's moon-coloured dress – trimmed with black velvet and little mother of pearl buttons. Sorel admired it, naturally, and my coat too – though when I said it was Madame Hanska's coat for driving in a berlin, she looked a bit blank.

October 18. Yes, materially life is becoming more and more difficult. One wonders what will become of us. Our big house is so demanding, more than we are. Thinking of life's difficulty reminds me of something Sem* said, twenty years ago. He had been to dinner with me in my little house in the rue de la Néva which I sold later to Princess de Broglie (Princess Auguste de Broglie-Revel was Jeanne Thylde, a mime at the Olympia when I was there, my friend and often my partner. Two princesses emerged from backstage at the Olympia. Sem was very perceptive but I don't know whether he foresaw that). Anyway, after dinner, when my electric brougham came gliding round to take us to the theatre, heated, and upholstered in white cloth, Sem gave me a look and said in his Bordelais accent: 'Life doesn't half treat you well!'

The Olympia, Thylda, Sem, Otero! Otero and Liane de Pougy, the two stars. Thylda was a good performer but she wasn't a star. Otero and Liane . . . stars, rivals.

Two years ago, on the Champs-Elysées, I suddenly noticed a fat lady with a very lovely face and a good deal of style, wearing sumptuous furs, with enormous pearls in her ears. It was my Otero! It really is true that every age has its beauty! She was quite roly-poly in her fat, but she looked radiant and her marvellous face was still the same.

Cavalieri, too, was among the Folies-Bergère stars of that time. She was as pretty as a cupid, with a piquante, subtle expression, but she didn't have Otero's splendid presence. One day a journalist asked me 'What is your opinion of Otero and Cavalieri?' For answer I gave him this little comparison which depicts them both: 'It's like this: when Cavalieri wears real jewels they look false, and when Otero wears false jewels they look real.'

Cléo too, dear, sweet little Cléo was on the same bill with us. I saw her in Monte Carlo when she was almost forty. She was still absolutely a little girl, tiny and nimble, smiling and fragile, fresh in spite of a few silver threads in her long plaits. She had just been

* Sem was a well-known caricaturist whose real name was Georges Gourset.

dancing very gracefully in a ballet of Paul Franck's. I congratulated her and we chatted for a minute or two: 'I have to go now,' she said in her little-girl's voice. 'I want to go back to the hotel to play with my dolls before dinner.' It wasn't a pose. Genuine puerility – not that it hadn't served some very dubious ends with men . . . but let's not go into that.

Max Jacob came with a friend of his called Herz, a writer and critic, rather scheming, who wants to undertake the sale of my house. Max looked well and was in very good form. Among other striking things, he said that there is something 'metallic' about Jews. He talked with me, too, about God, Jesus and the Church. He is very much a practising convert, but it is odd how when he talks to me about those things I feel embarrassed and a bit pained, as though he were making me an accomplice in a sacrilege.

. . . .

November 8. They are doing quite an interesting play of Jean-Jacques Bernard's at the Théâtre-Libre. It made me think of our friend Count Roman Potocki. When the Cossacks overran his estates (Lansut in Austria) they found everything they could wish for in the castle. Roman was already old, but great nobleman that he was, he received them generously, simply and without bravado. When they left, they damaged nothing. Most of the neighbouring land-owners had panicked and run away. Their properties were razed, looted, burnt. So the Austrians put their heads together, decided Roman must be suspect, and had his castle searched. He had to endure the sight of his beautiful Lansut taken over by the police who cruelly and systematically demolished the panelling, the floors, the chimney pieces, the ceilings, knocked down walls, took a criminal and brutal delight in ruining everything. Poor Roman was unable to stand the affront and the commotion. He quite simply died of it, victim of the war and of human stupidity.

He was a really great nobleman: such distinction of appearance, such charm! Roman had enormous chic. He was big in every way. A gambler! and he knew how to play. He adored Paris. He appeared there every year, the clubs welcomed him with delight. He used sometimes to play at Monte Carlo, too. I remember that when I was starring at the Folies-Bergère he appointed himself my *cavaliere servente*. Every day he would put aside five thousand francs from his baccarat money for the whims and the gloves of his little Lianon. He came to pick me up at the stage door and took me to supper at

Paillard's, saying: 'Lilisky, bring anyone you please: actors, actresses, writers, friends, whoever . . .' Sometimes there were twenty of us. Henri d'Orléans would rub shoulders with Sulbac, Mayo, Mimi Saint-Cyr. And Roman himself would help the waiters hand round the oysters and champagne so that the service could leave nothing to be desired. It was at Paillard's, and in that same room, that I wanted to have our wedding breakfast. To celebrate and bury the crazy life I had led as a dancer.

I loved him with an affection sincere enough to extend to his family. When I was in Lemberg I wanted to see their ancestral home. There was a great entrance on a beautiful cobbled street, and opposite it another great entrance. Their house, his house, a pair of beautiful, aristocratic old residences. Countess Yaworska, who was acting as my guide, told me: 'On rainy days, when the Potocki family wanted to go from one house to the other, they had themselves carried so that they wouldn't muddy their feet. You would see the old Countess coming out first in the arms of two footmen, followed by her green dwarfs, also being carried by two stout fellows; then came Clementine, Beta, Roman. A whole liveried household carrying Their Lordships, nonchalant and refined, dreading mud as much as a blot on the escutcheon.'

. . . . Roman's mother was a redoubtable old Boyar. Even in the years just before her death, her children still trembled before her. Very much a figure from the past, very grand, she lived shut away in her palatial house with some thirty servants and the two dwarfs dressed in apple green who never left her, slept in her bedroom and kept her amused. She spoilt them and tormented them by turns. They played tricks on everyone and the old Potocki adored them. I rather like the idea of that, I'd have enjoyed it. I made do with three Moors. The truth is that it was rather awkward, it can't work in our country. When my little Halima tried to poison my two Italian greyhounds, Madame Garat and my husband, I wanted to take a strong line and have her locked up. All Roscoff rebelled: there was talk of illegal restraint, tortures and cruelty. I fell back on a diet of dry bread: the men slipped her chocolate on the sly . . . Finally, quite discouraged, I sent her back to her family, her poverty and her rags . . . .

November 10. . . . . An excellent *choucroute* bubbling away with its hambone and its sausages, its aroma wafting up the stairs. In comes Georges, and starts giving orders, carping, disapproving and pulling a sour face into the bargain. I turned him out pretty smartly. He really does lack tact, that boy. He nags us pitilessly for misuse of the subjunctive and for the smallest domestic failing. Why isn't he sculpted in old wood? He'd give us much less trouble and the state of my nerves would improve!

. . . .

November 17. Little Maurice Rostand, as no one can fail to know, lost his father to the Spanish influenza last year. This young man is very exaggerated in his manners, his morals and his speech. One of his acquaintances invited him to a musical evening, highbrow, rather tempting. He hesitated, thought it over, and decided, 'No, my dear, I can't. I'm *madly* in mourning.'

Our cold baths have driven away the last signs of our colds. They are really marvellous if you can bear them. As the hour approaches we begin to paw the ground, nothing could rein us in, not the icy house, the pleading of our friends, our aches and pains – we disregard the lot. Undress very quickly, in and out! You emerge merry and brisk, refreshed and ready for anything, rather proud of your heroism. . . . .

. . . .

November 21. Salomon dropped in this morning. He brought us the latest volume of the *Chronologie de la guerre.* He is very upset by the behaviour of the Americans who are refusing to ratify the peace treaty and no longer want to belong to the League of Nations. The idea of which – so difficult to put into practice! – came from them. Evidently this young America is lacking in tact.

I distrust Americans. They are a bit childish. When they arrived in Vittel in August 1917, we happened to be there. It was the height of the season. They had been billetted pretty well everywhere and they were scattered all over the park, near the springs and in the restaurants. They received a fraternal welcome. People smiled at them, greeted them, overcharged them in the shops! One evening my husband was walking his little dog round the hotel when a charming Sammy came up to him and drawled: 'That's a very pretty little dog you have there, sir.' Georges smiled, much touched. Thus encouraged, the Sammy went on: 'You have also got a very pretty wife.' At that, Georges laughed aloud. They shook hands. The next day Lorenzo Thomson was waiting for us at the springs, introduced himself formally and became my *cavaliere servente.* Eight days later he asked me to divorce Georges and marry him. He might well have said to me what that rogue Goldschmidt said when I mentioned my age in order to discourage him. 'I prefer a woman of forty to two women of twenty!'

. . . .

November 25. No more punctuation! The literary pundits of futurism and cubism want no more of it!

Saw in the paper that Madame Jacques Goudstikker – fat old thick-lipped mother Goudstikker who guided me through the labyrinth of precious stones in the days of my youthful independence – is dead. Sarah spent many millions with them. I myself must have had about three million-worth of jewellery from them.

Lazarus, to whom I offered a beautiful copy of my *Idylle saphique* printed on vellum, has paid me huge compliments. He says that it is a very important document and very well composed. He was so caught up in it that he galloped through it in two hours, only to read it again in minute detail from beginning to end, immediately afterwards. It comes off, but because the subject is rather improper I fear that the only reason why it pleases sóme men so much is that it awakens the animal sleeping within them. . . . .

. . . .

December 1. My garden looks like a marsh and smells of mould and desolation. I don't know which saint to call on. Life is sad and difficult. Georges is very far from being a support. He has no strength. Nor has he any guile.

December 2. At midday it was five years since my child died for his country . . . I had gone out, I remember, to buy something for a layette we were putting together for a poor woman whose husband was at the front. Marguerite Godard was with me. Suddenly I felt the most violent pain in my bowels. Almost fainting, I gasped: 'Margot, I'm ill – take me somewhere quickly – into some concierge's, anywhere.' Margot, frantic, said: 'Princess, you are quite near home. Try to get there.' I got back into the house as mid-day struck (I have my son's little gold watch, found on him, half smashed and stopped at two minutes to twelve). I rushed into the bathroom; the pain had gone. I felt so tired and unstrung that I went to bed. I was knitting some little socks. At six in the evening the telephone rang. Georges went down, spoke, and came back, *green*!

He said: 'They want me to go to the town hall, straight away.' – 'Why?' – 'Something about – Marco.' He went even greener. 'He's dead!' – 'They didn't say so. He has had an accident.' – 'Go quickly . . . quickly!'

He left and my heart beat and beat enough to break. Mesdames Pernet (billed these days as Tonia Navar) and Gregory were with me. We kept saying it might be this or that – something less cruel. We waited. The two ladies got on my nerves, combing their hair, powdering their noses, watching my pain. Georges returned, staggering. 'Dead!' I exclaimed. 'Yes,' he said, hanging his head. 'Poor kid!' – and that was all I was able to say. Everything inside me was knotted and tense. No tears, no screams. I was bent double and couldn't straighten myself. Haunted by grief and every kind of regret, I suffered agonies for fifteen months, it nearly killed me. Ah! When it came to grieving I was a mother.

And what a way to break the news! No trouble taken, Georges summoned to the telephone and then to the town hall so that they could stun him by brutally thrusting this telegram at him: 'Inform Princess Ghika that her son, the aviator Marc Pourpe, fell gloriously on the field of battle at midday today and that the burial will take place at ten o'clock on Friday morning at Villers-Bretonneux.' Poor Georges, laden with his own despair as well as mine, could hardly stagger home.

Yesterday Salomon came in with a bunch of carnations for my hero. Fatoum and Rose followed, each with chrysanthemums. Georges has ordered a pot of flowers and I am going out to get another. He will be garlanded. His bedroom has to be his tomb because it is still impossible to move him and he lies down there in a vault belonging to strangers.

December 5. Joncières is having a bad time at the Comédie-Française. The papers say that it will be Ventura who will star in his play. Ventura, not Piérat, his beloved, his muse, his friend, the one and only, the most beautiful, the most inspired. There's been a falling-out, that's for sure; his heart must be bleeding. Not that he will lose by it with an interpreter like Ventura; subtle, very pretty, elegant, full of talent, better quality in every way than Piérat, and – a foreigner, which, with us, is always an added attraction. Ventura is a Roumanian Jewess, charming and much admired – and as for me, I acquire great merit by singing her praises because she used to be Georges's mistress. Oh, it was long ago – two years before we met, he and I. She was one of my friends. Retrospective jealousy? Once I knew Georges I never again wanted to look at her. Of course I'm silly to be jealous of Ventura, but even hearing her name spoken suffocates me! Is this stupid? I have to admit that it's the same with all of Georges's mistresses known to me.

These days the Americans consider D'Annunzio the greatest (or rather the most famous) man who ever was. During the war he was brave to the point of gallantry, for which he is forgiven a great deal.

I met him in Florence when I was dancing there. It was in 1902. Yesterday I came on a book which he gave me then: his *Francesca da Rimini*, bound in parchment tied with green ribbons, and copiously inscribed. I remember . . . he praised me for my corporeal grace – his expression – and invited me to visit his Capponcina. I accepted. He sent his carriage for me, filled with red roses. It was May 1st, which is the date of the rose festival in Florence. On my arrival I was greeted by workmen and young boys making a hedge between the gate and the front door of the house, all holding hand-fuls of roses which they threw at my feet. Inside, a 'poetic' décor, rather rubbishy and designed to impress. His conversation was marvellous. But there before me was a frightful gnome with red-rimmed eyes and no eyelashes, no hair, greenish teeth, bad breath, the manners of a mountebank – and a reputation, nevertheless, for being a ladies' man, and a man who was, to say the least, ungrateful to the ladies. I used every possible trick to resist him, and escaped by promising to return. Two days later he sent the same carriage for me. I substituted my maid for myself, with a note – a long note – saying: 'Stellio (the name of one of his heroes), that which has not been done is still to do . . . one day, no doubt, and why not . . . One cannot get used to such happiness all at once' – agreeable and un-compromising clichés. He had flown to the door to greet me and recoiled in furious dismay at the sight of my sniffy old Adèle. He pulled himself together and showed her the dinner which had been prepared, the table, the lit candles, the path I would have trodden spread with embroidered chasubles and scattered with rose petals (from the roses of two days earlier, no doubt). He gave her a folded paper for me containing these words: 'You light candles from afar, as well as near by. Take care. Stellio.' . . . .

It has happened – Carpentier has knocked out the Englishman. Splendid victory. Paris delirious with joy!

December 7. Here I am in bed for two days. Balthy calls it 'having your baddies'. She says it with a tiny touch of a Midi accent, which is irresistible! But like all women approaching old age, she speaks of it much more often than every twenty-eight days.

When I, a young Manon, arrived in Paris in 1890, Mademoiselle Balthy already had wrinkles, a public, a reputation, a tiny place of her own on the rue de Chazelles, a carriage and pair. I lived with a friend opposite, at number 34, two ground-floor windows and two rooms. I slept in the living-room (where we also ate) and used to fly to the window to admire Balthy as she came and went. The jingle of her horses' harness used to alert me. I remember her in a glossy, tight-waisted astrakhan jacket with velvet leg-o'-mutton sleeves. Oh, how beautiful I thought it! As soon as I could afford to buy myself something chic, that was what I started with. How proud I was to sport a garment costing more or less the same as Louise Balthy's! I was not yet twenty. As for the famous Louise, she must have been at least twenty-eight. And now . . . she is ten years younger than I am! And she says as much even as I quiz her with an indulgent smile. Afterwards she takes my hand, pulls a naughty face, looks me in the eye and pronounces in her beautiful contralto: 'Darling, how I do admire you!'. . . . .

I sent a pretty shell to Cocteau, who loves them. That was ten or twelve days ago, and still not a word. Poets are absent-minded – yet Cocteau is very fond of us.

Last April I invited him to dinner with my mother-in-law in Paris, at the Jean Simmonds's apartment which they lent us while they were in Haiti. Cocteau spoke of foreknowledge of events as though it were a scientifically established fact, explaining himself in these terms: 'For you, who don't know, it is folded up. I know, and for me it is unfolded. You understand?' Well, yes – we understood, but . . . what did it amount to?

Cocteau is a dazzling talker, passionate, ironic, vigorous, elegant and abundant. He is delicious, slightly . . . repulsive, and very disturbing. He will kill with a word, is immeasurably and ceaselessly wounding. His mockery is sharp and cruel, respects nothing, plays with everything.

December 8. In *Yvée Lester* I wrote: 'Friendship gives and receives.' Friendship does demand a reciprocal honesty and a certain amount of esteem. I admire the Rochegrosses. I thought I was friends with the Poirets, but it couldn't last. Salomon? I admire him, I adore him – is that friendship? Camille? Rather like Joncières – lost dogs – mangy dogs, adoption and pity. The Isch-Walls, yes. The de La Jailles, even more so. The Jean Simmondses? No, distrust reigns. The Rouveyres? Almost. My Flossie? Less and more. The list is open, never closed and often revised.

And then there is Lewis the milliner, whose flourishing career I have followed and fostered. He's one who has become a habit. I knew him at Nice; in the morning he himself would bring round two or three huge boxes of the exquisite hats he had made the night before. The creature had taste, and made us laugh. What a gossip he was, and how he laid on the flattery! One day he brought me a ravishing beret of plaid velvet. I was nineteen years old . . . I ordered six, in different colours, and coquettishly I flaunted them. Everyone wanted one!

My Lewis, who was living in the attic of a tenth-class boarding house, had to take on an apprentice and descend to the ground floor. Customers came in droves and remained faithful. His skill and his funniness kept them happy. He spread to Paris, rue Royale, could turn his hand to anything, travelled, was always there on great occasions and became 'fame-valet' (to borrow Jean Lorrain's title) to all the celebrities. He stuck by me, insinuated himself into Otero's favour, achieved Sarah, knew how to take advantage of everything, broadcast what he was meant to and concealed the rest. He became the indispensable confidant, the familiar.

He ran faster and faster, sped to Italy to make hats for queens and great ladies, then to Spain, followed the season wherever it was. He has become formidably rich. No one could possibly be more obliging, provided it costs nothing . . . but if it does his feathers ruffle, his buzzard's eye grows beady, his voice goes edgy and gruff, his words become stinging and perfectly clear. Taking shelter behind the solid defences of his greed, he backs out of sight for ever.

He has remained rather faithful to me, even though I never buy his hats any more. They are too showy for my age and my situation. He was a witness at my wedding. He gave me my big Louis-Sixteenth black straw hat, trimmed with a cluster of aigrettes. A week later he came to call on us. 'Princess, keep the hat, of course – but take off the aigrettes and let me have them back!' – 'Nuts to you, of course I won't' said I, quite the princess! 'But they are worth 1,200 francs. I told them to use only the best. Ah, if I had only known . . .' He looked so woe-begone that I laughed till I cried.

December 10. My niece Aimée writes to say that she is expecting a baby at the end of April.

Yesterday some people came to view my tapestries, panelling and groups of stone figures. I need to raise a hundred thousand francs in order to increase my income by six thousand francs and pay my new taxes more easily. I entertain my friends freely but modestly. In the past I served them peacocks dressed in their plumes, exquisite foie gras, champagne. Now everything is planned, costed and prepared economically, though pleasantly, because the exchange has ruined my husband and enraged my mother-in-law, who keeps her purse-strings knotted. The value of the shares I hold has dropped. Some – the German stock for example – bring in nothing. I find myself much impoverished, while still having the same needs. Before the war butter cost 1.40 francs a pound, now it costs 9 francs. I used to pay my cook 100 francs a month and that was a good wage; today I pay 300 and get little satisfaction for it. Everything else is in keeping, which is why we want to sell this big house, this lovely garden in which we are not happy, and adapt our way of life to the style of the times.

December 11. Salomon teases me rather about my religion which, according to him, is full of error and most untheological. I may not be a woman of great faith but I know I'm one of good faith. Marie Bashkirtseff believed deeply in God, which did not prevent her from consulting fortune tellers. That I do not tolerate. I don't deny that during my wild years, influenced by my friends, I have tried it. I came away sickened, feeling diminished, despising myself. Oh that visit to Madame de Thèbes, in that filthy, smelly little place on the Avenue de Wagram! Old house, dirty stairs, smell of frying. I could have cried! Common, crafty woman with a vulgar, snub-nosed face, foxy eyes, a gift of the gab, sly and pushy! Jean Lorrain wanted to be friends with her, more or less, in so far as someone of his intelligence can be friends with such a person! At least he used to see her quite often. She plumed herself on having been very close to Alexander Dumas. Lorrain inflicted her on me several times, among others at a dinner which took place at la Cascade, when Jean had primed her in advance about the lives of his guests. The prophetess held forth at length and told us extraordinary stories. There was a great admirer of Jean's there, the Baroness Boulard, a very rich widow fresh from the fields of the Landes. She had been married to a young lord of that region. The Thèbes woman, warned, could play that situation with one hand tied behind her. She did it so well that we were all overcome with admiration and the Baroness fainted. Complete success!

When I was taken home after two weeks in hospital, at the time of my car smash, all literary and artistic Paris came processing past my bed. The Thèbes woman got wind of it, and two days running she installed herself in the boudoir next to my bedroom. She clutched at people as they went by, introduced herself, intrigued them. One or two took off their gloves there and then, others made appointments. I was furious. She wanted to force herself on me and I was obliged to have her thrown out. Lorrain had died a few months earlier so I was not afraid of offending his friendly feelings for Madame de Thèbes – feelings which, in my opinion, didn't exist anyway, because Lorrain knew his world, manipulated it and made it dance to his tune like the clever Norman that he was.

December 12. The Prix Goncourt has gone to Marcel Proust. *A l'ombre des jeunes filles en fleurs* took all the votes. I am in the middle of reading it. It is dense, heavy going, elaborate – it's very good. One can point to something masterly on every page.

I once met Marcel Proust. He was, and no doubt still is, a friend of Reynaldo and of Madrazzo. He was always ill, shut away indoors, working without cease on the books he has published since then. My friends adored him. His delicate health and his retreat from the world made him seem a rare being in an ivory tower. It was the first night of Reynaldo's *la Carmélite* at the Opéra-Comique. I was there, very excited. Reynaldo, all in a twitter of nerves, had the kind thought of sending Marcel Proust to me in every interval (Proust had departed from custom for this great occasion) to give me his news, collect mine, learn what I was thinking, what my impressions were and those of my entourage. Proust brought the notes with a kind smile, transmitted my messages cheerfully. Everything went as well as could be. He gazed at me with his deep look, his deep blue look, very gentle and thoughtful. I knew the poetic and melancholy legend which surrounded him, and welcomed him with the most affectionate sympathy. I never saw him again, but I am very happy to have his talent and his success confirmed, and to learn that apparently he has overcome the illness which kept him down, isolated him and worried all his friends: bad nerves, persistent weakness, lack of vitality in short. A sort of 'brother-in-suffering' to myself.

December 15. I was not able to go to Mass, so to demonstrate my good will I went into the church during the afternoon. A priest was in the pulpit addressing the large congregation. I got only a confused impression of his words, but the sound of his voice prevented me from praying; so I left after making a short little act of deference in honour of my promise.

It's at night, in bed, that I pray best. I feel nearer to God's presence then. Yes, sometimes in the solitude and silence of the night I am able to pray with fervour. Out of doors, too, under the sky and among trees, in the wide open spaces, words come to me easily and soar upwards. At those times it seems to me that God is present and hears them at once. In church – that is something else again. The music, the flowers, the beadle, the handsome Swiss, the scraping of chairs, the organ . . . I am no longer there. For me, church is a duty which one has to perform. I am able to feel neither fervent nor attentive, but I know that it is good and necessary to be there, as our Church directs.

December 17. Gaby Deslys, the pretty Parisian doll, the richest actress in France, the one with the most pearls and doubtless the most enviers, is at the point of death.

Madame Charron, my new caretaker, is going to help in the house. She is the cousin of Madame Martet, wife of the Martet with whom we had our famous 'little hat' row and who perhaps was the cause of my getting married. I must tell that story once and for all.

It was Easter Monday. Georges, Liane de Pougy and la Gigolette [Blanche d'Arvilly] had lunched in Saint-Germain, done the rounds of the antique shops, and were proceeding sedately along the rue au Pain to take a four o'clock cup of chocolate at Jousset's. I was wearing a little black hat trimmed with coarse white lace, very simple, today's sort of hat although it was 1910, that swashbuckling period of wide brims, etc. We passed two stout parties beplumed with ostrich, who pointed at me, burst out laughing and said in a loud voice: 'Just look at that hat! It's Liane de Pougy, the Paris tart.' Georges heard, stared at them and exclaimed 'You should take a look at yourselves before insulting other people.' Their two husbands were behind them. One of them, Martet, threw himself on Georges swearing blue murder and punched him on the jaw. Georges, stunned, was unable to defend himself because in one hand he was carrying two ravishing East India Company salt cellars and in the other two pretty Directoire miniatures. Blanche called for help. I must certainly have done the same. A policeman appeared at last and took us, at our bidding, to the station. Explanations, reports, legal action. Georges was bleeding, old Martet was frothing at the mouth. He was quite a drinker at the best of times, and had been celebrating Easter Monday with friends. The fresh air, and rage, had undone him. We all appeared in court equipped with lawyers, the Paris press attended in full strength. It was there, in front of the magistrate, that we became acquainted with the talented humourist Géo de La Fouchardière. There were witnesses a-plenty in our favour; we won. I shared the money out among the poor people of Roscoff, where I was when it arrived, having no wish to pocket my dear defender's 'blood money'.

The papers snatched at the chance to spread themselves in nasty gossip about both our exposed personalities. They poured out low envy, old grudges, every sort of spite to their hearts' content. Our allies joined battle, which prolonged it all. I was often irritated and saddened. Georges, who admired me as much as he loved me, said to himself: 'It is not fair, I am going to put matters right with one gesture which will place her above all these allegations.' Six weeks later he married me. Naturally there was a veritable storm of articles, gossip from dear old pals, gloomy predictions from our friends. We received a number of coarse and threatening anonymous letters.

Time passes . . . My private happiness endures in spite of all, in spite of everyone! Basically that disparaged, vilified, much-sued Liane had all the makings of a good wife – credit which I must now share with my equally abused little companion.

Georges has invited Cocteau to come to lunch on Christmas Day. Jean answered with a friendly, charming, affectionate, even tender note which said in effect: 'I will come if I have nothing else to do and if the Christmas Eve party to which I may be dragged doesn't tire me too much.'

As for Max Jacob, he writes: 'Ought I to bring holly or a poem? Cocteau says I should bring the poem, I have written it.' They enjoy our company and are happy to see us, but not if they have to catch a train, so tiresome! Saint-Germain is remote, in the provinces – in the eyes of a cool, calculating friendship. Coming here is a proof of attachment.

December 22. First day of winter. It is mild. Yesterday evening the storm started up again, very violent, making me think of my fierce Roscoff.

I have had a horrid accident. I was combing my hair in Georges's study, using the comb from my chignon. As I smoothed the hair over my temples the comb hit the corner of my eye. I went into my boudoir, looked in my dressing-table mirror and saw something horrible: the corner of my eye was nothing but a great bubble of blood which was swallowing up all the white. We telephoned Venot who came running. I really have wounded my eye, but not in a way to affect my vision. The blood has spread right over the eye and will take a long time to clear away. I see clearly, praise God, that is what matters. Only my beauty has suffered. It is impressively hideous.........

December 24. Dear Father Christmas, heal my eye! Father Christmas of my childhood, of my ancestors, of my church, bring me a brand new eye, all white and purified, or else the great courage needed to accept it cheerfully as it is! It is ugly and disgusting! I'm starting to jib a little.........

The turkey has arrived, superb, fat, heavy. Raoul [de Galland] has brought three magnificent truffles from Paris, so we are going to give it the treatment it deserves. Let us console ourselves with food, which is also a gift from God. Raoul has also ordered a hundred oysters from Prunier's. I supply the traditional sausage on a bed of sautéed apples. Georges has bought a beautiful plum-pudding which he will set alight with Simmonds' rum. The champagne comes from Mariette, who would be enraged to know that something of hers was contributing to my little family reunion. Particularly as we shan't drink her health!

December 25. Father Christmas!!! My eye is pure tomato sauce. Too sad! We gave our presents yesterday evening. Great excitement over wrapping them up and keeping them hidden from each other. After dinner we set off in single file on the hunt for our shoes. So that is the modest Christmas of 1919's New Poor! ....

A mild, snowless Christmas. An intimate Christmas. I wore a dress of mouse-grey velvet. Max Jacob arrived with a beautiful holly tree. I feel as grateful to him for having transported it as for having chosen it. The dear boy is earning money and delights in spending it and in spoiling his friends. He went into the kitchen to wish Rose and Fatoum a happy Christmas, and scattered them with hundred-sous notes. He is selling his paintings. He is getting masses of orders and opened his wallet to show us with evident enthusiasm that it was stuffed with banknotes. He said: 'Look how many I have! I have heaps of them, and I'm going to get more!'

Cocteau didn't come. A long telegram at about four o'clock explaining that after celebrating Christmas Eve he woke late and harassed, and demanding that we send him word that we forgive him.

Max surpassed himself. Raoul played the piano, improvising on themes he set, and Max, in the artificial kind of voice used by masks, recited very funny little burlesque verses which made us roar with laughter. He was in a mood of boundless and amusing vitality. After 'The Jealous Vizir' he gave us 'The Little Cabinet Maker in the Forest' and 'The Aristocratic Motor Car with the Drawn Blinds', etc. Then he invented snatches of conversation between two dancers while Raoul played a slow waltz.

Max had an important engagement in Paris at six o'clock. He remembered it – at ten past six! So he stayed to dinner with us, was charming all the time and told us a play of his which is soon going to be put on by Barbazanges, Poiret's tenant in the faubourg Saint-Honoré. Our Christmas was gay, witty, graceful and affectionate. Georges was witty. Speaking of Baudelaire he called him 'the Musset of horror'. Neat? But a bit unfair.

December 29. Gaby Deslys becomes iller and iller. Perhaps it will be her fate to be spared old age and an actress's retirement, which is like burial.

I am reading Pascal's *Pensées*. I have begun his 'conversion of a sinner'. It could well be applied to me . . . but why are these pages, and all writing concerning religion, so full of exhortations to humble and abase yourself, to fall on your knees and smite your breast? Does God really want that from His creatures?

They say that D'Annunzio, like Napoleon, has been abandoned by all his friends. He continues, nevertheless, to live in Fiume.

December 30. I have read Max Jacob's *la Défense de Tartuffe*, which has just been published in its complete form. It is good. The passage about humility which I already knew is certainly the best part of it. The book is meant to be religious, but is it? The faith which Max has inside him fails to inspire him with a very sincere tone. One is always being shocked. I think he's aiming for 'the primitive' and one wonders if he is being serious, if he is being ironical. To my mind his writing is full of double meanings, dishonest, studied and without passion. Some of the prose is fine – is magnificent. He has made me think. According to him, too, it is necessary to humble oneself because of the sin one is constantly committing.

Confession bores me, and the mass, too, costs me an effort – I am not making progress on that road; I reproach myself for it. I am a poor soldier, at the least excuse I swing the lead. I don't rally properly to my flag, and I take the punishment for it inside myself: I am not happy.........

....

1920

〜〜〜〜〜〜〜〜〜〜〜〜〜〜〜〜〜〜〜〜〜〜〜

Saint-Germain – January 1 to March 14

January 1. My God, I ended the year straining towards You, and that is how I want to start the year which begins today. My God! Bestow Your blessing on me and mine. Give us the strength to stay upright when it is stormy and good when we are happy.

Georges wrote me a beautiful letter. In the small hours of the New Year he came to kiss my forehead, my hands and my feet. Then we both went back to sleep. On waking I said my prayers, in my own way as always. Then the little ones came in to kiss me and give me their good wishes: I gave them presents of money.

January 8. Gaby Deslys has been saved: I wonder whether her near approach to the great mysteries will change and convert her? What an example she would provide if she sold her pearls and her real estate in order to give to the poor.

The really poor? They no longer exist! Washerwomen wear silk stockings, my butcher has bought herself a car. At Christmas and New Year my husband's barber sold his whole stock of madly expensive perfumery, above all Coty's which is prohibitive, to work-men. They eat roasts at forty francs, and the best poultry, go to the cinema several times a week, etc. Most of them, particularly the young couples, don't want possessions and choose to live in furnished rooms. They have got their insurance, haven't they? Their pensions, the backing of the boss? It is a change in the French character. As Lazarus wrote to me yesterday in his witty way: the shoemaker is getting the pleasure of the financier's money without the worry of it.

January 9. The Austrians have enough supplies left for only three weeks. After that it will be famine and people are saying that it could spread like an epidemic. At the word 'famine' I prick up my ears and hurry off to the grocer's. I do not approve of people who hoard too much, but one must have a little foresight. Georges laughs at me.

January 11. Like every morning I have had my enema, in order to preserve a clear skin and sweet breath. It is a family habit, approved of by Dr Pinard. One of Maman's old great-aunts, the beautiful Madame Rhomès, died at the age of ninety and a half with a complexion of lilies and roses, skin like a child's. She took her little enema, it seems, at five o'clock every evening, so that she would sleep very well. She did it cheerfully in public. She would simply stand in front of the fireplace; her servant would come in discreetly, armed with the loaded syringe; Madame Rhomès would lean forward gracefully so that her full skirts lifted, one two three, and it was done! Conversation was not interrupted. After a minute or two my beautiful ancestress would disappear briefly, soon to return with the satisfaction of a duty performed.

Salomon told me a very charming saying of Flossie's. When Rita Harry, a woman of letters, asked her for an interview, Flossie, who detests curiosity, hit on this delicious way of answering: 'You must forgive me if I refuse to disappoint you.'

. . . .

January 16. I have taken a grave decision. Georges is stunned by it. I no longer want to sell my house. Yes, that is it! I have made a thorough examination of my feelings and I have come up with the following scheme: sell ten thousand metres of the grounds. That will abolish the cost of a gardener-caretaker. All I shall need then will be a man one day a week. What is more, it will reduce my taxes, augment my income. It is common sense. Because I cannot find the maid of all work I am looking for, I stop making use of my third floor. My little ones' work will become much lighter and easier with seven fewer rooms to keep up. I will arrange the rooms thus: kitchen, maid's room and boxroom, dining-room, drawing-room (these two delightfully proportioned rooms opening onto the beautiful terrace which overlooks my rosebeds), one big bedroom, one small one, a hall and a W.C. Every summer I will let them furnished for three months. That will cover my taxes.

No sooner decided than done. I hurried off to see a letting agency. Like Diogenes I set about looking for a man – that is to say, an upholsterer-furniture-remover-handyman – and I have found one Souris, with whom I have made an appointment for Monday. Georges is dumb with disapproval. What a wet blanket he is!

Furniture has been dancing in my head all night. I am happy, agitated, in a fever. I feel strong and resolute; I crush Georges with my scorn; I win him over to my cause. He has started to move and measure furniture. It is the thought of a tenant which ruffles him. Yet it is reasonable and carefully thought out.........

January 17. We are busy; we are exhausted. I have stripped my Marco's room. It wrenched my heart. Five years, and already I am demolishing – I am displacing his memory. I am putting it in the forgetting-box which, no doubt, I shall be unwilling to open ever again. And that is life, and that is for the best.

January 19. France has a new president: Deschanel! Father Clem has resigned on the eve of a set-back, rather angry. The preliminary scrutiny which took place yesterday revealed that he had a minority of nineteen. An inexplicable minority, but undeniable.

January 20. The house-moving has begun. My well-kept house in which we use so much bees-wax, so much turpentine, so many dusters, so many brooms, as soon as we start moving furniture my poor house reveals great clots of dust! It's heart-breaking.

This morning, when my face was dirty, my hair was a mess and my hands were black, Salomon suddenly loomed up before me in the open doorway. Pleasure equalled embarrassment. He understands this kind of thing and approves of the effort and the trouble we are taking. His visit relaxed me a bit. He talked to me about Flossie, whom he finds slightly tired, and about the election of the President of the Republic. In his opinion the right thing would have been for us to elect Clemenceau and then for him to resign after a few days. Concerning Flossie and her return from America, her friend Madame de Clermont-Tonnerre who travelled with her has given an interview in *Excelsior* about her impressions. She seems to have been wonder-struck; hardly surprising, in Flossie's company. She was enchanted by all the little details. For instance here, when we go for a drive in a motor-car, we are condemned first to bad roads, then to stopping in villages and getting out to ask the grocer who is sometimes kind enough to come and empty smelly cans into the fuel tank. Over there it is done as though by magic. You stop in front of a building, put the necessary money into a hole, turn a tap, and the liquid pours itself just where it ought!

I have begun a book by Rudyard Kipling. The brutal strength of his new ideas cracks my brain. I do like progress, but you need to slip into it gently, install yourself comfortably without being deafened and shaken up. No doubt I belong to my time, I mustn't be hustled too much. Certainly the wood fire which crackles in my room every evening, throwing its pretty lights, is much more to my taste than some disgusting stove! ....

January 23. .... This day, the anniversary of the death of Louis XVI, brings back memories of my childhood in that corner of Brittany where all the old, right-minded families indicated their respectful mourning by keeping their shutters closed all day, going to mass dressed in black and doing penance to compensate for France's criminal gesture. My mother, my old aunts and their friends set the example. My youth and cheerfulness were put to a hard test. Faces had to be long. Only the humble folk were allowed the privilege of passing this day comfortably, but they were regarded with an indulgent and disdainful pity.

I once knew an indirect descendant of Louis XVI, even knew him quite intimately. He was the eldest son of the Duc de Chartres, that charming Prince Henri d'Orléans who went exploring in Africa in the direction of Abyssinia. Sadly enough, he died down there, like the young Duc Jacques d'Uzès who preceded him by some years. Henri d'Orléans pursued me and loved my beauty, my wit and my delicacy. True descendant of Henri IV that he was, he had heaps of passions, but his faithful friendship gave the little dancer-mime at the Folies-Bergère a sort of halo. He used to write to me from those distant lands, tell me his exotic experiences, give me his books (he published several accounts of his travels). One day he sent me some heavy bronze rings and some circlets of old yellow ivory, saying: 'I have brought you back bracelets from your Abyssinian sisters, you won't think them very elegant. Use them for paper-weights.' I still have them at Roscoff; they are precious on the days when the wind rages.

Another time he gave me a white poodle from Syracuse, bought from a circus trainer. I couldn't keep it, it was so vicious. The mountebank must have beaten it dreadfully. Henri sent it to me washed, combed and tied with sky-blue ribbon, accompanied by these words in a letter: 'I belong to Liane de Pougy. I want to live for her. I know how to jump very high through a hoop of flaming paper, climb a ladder and count to twenty.' At first I was enchanted – then I had to think twice. The animal went for people's throats. It knocked down Emilienne d'Alençon and bit my butler. He opened the door for it and the animal flew out and ran away – to the house of the Duc de Chartres! Henri caught it and sent it back, thinking that it had escaped. Then I told him everything and begged him to rid me of it. He took it back, a little vexed I think, and after that gave me easier presents.

January 24. I slept badly and I prayed. I prayed to God and to Saint Anne of Auray. I consider her kind and merciful; God seems to me severe and alarming. My heart shuts against Him. The opposite of the state of grace. Instead of blessing, I curse, instead of praying I argue. Then I lament over myself and cry: 'Saint Anne, lead me to God bound hand and foot, grant me the blind faith of the simpler people whom I envy.' My God, I perceive You dimly, through trouble and discontent. I want to come to You, so do not hold me off like this!

Organizing all this furniture-moving, and actually doing it, is good for the nerves. My little kitchen is nearly done. It will be ravishing. The walls will be painted a sunny yellow; soon the windows will open onto a cloud of Persian lilacs which will fill the room with their scent. My tenants will be enviable!

January 30. Something strange is up: for some time the wireless telegraph has been registering mysterious signals. Our learned men wonder whether we are in communication with a planet – Mars, it would be. Oh, how wonderful it would be to see that in one's lifetime! There are people who laugh and think it's a hoax, but I prefer the explanation which gives my imagination play.

January 31. Henry Bataille has just put on a play, *l'Animateur*, which everyone is talking about. His beloved, his muse, Yvonne de Bray, plays the leading role. It is a huge success, the reviews are glowing. Bataille never writes anything commonplace. Yvonne is at the top of her form and has talent, certainly: their union is a fortunate one for them and for the public too.

I no longer care much for the theatre. In the last five years life had given us so much drama! I prefer the entertainment of a café-concert, amusing numbers, good, silly, funny popular songs. The variety programme at the Olympia attracts me; I shall try to get to a matinée some time this week. A new attraction, a Spanish woman, is spoken of very highly: Madame Raquel Meller.........

Sacha has a new play on: *Béranger*. Yvonne Printemps gives a clever performance in it as Lisette. The great Lucien Guitry plays Talleyrand; Sacha is Béranger. I am very fond of them in a sort of way, based on a sort of admiration. I know their defects and am indifferent to them; their good qualities interest me to the highest degree. They have always been charming to me. The father calls me 'Beauty'; the son tells me 'Nothing is prettier than you are'. Little 'springtime' smiles nicely at me. They make much of me and send me seats. At the time of Georges's operation they made the touching gesture of sending me a *pneu* as full as could possibly be of affection.

February 1. Salomon came and I had him to myself almost the whole time. He talked about Flossie: she is preparing two books full of marvels.

Salomon is not pleased with my poor little naïve faith. He thinks it is a pity that a soul of my temper should be so given to nonsense. He quotes passages from the Bible and makes me put my finger on errors and contradictions. What do I care for the Bible, sermons, conventions? I draw my consoling faith from the vanquishing of my own strength. Dear Salomon, don't blow away my pathetic conviction, so frail and weak. I have had so much trouble bringing it to this point. All my family believed in God, and served Him; I choose to stand beside them.

. . . .

February 6. A lovely time at the Olympia. Good, amusing, varied programme: acrobats, shadow-play, songs, dances and Raquel Meller who was worth the journey. She is fragile, tall and magnificent, taking, touching. One's heart aches for this frail and slender creature whose whole being lights up at the word 'love', who shudders so painfully at the sorrow of love, who is left shattered by the beloved's death. A great artiste. She deserves her reputation. Her Spanish costumes are ravishing and underline her performance. She has fine, elongated features, eyes which are large and luminous, a rather poor mouth, sad when she isn't smiling, and very sober gestures. Her voice is fluent and pearly, grave even on the high notes, effortless, as though she knows profoundly well how to project it. Bravo Raquel Meller! It's a pleasure to have seen her.

Ozenfant writes to us on behalf of Max Jacob who is at Lariboisière afflicted with two broken collar-bones and a congestion of the
lungs. The poor dear was on his way to see the Russian ballet at the
Opéra, in top-hat and tails, when a car ran over him and now he is in
a public ward with his top-hat and tails perched sadly on a chair
beside his bed, his body mangled, his fever high, reduced to pain
and immobility. He is thinking of us. He knows that we will feel for
his sufferings. I am about to despatch a messenger with letters and
fruit. We are too fragile to risk going there ourselves. Georges and I,
who sped off to see Raquel Meller, haven't the energy to visit Max
and I know that we are not going to have it. We are going to write
to tell him that we love him and that we have caught colds.

We will take trouble for him. I have just prepared a beautiful
basket of choice, juicy, golden fruit for him. He has my affection and
some of my anxiety, but I shall not go to see him. I am woman
enough to take him in to my home and nurse him through his
convalescence if necessary, but not to go to that place. I really do not
understand myself. If loving is preferring another person to oneself,
as Tolstoy says, then I don't love him; and yet his fate, his
appearance, often move me almost to tears.

February 8. Yesterday my little Charron went to Lariboisière. He
saw Max Jacob who was talking to a friend. He was short of breath.
He has been forbidden to tire himself and his oranges have been
confiscated. Tomorrow I will send him some huge grapes, with a
note.

I am exerting myself to make him feel that our friendship is on
the alert, but . . . we do not budge. He will need at least a month
in hospital. Then it will be less cold, and if he wants to come and
convalesce here I shall invite him and look after him to the best of
my ability. I have already had him at Roscoff for two months. He
was calm and good-tempered and buried himself in the library –
and managed, nevertheless, to make himself insufferable. Sharp
words, quarrels, sulks . . .

February 10. At this moment I adore Max Jacob. I will be judged
inconsistent, changeable, crazy. I have fulminated against the poor
devil in my time . . . Everything is different. I am sensitive to a
fault, influenced by the day and the event. This poor, crushed Max,
I love! I began to love him when I saw him again last year and he
had risen somewhat above his material misfortunes, had started to

earn his living – and his socks. Before that he used to wear his friends' socks and underwear, their old clothes. I was sorry for him but I found that ignoble and it hurt me to see a gifted man so bogged down. I found him repugnant and turned away from him angrily. Now he has freed himself from Picasso and his charity, from Poiret and his old neckties. Since his painting sells, he has been painting and has thus been able to continue the philosophical and poetic lucubrations which bring him in nothing beyond admiration. His accident has moved me very much and I am going to prepare a pretty, sunny, white and red bedroom for him on my second floor, for a sweet, affectionate convalescence in the fresh air. I will plan meals and flower arrangements for him, delights, instant satis-factions; in fact I will take – with a great deal of pleasure – a lot of trouble for him and he will not feel the effort in it.

. . . .

February 12. Letter from Max, highly delighted about coming here for his convalescence. His accident was dreadful. He was crossing the boulevard de Clichy on his way to the Russian ballet when he found himself threatened by five or six cars, took fright and clutched at the headlamp of the one nearest him. The driver didn't stop, Max fell, the vehicle went over him, he fainted after seeing 'all the under-parts of that car', he says jokingly. When he came to himself he was lying in the Place Pigalle surrounded by three hundred people. He was rushed to the Lariboisière. The brutal driver was chased and caught, he will be sued. Max is happy in hospital, he is drawing a little with his undamaged right hand; he has lots of visitors; he makes jokes; he wins hearts. He is allowed one visitor a day and more on Sundays and Thursdays. His friends come crowding in and spoil him. He prays; not for a minute does he complain. I have written a rather reassuring letter to his mother because in spite of their incessant arguments the old lady will be anxious. Of course I know that distance lends enchantment, but I am infinitely fond of Madame Jacob; she may not be the mother he would have chosen, but his mother she certainly is.

February 13. Gaby Deslys is dead. Never will she know the wrinkles of old age, and all they bring, and all they drive away.

. . . .

February 16. . . . . Lazarus informs me that I ought to sell at once in order to buy more Royal Dutch, and some Central Mining. I had said to him: 'I never touch anything of yours any more, life is so expensive.' [Lazarus dealt in jewellery] – 'All right, how much do you need a month?' – 'Not much, I could make do with twenty-five louis.' – 'Very well, you will have them, and without loss of capital, you are reasonable.' He explained to us that Tanganyika is a lake in the Belgian Congo surrounded by a very rich subsoil and that it has a tremendous future in the production of copper, coal and tin. The way he spoke inspired confidence.

. . . .

February 21. The town of Tourane has sent me a very beautiful letter of thanks. At Lorient, where my son was born, there was to start with some question of naming a street after him. There were man-oeuvrings and discussions. Finally this is what they came up with for me: 'We will wait for the end of the war so that we can choose among the heroes of Lorient.' Then last year the mayor came to see me and gave me to understand with considerable clumsiness that all I had to do was make over a hundred thousand francs to the town of Lorient and the thing was done. I gave this person a vague – oh, a very vague! – answer, showed him out and left it at that. I have absolutely no intention of stripping myself because my child died for France!

February 22. Yesterday, day in Paris.

We trooped off to the Champs-Elysées theatre, a pretty theatre up on the sixth floor. Cocteau's show has the very latest thing in music: overture by Poulenc. We expected something eccentric but it was charming, a flight of elegance. Then came songs by Cocteau interpreted by Koulitzki in a beautiful voice slightly muffled by influenza, to pleasant music by Auric. That was all. Childlike word-play by Cocteau: '*Miel de Narbonne, bonne d'enfant, enfant de troupe*, etc,' ending with this phrase dropped as though at random: '*Le trapèze ensense la mort*' – felicitous, and impressive. It was madly crowded. Friends came up to congratulate me on my appearance. I was the smartest: sable coat and shift-dress of glittering silver material with a large black pattern: a simple style with a touch of the medieval, clear-cut lines. It suits me better than elaboration and it's never out of fashion . . . . Saw Henri Bernstein and his wife whom I couldn't find pretty however hard I tried: little shopgirl's face, badly proportioned features, not ugly, not handsome, insignificant.

Women nowadays are so commonplace! Monsieur and Madame Valette (she is Rachilde of the *Mercure de France*) were sitting in front of me. We exchanged opinions, ran down Ajalbert, admired Flossie whom they see often, and waited for the rest of this charming and revealing show. Two clowns dressed all in black did marvellous tricks to music by Auric. That was good. The very young leader of the orchestra was extremely good looking and graceful. I leant forward and said to Rachilde: 'Look at the leader of the orchestra, he's the image of my son.' – She answered: 'Your son must be better looking than that.' – 'He was killed in the war, alas.' The little shock made her give me a very quick kiss on the cheek, then she sat back, thoughtful.

And we felt the same about Colette Willy, too – her insincerity, her affectations, her talent in spite of all, and her infernal spitefulness. The next part of the show was three pieces by Eric Satie, encored and much applauded. The composer had to come down into the auditorium. I had met him before. He pressed our outstretched hands warmly, thanked us for our compliments and withdrew, happy at his success. He was first introduced to us on a less triumphant occasion, at the Ballets Russes, that famous performance of *Parade* – Cocteau again – which was whistled, hooted and shouted down so that we could hear nothing of the music. To end with, a coarse farce entitled *le Boeuf sur le toit*, the characters in carnival costumes with enormous cardboard heads. It was coarse, childish, not new, not funny. I'd much rather have *Parade*. Darius Milhaud's music, which was played alone at first, was pretty and alive and could only lose by this buffoonery. It had its longeurs, but it gave the impression of a crowd, a multitude, masks, tragedy, comedy, which the action spoilt and diminished. To sum up, the musical side of the show was brilliant, full of charm and talent; but Jean Cocteau's side of it, to be honest, was deplorable. Parts of his books are admirable. There he has a dazzling gift, a new and bizarre kind of talent. He touches the sublime and overleaps good sense. He should stick to that. But . . . he is so completely *Parade*! He needs the stage, the scenery, the noise, a tickled public. Rachilde said: 'He knows his public and what it likes, he's rubbing our noses in absurdity.' These words and her amused attitude enraged Georges. But there was something in it, all the same.

February 23. Read in the papers yesterday that my friend the Duke of Oporto had died at the age of fifty-five, an exile in Italy. I was assailed by a thousand memories: my travels to Portugal, staying in the palace at Ajuda, the friendship of that good fellow, that bear not quite licked into shape with his simple emotions, our evening drives in the country, along the banks of the Tagus. He drove a phaeton with a team of high-spirited and beribboned mules, and their bells were muffled (see *Idylle saphique*) because the revolution was brewing, anarchy was grumbling. It smacked of ambushes, assassinations. Alfonso had preserved the spirit of a child in his sportsman's body. I remember noticing one day that his ears, cheeks, nose, fingers were covered with thousands of tiny pricks and scratches. When I asked him what they were, he told me: 'I'm raising rats, twenty of them, and sometimes they hurt me.' – 'But why are you raising rats?' – 'Because on Easter Day I'm going to send them to old Countess X, hidden in a basket of flowers.' – '?????' – 'She has said very nasty things about my mother (Queen Maria Pia), my brother (King Carlos, who has been assassinated since then) and me.' A prince's revenge! A courtly pastime!

I saw him carrying a wardrobe on his back when two of his servants had been unable to lift it, and freeing the mule-carriage by putting his shoulder to it when it was stuck in the mud. In civilian clothes he looked like any fat bourgeois. It amused him when he was not recognized and could fool about without constraint. If he met a pretty theatre colleague at one of my tea parties or receptions, and I asked him next day if he had liked her, he would answer candidly: 'Yesterday I liked her a lot; I had supper with her. Today she doesn't look so good.'

He was unable to come to Paris, the Paris of his dreams, very often; his means were limited. But they would send him to the English court with a wedding present, to the German court with a christening present, and that gave him delightful holidays. He pinched and scraped out of his travelling expenses so that he could stay longer in our capital. We often had a good laugh together, going over his accounts and the risks he took with them.

Once he made me come to Lisbon. He was not at the station, as he usually was. He was not in the hotel suite which he had reserved for me and filled with flowers and chocolates. They brought me a letter: 'I've got rather a headache, I'll come in a day or two.' I was so vexed that I was thinking of catching a train home after a short rest, when I was summoned to the Ajuda palace. A closed carriage was waiting for me. I jumped into it, arrived, and there was my Alfonso with his forehead laid open, minus the lobe of one ear, his face wrapped in bandages, one eye closed. 'What on earth . . . ? An assassination attempt?' – 'No, something in my motor-car blew up in my face.' He called that having 'rather a headache'.

He was my sincere and devoted friend and could refuse me nothing. He would have made a detestable lover, chasing any skirt which passed. When he was in Paris he indulged in it to his heart's content and every morning at ten o'clock he came to my little house in the rue de la Néva, sat beside my bed, listened to my news, gave me his, read me the newspaper and took my commissions. He adored his mother and always felt like a little boy when he was with her . . . .

February 25. It's going wrong with Max Jacob. He is becoming impertinent. He feels that I am cossetting him and he is taking advantage of it. The other day he wrote complaining about how disgusting the hospital food is, and saying: 'I'm longing to eat some meat cooked by *people*.' I went off to the butcher and bought pork at 8 francs a pound, to the poulterer and bought a chicken for 18 francs, to the other butcher to buy rump steak. Fatoum roasted it all during the afternoon. We cut it up and arranged it in a charming china dish which we will never see again; we despatched young Marcel Charron who has to be paid for his trouble, he took it there, handed it over, Max opened it and pushed it away saying: 'But it's Lent, I can't eat that.' He distributed it round the ward. I am not complaining, but what manners! That renegade Jew is more Catholic than the Pope! A sick man, crushed, with congestion of the lungs, doesn't have to fast – and a man should always remember his manners!

. . . .

February 27. Max Jacob got Ozenfant to telephone us and let us know that he was very ill, that they have given him two punctures without much success and that they are going to give him two more. A pulmonary complication.

The poor boy must have had a temperature when he wrote us that vehement letter. I don't hold it against him, but I would rather not have someone to stay who is so irritable and still so delicate. Above all I owe it to myself to keep well so that I can care for my family, those nearest to me, those whom God has chosen to collect around me and in my house. The latter has become very precious to me since it escaped the profanation of being sold. I think it more beautiful, I adorn it, move the furniture around, take pleasure in it, embrace it symbolically, air it, warm it. It smells good, it is spacious and light. Every corner is tidy and clean. It was in ruins when I bought it, and I restored it. It is mine, I shall keep it.

. . . .

March 2. The spring doesn't suit Georges: he is grumpy, discontented, languid, disagreeable, boring. He will read these lines and learn what I think. I think this stupid boy eats enough for four, takes no exercise, that at this time of year it is a good thing to take a purge and that he's sticking in his toes. To think that the happiness one expects from a man depends on castor oil or some sort of pill or salts! . . . .

March 3. Max Jacob is calmer and seems to be sorry for his outburst. He's almost apologizing. I have sent him an affectionate answer. Poor Max, he really is too weak and wounded to return to the usual course of his bohemian life.

March 4. Yesterday morning I went out early, exasperated by Georges's tiresomeness.

I bought some thick English tweed with a black stripe making a large check in the latest fashion. Rose will make it up into a skirt for me, and I'll wear it with a black silk sweater and cardigan. It will modernize them a bit.

On my return I had the nice surprise of finding my Salomon. I had been to see a delicious little old house which is up for sale. I like it immensely, but it's Cadet Rousselle's house without floors or ceilings. The price – including the most urgent of the necessary repairs – would come to between two hundred and two hundred and twenty thousand francs. It encloses a square courtyard, there is enough garden, a cedar tree, a splendid wistaria, old panelling, four ancient mirrors, five or six old chimney-pieces, and a roof of mellow tiles which any collector would love to lay his hands on. The roof is collapsing, of course. The whole thing is in a lovely countrified style, very snug, well planned, designed for a peaceful life in well-earned comfort, and it would all have to be done over.

Salomon admired my material; Georges too, but he doesn't like the idea of a home-made skirt at a bargain price – the dago!

Salomon teased me about the versatility of my decisions; not to sell my house, to sell it, to buy another. Look: if someone will pay me a very good price for my house, 700,000 for instance, I'll sell it; I will invest 500,000 francs through Lazarus and I'll buy the old house which is better proportioned, more secluded, more intimate than my Noailles folly which is only a small bit of a castle chopped off when the road was built, nothing more, really, than a stub-end of a house.

March 8. At about five o'clock the bell gave a feeble tinkle. Georges hurried to look out of the window and came back quite overcome: 'It's that poor Max clasping a sheaf of flowers in his damaged arms!'

I flew to let him in. The poor dear boy, thrilled to see us again, thinner, nervous, out of hospital on Friday, had made the great, the beautiful, the touching, the elegant gesture of staggering all the way from Paris with a heavy pot of azaleas in his arms. There are simply no words to depict what I felt at the beauty of it. He wanted to thank us again, to apologize for his feverish note.

He looked well. Apart from the damage he underwent, he has been able to rest his organism and has been cosseted. Life seems sweet to him. He took great pleasure in the train's progress through the fresh springtime greenery as it carried him along between the flowery embankments. He had his own little tea-tray, just for him, near the fire. And my heart throbbed, and I felt infinitely sisterly and loving towards him.

March 10. Cold, melting snow, a bit of hail. The workmen break their promises. They don't turn up, or else they begin their day at midday; they have forgotten most of their tools, they roll cigarettes. They stop giving a damn as soon as you stop chasing them.

Cocteau telephoned. He is enchanted by his success as author-backer. Houses have been so good that he has got to give an extra performance on Saturday. It's all too much, his voice takes on a dying fall. The Opéra is going to do *Parade* again. He has a new piece in preparation; he wants to visit us. Yesterday he went to see Max Jacob's play. Is it good? 'Ye-e-es. It's Maxish . . .' And no more need be said.

March 13. Sent Max Jacob proof of my restored affection: a pot of goose-liver paté and a delicious cake. Will he perceive my tenderness in it? I don't usually have much luck with my inspired gestures.

Yesterday I was reading about Heinrich Heine and I couldn't help comparing him with Max Jacob when it came to family feeling.

Like Max, Heine had it in for his family, loathed them and ran away from them. One day he even had the elegant cheekiness to write the following words to an uncle of his who was a millionaire and paid him a fat allowance (unlike our Max in that, alas!): 'The only good thing about you is that you bear the same name as your nephew.'

Paris – March 23 to 24

March 23. Hotel Terminus, room 142, second floor, looking onto the courtyard, twin beds, 34 francs a day, 39 because of the little dog. Twin beds! Snores, promiscuity, invitations, arguments, sulks! We have been here since yesterday. We were welcomed and installed with the manners refugees have to put up with.

We leapt helter-skelter into a taxi to go to Max Jacob's exhibition at Bernheim's. No luck, it was over.

. . . .

Saint-Germain – March 25 to August 21

. . . .

March 29. Yesterday Max Jacob arrived late; the asparagus soup had thickened, the risotto was over-cooked; he was impertinent, demanding, mischief-making, started smoking during the meal. He has his pockets full of money and a first-class ticket, if you please, for the Midi. Money doesn't suit him. He wasn't even funny. . . . .

. . . .

April 2. A portrait of me with the famous dancer Régina Badet. That young person is still thirty-two years old! She avoids me as though I were the devil and occasionally admits: 'At the very beginning of my career, when I was a little girl, I once danced with Liane de Pougy.' Without being spiteful, I do feel obliged to state that for a little girl she had very big arms, bottom and bust, not to mention a solid career at Bordeaux where she had achieved the status of *première danseuse*.

. . . .

April 4. Easter! Christ is risen! It's going to be a grey, rainy day. Joncières is here, unrecognizably good humoured and charming, he has suffered a lot.

I must say in his favour that he shows no bitterness against Piérat. He simply reveals the facts. When I complimented him on this he answered: 'One should never tear oneself to pieces. Piérat was sixteen years of my life, after all.' He added: 'The other day I was having dinner at Madame Gillou's with Colette – who, by the way, rules the roost at *le Matin* on the literary side – and she started to malign Willy* quite terribly. She was really out to get him, omitted nothing, exaggerated everything, swore that he had never written a line of any of his novels, gave the names of the writers he exploited, burrowed in her handbag for revealing documents. It was painful.' A clever woman, certainly a glib one, talented, knowing the right people – but ill-bred and with a streak of silliness which prevents her realizing how odious and even ridiculous she looks in this role of hatred and disparagement. Her marriage to Monsieur de Jouvenel who she pinched from one of her friends, the beautiful Ida de Comminges – a brilliant marriage which gives her a high place in the world of letters – ought to have raised her above this low kind of bitterness.

Ah Colette! Of what metal is she made? She goes on being just what I, from unhappy experience, always thought her. Life neither softens her nor makes her more beautiful. It is rumoured that she is not very happy, deceived, rejected, ill-treated . . . Perhaps she still loves Willy who was her first victim, and her resentment is exacerbated by his sad fate. She believes in neither God nor the Devil, she fears neither sin nor death. I have watched her dancing and guzzling, with the corpse of a woman she loved lying in the room next door, shouting at the top of her voice: 'That's how we'll all end, the dead mustn't depress the living!' Poor, poor Colette, swollen with fat, puffed up with bitterness, envy, ambition. They say she's manoeuvring for the red ribbon.

. . . .

April 10. I have migraine. Georges is reading Nathalie's book and criticizing it heartily. As for me, I'm prejudiced in its favour, but I admit that it could be tedious to read all those fine phrases from

* Henry Gauthier-Villars, Colette's first husband, who exploited his wife by publishing her early work under his own pen-name.

end to end. Rather like eating too many delicious sweets, a bit sickly.

My park is ravishing. A real bosky grove full of birdsong which irritates Georges quite as much as Nathalie's book. I believe Georges would like to stay indoors for ever, his window bricked up, and could forget the rest of the world for the interest of watching a spider at work.

April 12. Lewis arrived late. He told us a thousand bits of tittle-tattle from his world: how Emilienne d'Alençon has 'debauched' one of his little mannequins, very pretty and young, for two thousand-franc notes. Emilienne rigged her out, did her up, trained her, introduced her to old Hennessy, took her to Monte Carlo and gave her the name Liane de Reck! She loves the name Liane, which I was the first to assume. She likes to speak it, to propagate it – in memoriam, no doubt. I spent so much time gaping at her in admiration between the ages of eighteen and twenty-two. She played so many wicked tricks on me, all of which I forgave as soon as her fresh and charming face appeared before me. Emilienne dances, tangos, dresses up as a naval officer in shorts (!!!), has her little curly head dyed red with henna, visits scandalous bars patronized by inverts, carries on with her vicious and fantastic little life, pays no heed to nature or to the Creator, enjoys herself according to her whim. She's a philosopher in her way.

Lewis told us how Gaby Deslys died after four months of suffering. A priest came to talk to her and advise her; a statue of the Holy Virgin was placed where she could see it; she made her confession, took communion, prayed. Religion gave her comfort.

Lewis wastes no time on sorrow or regrets. He says: 'Gaby was finished in America. They wanted no more of her, they'd soon had enough of her! People exaggerate the size of her fortune. She had a nasty illness in her blood,' etc.

Poor Lewis. His visit left us with an uncomfortable feeling of embarrassment. He explained quite naturally: 'Gaby left a life annuity of 18,000 francs to Harry Pilcer. Harry is very chic at the moment; he has just bought 300,000 francs worth of furniture; he's kept by a very rich old Greek.'

. . . .

April 14. The other day Lewis and I spoke about Mata Hari. I deny that I was ever a friend of hers. She was brought to my house by

Hector Baltazzi, a gentleman of Greek origin transplanted to Vienna and washed up in Paris. Hector was an uncle of Marie Vetsera, heroine of the Mayerling drama, and a friend of the Empress Elizabeth. He used to ride with her and she nicknamed him 'my little pocket-handkerchief'. He was dreadfully small, very dark. My name for him was 'the Havana cigar-butt'. He was 'wagons-lits', always on the move, surrounded by foreigners, very international. Ruined, he lived luxuriously, was received everywhere and used to introduce well-born foreigners to the most charming of the Parisian actresses. Nothing has been heard of him since the war.

This photo of Mata Hari, so beautiful in her body and so ugly in her soul, who simply for love of lucre betrayed the France which welcomed her so kindly – this photo reveals her slyness. Though her eyes are beautiful her look is glowering, her expression is shifty, her countenance is hard and vulgar. I said that never was I able to feel friendly towards her, and it's the truth. There was something too hard in her which I found tedious and off-putting. She had a loud voice and a heavy manner, she lied, she dressed badly, she had no notion of shape or colour, and she walked mannishly.

. . . .

April 22. Long talk with Georges last night, from bed to bed. I made my way of thinking perfectly clear to him. It will do no good: Georges is a stupid and ceaseless bungler. He becomes more like Mariette every day. I really can't stand any more of this dismal, bad-tempered, discontented, hostile and disapproving spirit of contradiction. When he assured me of his profound and faithful love I ended with these true and conciliating words: 'I don't mind about your love, just give me a little sympathy and kindness. That is what I need and that is what my conduct, my bearing and my efforts have earned me.' Sympathy and kindness! Those two words contain the whole secret of domestic happiness.

Royal Dutch have fallen to 61.000 francs after having risen to 66.400! We are very dejected. Georges telephoned Lazarus who doesn't care a jot for us. These fluctuations are the coquettishness of value, allowing clever speculators to play with it and grow rich. The carrot is dangled, then withdrawn.

April 23. Saint George! Happy feast-day to mine! Among the gifts I wish to bestow on him are sympathy and kindness, the two best of household fairies Everything is all right so far as it goes, but it doesn't seem to be going far – not at all far! I give warning in order to avoid trouble! I wrote him a dada letter which amused him very much and gave him a box of sultanas from Ma: quis and enough cigarettes to provide him with his eight a day for about the next two years. Tobacco is becoming scarce.

May 9. The day before yesterday Georges and I laughed for a whole hour till our sides ached, till we couldn't draw breath, till we cried.

We don't often get carried away by that sort of laughter. It hurts. It's the good old giggles of childhood, which you can't stop, which you suppress a little and then it bursts out even louder and harder. 'Laughter is characteristic of Man.' But I also say that 'Clothed, Man buckles on his principles. Naked, he is an unreliable animal, almost always dangerous.' Georges adores being naked, sauntering about naked in his bedroom and the bathroom. Savagery . . . When I was small my mother made me wear a chemise when I was taking my bath, for the sake of modesty and good breeding. When I began to fly with my own wings, at about sixteen, after my marriage, I deliberately left off the chemise on these occasions – which were rare enough, as it happens: three or four times a year. It caused a scandal in the house, scoldings, predictions of disaster. Modesty, even if only in her own eyes, was a woman's loveliest quality; losing modesty, she lost everything, even her husband's respect.

. . . .

May 12. They say that today the strikers want to come out and prevent the non-strikers from working.

Ever since April 13 there have been strange-looking beings strolling the streets, idle squat males in thick corduroy trousers and flat caps, with their sturdy, weather-beaten, hatless ladies – what magnificent heads of hair these women of the people sometimes have! – and it needs no more than the appearance of a group of them, or a family, on the terrace and in the elegant places we give up to them on a Sunday . . . it needs no more than their undesirable and unaccustomed presence to make us feel threatened and flouted. One pretends not to notice them, but one sees and senses them, and terror is not far off.

I am reading Madame de Boigne. Naturally she knew that she was pretty, her portrait shows that she was, and she says as much. 'I was first made aware of it by the exclamations of working-class people in the streets.' It's a long time now since young men in the street have exclaimed at my beauty. It did use to happen, a bit. I went by quickly, in a carriage. Nowadays there are a lot of pretty girls, cosmetics diminish the gap between beauty and mediocrity; and anyway the working people have other fish to fry. My kind of beauty made its impact from close-up, in intimate situations. Above all I was distinguished. My beauty wasn't striking at a distance like that of Otero, Cavalieri or Emilienne d'Alençon; its action was delayed. Meilhac once said to me: 'You are so subtle, so perfect, it's comparison that reveals your prettiness. The greatest beauty ceases to exist beside you.' Reynaldo Hahn often told me the same thing and so did Helleu and Coco de Madrazzo, for whom I often posed.

Emilienne was the great object of my admiration. I spent hours gazing at her. Her looks enchanted me. The freshness of her complexion was dazzling, you could see the blood running under her skin. I have got her portrait wearing a petticoat. Because I wanted to be like her, I said to Reutlinger one day: 'Take a picture of me in my petticoat, like Emilienne.' He looked at me and started to laugh. 'Oh no,' he said, 'you are not at all the type, it wouldn't work. You were born to play princesses! Resign yourself to being a princess.' He was nearer the mark than he knew. Far from being flattered, I was very cross. I knew I was slim, incredibly so; I was always being teased about it in the gossip columns and I thought he had refused to do me in that pose because I was too thin. I returned to the charge a few years later. To please me, he draped me in a large shawl and did a semi-nude of me which came off quite well.

. . . .

May 17. My son's birthday today, he is thirty-one. I longed passionately for a girl because of the dresses and the curly hair. My son was like a little living doll given to a small girl. I was very proud and forgot all the suffering I had been through. Yet fate was to make me a hopeless mother; all of life called me, all the different countries drew me away.

My Marco, who was not loved enough and who didn't love me enough! During the last three years we understood each other better and drew nearer to each other.

My God, thank You for awakening me under the spur of pain. I bless You for all the suffering which turned me into a real mother for my Marco. . . . .

. . . .

May 25. Spent the day, yesterday, in Henry Bataille's roost. Roost is the word, it's at the top of a tremendously steep path: a rustic and ugly villa called 'Paradise'.

The lord and lady of the manor were still in bed at midday. We had a look round as we waited for them. Yvonne de Bray appeared, fresh and smiling, prettily dressed in black satin embroidered with gold. We kissed, gushed over each other, exchanged compliments on each other's dresses and looks, etc. Then Henry made his entrance, stiff and large, pleased to see us and complaining about his health. He says that he can't walk, has tachycardia, is getting fat, sleeps well, eats hugely and works. His poetry and his plays bring him in an income sufficient to keep up his house at Vivières and pay a big rent for a handsome unfurnished flat in the Avenue Bois-de-Boulogne belonging to old Doucet, the couturier.

Henry and I, akin in suffering, talked about illness and doctors. Yvonne and Georges jokingly posed as the victims of our nervous systems – victims quite happy with their lot.

The day went quickly; we had so much to say to each other. We are very fond of each other: each of us embodies for the other something of his or her youth; we have survived so many vanished friends, been through so much, and we see each other so little, I really don't know why.

We promised them that we would spend a few days with them at Vivières. Georges can have a mattress on the floor at the foot of my bed, they invite our dear Lolotte as well and they urge me to bring Fatoum. They were so ready to meet all our conditions that finally I accepted in principle. They are our sort of people, and among the best of our sort of people. We speak the same language and share the same views. The only thing Henry and I disagree about is Flossie. He insists that she is spiteful and sly. I think she sided with Berthe Bady when Berthe and Bataille split up after twenty-five years.

May 26. In the middle of the night of May 23–24 some unhappy railway-track watchman had a horrible time. He met an old gentleman wearing white pyjamas who stopped him and said: 'I know this sounds very odd, but I am the President of the Republic and I have fallen out of my train.'

Malesherbes, with its lunatic asylum, was quite near, so there was our good man scratching his head and wondering what on earth to do. To his great relief the gentleman, having spoken, fainted. Our railwayman summoned whoever was available at that time of night and in such a place – his wife among them – and Monsieur Deschanel, for it *was* him, woke up reposing comfortably under respectful surveillance in the level-crossing keeper's house. The wife, quicker in the uptake, had recognized him from his portrait which has already been much reproduced all over the place.

As my learned friend remarked yesterday, we will be the laughing stock of Europe! We are all sniffing the air for mystery, crime, assassination attempts . . . Moral: a President of the Republic in the twentieth century must not sleep or indulge himself in the comfort of pyjamas. I was once told that Cécile Sorel – my Superb – remains armed throughout the night, discipline having developed into a graceful habit: a smile on the lips, arm folded under head, expensive and elaborate negligée, ostrich feathers arranged in carefully dishevelled hair – ready, in fact, to charm and tame whatever insolent being might have the audacity to intrude without warning, through door or window, into the presence of Célimène: of Célimène, who must never, never allow herself to be taken by surpise . . .

. . . .

May 28. They announced the death of Chaliapin, hideously assassinated by the Bolsheviks. It seems that it's not true. Dear Fedia is doing well in Moscow, singing every evening and enchanting those people in their delirium. It was a French journalist, brave enough to undertake a journey to that terrible country, who told us appalling details and denied the many rumours. Our compatriots, detained until now, have just been allowed out. They are in a lamentable condition. There was a reception for them at the Saint-Lazare station, and the photographs of it in the *Excelsior* were very moving. They were crying; smiling nervously; faces were rigid in expressions of sorrow; some were on stretchers.

I am infinitely delighted by Plato's *The Banquet*. I'm proud of liking and understanding it. Modern philosophers use such a tortured and difficult vocabulary, you have to be initiated in order to read them, learn their language as though it were a foreign one.

. . . .

June 7. Tumultuous day yesterday. My menu was phenomenal. Our guests were Bouchor, unexpected; Max Jacob, appearing like a jack-in-the-box with a beautiful bouquet of roses; Lucienne Rouveyre; Raoul de Galland, who came by car bringing his camera; Margot de

La Bigne and all my shopping. For tea we were joined by our future tenants who have signed the agreement, my uncle and aunt Burguet, Steinilber and Lazarus with his little Pierre. Lazarus – oh dear, not so good. He was embarrassed and uncomfortable in my presence. On my side I smiled too much and couldn't help feeling hostile, also embarrassed and uncomfortable. Oh dear, money! Damnable and necessary money, up to its tricks.

Last but not least we opened our big gates to a ravishing grey motor-car from which Andrée de La Bigne emerged, all golden in a dress of blue Japanese silk – really stunning, that girl – and loaded with chocolate caramels. She was followed by André Germain, resolute but staggering under the immense weight of his literary productions. Finally a delicious little grey night-moth came flitting out of the car, alighted beside me, fixed me with its tender and luminous gaze, full of childlike curiosity. It was Madame Clauzel, and I was conquered. Our arms linked, our hands met, our enchanted thoughts mingled. She is exquisite, gentle, authoritarian.

The friends left, the night-moth stayed – the night-moth and the clothes-moth. André Germain is a domesticated clothes-moth, we choose to spare him. He read us his articles on dadaism, on D'Annunzio. Meanwhile the night-moth was in my arms: delicate touches, caresses, kisses, nips and scratches. This morning I still have little marks on my wrist. Like me, she adores Salomon, loves Flossie, admires Pauline. We evoked them, we compared our pearls and the textures of our skins. There were ripples of laughter, exclamations. Stern André Germain came to a halt and drilled us with a coldly indignant look; his nose became even more pointy and he told us: 'I can't go on reading while you talk.' So we kept quiet and our hands squeezed each other with increased intensity. She is like Eva Palmer, my Yvée, recalls a slender Liane from those bygone days of fragility and delicacy. I gave my *Idylle saphique* to the night-moth, who opened enormous eyes at the idea of reading something which, she says, Salomon has forbidden her. Oh, Salomon!

My 'Maintenon' dress exhausted me, I was the slave of that white collar which crushes so easily. Lianon! Organdy's victim! It's impossible to lean back. Poiret is decidedly impractical, doesn't know how to combine elegance with comfort.

June 13. My tenants moved in yesterday and I have sold my tapestries. I had to consent to a considerable rebate, 33,000 francs instead of 40,000. So much dust, so many moths and maggots concealed behind those lovely things. Like in people's minds, a mass of evil thoughts, bitterness and intrigue.

Yesterday I telephoned Lazarus to tell him that I needed 100,000 so he must sell my most valuable shares. He told me: 'You are a delicious friend, but as a client you are nervy, anxious, suspicious, cowardly. You are not up to it. A client who is, entrusts me with his money and doesn't give it another thought.'

June 16. Réjane has died of a heart disease. She was sixty-four, an immense talent, profound and moving. She could make me laugh and cry, make my heart thud while tears and mascara streamed from my eyes. Off the stage she was an exquisite being, passionate and not always very happy.

A big headline in *l'Intransigeant*: Paul Darde, former shepherd, received the National Prize for Sculpture at the Salon. I like that: a shepherd becoming an artist, a little flower-seller becoming a famous singer (Cavalieri), a prince marrying a dancer from the Folies-Bergère – it breaks the tedious protocol of life, it's a flash, a glimmer, a little triumph of fantasy over convention.

June 21. A delightful day yesterday. Max Jacob arrived at lunchtime with Georges Auric, a young composer much in the public eye, very futuristic, a protegé-friend of Cocteau's. He collaborated in *Boeuf sur le toit*. He's a mere boy, hardly twenty-two years old. He has a remarkable talent, plays admirably and fluently. His talent is geometric, architectural, I might say cubist. He has outstanding control. Long torso, fat hairless face, rather comic, a sensitive simpleton. He is massive with it, and unhealthy too. The war tortured and undermined him. He talks little – people say with difficulty. He has an acute look in his eye, but in spite of all this he seems to be very good-natured. A reserved creature, pouring himself into his abrupt and tango-like music. He charmed us all.

June 24. Auric has sent me his favourite piece, or ours at any rate, *Adieu, New York*, with a friendly inscription. That boy displays a gravity and dignity almost incompatible with his age. He sees a lot of Poiret – hmmm . . .

June 25. Salomon came yesterday and was cross and hostile. He works too hard, which wears him out and makes him irritable. He saw that I was mortified and finished me off with these words: 'Nathalie has one great advantage over you and over other women in general, she shows great steadiness of character.'

July 1. I've just been reading Claude Anet's *Ariane, jeune fille russe,* in which she tries to pass as a dissolute woman although she's just a foolish virgin, and it reminded me of a chapter in my own story.

At eighteen, when I sent the laws of society and the family flying, driven by my greed to know everything, by events and by my first husband's book-keeping which was very like Lazarus's – at eighteen I became the irresistible passion, the Ideal (so he said) of the Marquis Charles de Mac-Mahon. One day he was questioning me jealously: 'Tell me, my darling – how many men did you give yourself to before me?' I began to ponder, to count on my fingers, to recite whatever names occurred to me – names of countries, names of famous vintages. The twentieth was that of Lur-Saluces. Mac-Mahon was stunned: 'What, So-and-so Lur-Saluces?' (I forget the first name). 'Yes.' – 'But he's my brother-in-law! I would never have thought it of him!' – 'Oh, it was only a casual thing, very casual.' – 'Lur-Saluces! That serious chap! Sleeping with a little girl of eighteen!' – 'What about you?' – 'That's different, I adore you.' Rather disconcerted, I continued listing names. The marquis was spluttering with rage, swearing, suffering. When I reached forty-two I judged that I had made my little effect and stopped. 'That's all. The forty-third is you,' and I looked at him out of the corner of my eye. 'Little wretch!' (I gloated). 'Vicious little creature' (I was in seventh heaven). 'It's not possible at your age; forty-three men, it's appalling!' Now, I had in fact known my husband, my first lover (the ship's lieutenant Cronon) and the Marquis de Portes. Mac-Mahon was a mere fourth, but I thought it much smarter to create a whole list. For me there was nothing between being pure and being dissolute. After that I took refuge in the most absolute silence and refused to answer any more questions. So he suffered inwardly and his suffering exhaled great sighs. He gazed at me tragically, he shook his head, his eyes filled with tears: 'The forty-third! I'm the forty-third!'

One day he turned up and announced without ceremony: 'I've just been with Lur-Saluces: I spoke about you, yes, I said your name and he never even blinked.' I didn't blink, either. He went on: 'So I probed him a bit. He didn't give an inch, he admitted nothing.' Gravely I pronounced: 'All crimes can be denied. The man did right.' I was thinking: 'So this is how family quarrels begin! To think that I only picked on Lur-Saluces because I'd had some with my dinner the night before!'

Never did I grant him the only comfort he could have had, the truth. Perhaps he would not have believed me, perhaps he would have loved me less without that lie . . . Who knows? Anyway I didn't care two pins for poor Mac-Mahon who was too much in love with me and whom I ruined and embroiled with his wife (he had married Mademoiselle de Vogüé before he met me) as casually as I would have swallowed an egg. I wasn't faithful to him for a moment. I had a liaison, secondary to the one with him, with Evremond de Saint-Alary – the very same man who won the Grand Prix three days ago. Saint-Alary could outdo me in disloyalty, cunning, intrigue and lies! He took eight thousand francs – he was a gambler – out of a roll of ten thousand given me by Mac-Mahon, and never repaid them on the pretext that he had 'spent a lot of money' on me. That's a reason but it's no excuse. It will soon be thirty years since then. We probably wouldn't recognize each other if we met in the street, but when our paths used to cross in Paris I would give Monsieur de Saint-Alary a very cold look without bowing, while his eyes shifted in the other direction as he sketched the gesture of raising his hat.

The past, the ugly past . . . I am angry with Claude Anet for bringing it to the surface. My Giorgio! You alone have raised me above all that wretchedness.

July 5. We have quite given up the notion of staying with Bataille at Vivières. Delicate as we are, accustomed to considerable comfort and a healthy diet, we would adapt very badly to the hurly-burly of a house where grouchy servants are constantly giving notice. Joncières told me that there is one big bathroom in which people take turns. We need our comforts, our snug little corners all to ourselves. And then Bataille lies in bed till midday and makes up for it by staying up till midnight; that wouldn't suit us at all. I can't be up later than ten o'clock without risking a sleepless night. It would be better to stay where we are. We will not be moved however much they insist.

July 6. Torrents of rain all day yesterday, broken by a pleasant but too-short interlude: Salomon's visit. What an agreeable talker! What a charming reader! He read us Bossuet and tried to read Cocteau but threw the book aside, laughing. . . . .

Salomon has seen Flossie, who is not leaving her mother's side at present. Her mother, an eccentric old woman who can't be less than sixty-five and looks eighty, was reckless enough to marry – two years ago, I think – a young man of twenty-five. It didn't last. She has returned to filial love which will, no doubt, be kinder to her.

July 7. I am reading Lauzun's memoirs which Salomon lent me. Gallant and tender, rakish and charming. He sums up the spirit of his age in three lines: 'As was common at that time, I possessed very fine clothes to wear when I went out; at home I was naked and dying of hunger.' You don't see much of that nowadays, particularly not among upper-class people. They get themselves jobs in industry: Boni de Castellane is 'in antiques', La Rochefoucauld 'in cars', etc. They marry Jews and Americans more than ever. They are right, but the century loses charm as a result, and manners suffer.

July 12. Our little gathering consisted of Max Jacob, Auric, Joncières, Lièvre, Steinilber and Margot. We talked about everything. Auric played the piano, his *Adieu, New York*, then Chopin, Schubert, Glück, Spanish songs and dances. I dug out an old piece by Ketterer which Tamberlick used to sing, *Oh! Souviens-toi*, and he tinkled it for us in the wittiest way.........
    Lièvre and Margot found common ground. It was Lièvre's father who designed and made Valtesse's beautiful bed of many-coloured bronze, that famous bed which cost fifty thousand francs (and that was forty or fifty years ago!) and which was said to be the model Zola used when describing his Nana's luxury; that bed which is now displayed in all its glory in the Museum of Decorative Arts. I have often been in that huge bed, which stood on a dais and was surrounded by a grill. When I went to stay with Valtesse I had my own room and a comfortable dressing-room; but when morning came it was the custom to take breakfast in 'the Golden One's' bed. An hour often went by in cheerful, affectionate gossip. She gave advice, she drew one out, and she kept her own secrets. To think that I never knew she had a daughter! And she had two of them!

July 14. Yesterday evening I read Colette's new novel, *Chéri*, at one sitting. Salomon knows it and is delighted with it. Well, my dear Salomon, here's something else about which we disagree.
    I find this book of Colette's muddy, demoralizing, depressing. Every detail reveals vulgarity. It is lively, well observed I suppose,

well written. So I scold myself for withholding enthusiasm. I fear that it's due to my stubborn prejudice, my memory's inner voice, the insensitivity of bitterness in fact! I pick the book up again, I search, I reread, and again I reject it. I do not like it, it offends me, almost wounds me. Yet I admire Pauline, Madame de Noailles brings tears of enthusiasm to my eyes, Madame de Régnier moves me, Rachilde interests and amuses me, Lucie Delarue-Mardrus charms me. There are legions of women who win my approval and whom I'd like to equal. Colette . . . no! I look down on her with a grimace of disgust. And all literary and learned Paris, all my friends, are going to exclaim with admiration while I sit here crossly with my mouth shut. Is it just that I am unable to control my own unfairness? Colette appeals to her readers' latent sensuality, she titillates sex, shakes up the kidneys, goes to the head, tries to intoxicate, is well aware of the vulnerable spots and flavours her salad accordingly. It works; it works with everyone; not with me. Nor with Georges. I loved *Dialogue des bêtes* and was tremendously amused by her Claudine books; since then my enthusiasm has gradually melted away. Colette has beautiful cats' eyes, a comic look, vulgar, childish, rather catlike gestures. She also has the gift of the gab, wit, education, a lot of cleverness. It all adds up to a talent, a talent which her experience directs towards matters which I find hurtful. Let's leave it at that.

July 15. Anniversary of my first marriage.

The Mazerauds came back with a huge pot of pâté, an exquisite speciality of Pacy-sur-Eure. They overwhelmed us by offering it to us. They are such charming people, tenants such as we never dared to dream of! They also brought back an impresario whom I used to know: Theuret. His business is chiefly opera or operetta. He couldn't get over finding me 'so beautiful, so plump, so rosy, you who were formerly so slim, so pale, so long', etc. The truth is, his admiration of my full-blown charms turned the knife in the wound. In the days when everyone fancied big women, I was slender; as soon as everyone starts wanting slender women, I put on weight. No luck! . . . .

I have turned up a very funny and very incoherent note from my old dancing master in London, Daddy Espinosa who was about a hundred and seven and had once taught Mariquita. He paid homage to my suppleness and nicknamed me the Electric Shocker. This old boy with a nose as long as himself, small, appallingly dressed, absurd, red, bald, drunk, was the master of such an inimitable skill that with one gesture he could become graceful, airy, incomparable. He had danced before the tsars and all the kings of Europe between 1850 and 1870, and had collected proof of their admiring munificence: gold watches with royal ciphers, heavy chains, tie-pins, rings and portraits. I was very fond of him. He made me work very hard and managed to get some unexpected results out of me. Wife, sister, sons, daughters, the whole lot danced, worked at the bar, teemed, spread, scattered throughout every ballet in London and thereabouts. He was much in demand as a teacher and producer. His brilliant talent was recognized everywhere. Irving was always in his company – they were great friends. When I wanted to obtain some extra-ordinary favour I would mimic him and he would laugh and say: 'Cheeky! Why didn't you come to me when you were six years old and I could have given your bones a proper breaking!' His feverish and exultant letter proves that you are no less a man for being an old teacher!

July 27. The Duc de Morny died recently. He was the elder brother of our friend Missy, alias Mathilde de Morny. I possess a picture of her as Napoleon. She gave it to me with the inscription 'To my daughter, from her father-in-law'. It was Missy's way to call nice-looking boys her 'sons': Sacha Guitry, Auguste Heriot, Georges, were all her 'sons'. So when I became the wife of her 'son' she called me daughter and signed herself 'your father-in-law'. She wore men's clothes, cropped her hair, smoked big cigars – and would have let her mustache grow if she'd had one! She exchanged the name Mathilde for the debonair 'Uncle Max'. At bottom she was a charming, childlike creature, a bit simple, well brought-up but an exhibitionist and a worry to her family. We gradually let our friend-ship with her drop, which gave no pain to either party. Max-Mathilde loved dressing up and giving fancy-dress dances; her whole life was a masquerade.

Another of our friends, Sarah Bernhardt's niece Sarita who died some years ago, had the same little kink; although she used to wear skirts and was masculine only in the top half of her clothing, her manner, her style, her rings. She too favoured the cigar, which made her presence very disagreeable to me. Sarita who was intelli-gent – more intelligent than Missy – was very deeply committed to this line of conduct and used, between ourselves, to make a living by it, whereas Uncle Max was ruined by it. I ought to add that Sarah Bernhardt tried again and again to tear her beloved niece away from those circles and those habits, she reasoned with her, she gave her an allowance, she took her to America, she put her into plays. Nothing worked. Dinner jackets and love nests, short hair and the style of an invert . . . She was still young when she died of intestinal tuberculosis, after appalling suffering. Only when she was in the nursing-home found for her by her aunt, did she become more or less one of my friends.

I shall never understand that kind of deviation: wanting to look like a man, sacrificing feminine grace, charm and sweetness. To help the illusion, Missy used to flatten her breasts under a wide rubber band. How horrible to crush and damage such a charming gift of Nature! And cutting off one's hair when it can be a woman's most beautiful adornment! It's a ridiculous aberration, quite apart from the fact that it invites insult and scandal.

July 31. Cocteau has sent us a little pink compilation on which it says in black lettering: 'Carte Blanche'. A collection of all the articles he has published in *Paris-Midi*, lively, witty and biting. He never lets anything go to waste and collects even the least of his charming outpourings. In it he praised my friend Mistinguett with her un-failing, subtle, moving talent, so very Parisian. I'm glad. 'You need to come from Paris to understand that battered little girl's face, that drawling voice. Does Mistinguett sing out of tune? I don't think so. Whenever I'm in exile the memory of that voice pierces me . . .'

Mistinguett! When we last saw Bataille he fulminated against her: 'She's an evil woman, a bitch! It's shameful for an artist to be on the side of the police.' First, it has not been proved. It was made public, then it was emphatically denied. Mistinguett is good and very intelligent. Her adored lover, the excellent clown Maurice Chevalier, was a prisoner of the Germans and very badly wounded in the chest. Mistinguett went even so far as the King of Spain to get him returned to France. She achieved it; Chevalier was sent back. She nursed him with matchless devotion. Slowly he was restored to life. She got him wonderful engagements in the shows she was in. He repaid her by deceiving her with seductive little chorus girls and enthusiastic members of the audience. It broke Mistinguett's heart, but every night – oh what a cruel and ironic fate – she had to smile through her tears side by side with her unfaithful betrayer, because their contracts were unbreakable. She kept it up, and I hope she has consoled herself by now. She's such a dear little Paris guttersnipe, a real sparrow, a character. Her envious friends put their heads together and said: 'If Mistinguett could rescue Chevalier like that, she must have been a police spy . . .' and the rumour got going. Personally I believe that if Mistinguett, always surrounded, always in the public eye as she is, was ever able in the course of one of her tours to do France a good turn, she did it, and she did it well.

We met each other more than twenty years ago. I was the visiting star at the Scala, and she was the established one across the way, at the Eldorado. Generously she came to see my act and gave me fervent applause and flattery. When I left she flew to the producer we shared, Madame Marchand, and said ingenuously: 'Oh Madame, please keep Liane's costumes for me, let me wear them in the next review!' Since then her indisputable talent has carried her far. Any number of beautiful costumes have been dreamt up, designed, created for her out of gold and jewels, fabulous period pieces, sumptuous elegance! – She knows how to wear them, how to 'manoeuvre' them as Cocteau says, with an incomparable chic that sparkles with wit. All in all, she is a great great artist. It does Cocteau honour that he wanted to say as much, to capture her in these eccentric and capricious pages which are rather like she is, unique Mistinguett whom I can't approach without my heart's beating faster.

August 1. . . . . Henri Régnier, a very old friend, has written a marvellous article about Colette, certainly far from impartial. On the other hand it appears that the well-known critic Henri Bidou has given her the most scathing review. So I am not alone; I am pleased about that, I was beginning to doubt my judgment.

Yesterday's conversation took a rather risky turn. In the course of it I learnt that the town of Bordeaux gave its name to the 'bordello'. I have visited them in many countries, out of curiosity and also because everyone else did. Each time I left one I experienced a feeling of disgust with human nature and hatred against men.

When I was at Bou Saada I passionately wanted to rescue that wonderful little Fally of the stormy eyes, slender and agile as a young gazelle; and her grandfather, like a good head of the family, refused to be seduced by even the most tempting offers. Finally, to convince me and get rid of me, I suppose, he told me: 'It is of the utmost importance that Fally should remain four or five years in the house of prostitution where her sisters, her aunts and her mother spent their youth.' I recoiled in horror. I tried to reason with him, to no avail. Nothing would shake him, sure as he was that he had made the right decision about the future of his wonderfully beautiful little grand-daughter who was alarmingly thin and shaken by a stubborn dry cough; his grand-daughter who at the age of eight was already dancing naked every evening in front of strangers. I sought out the commandant of the place, explained the situation and told him how I wanted to save pretty Fally's body and soul. He looked at me askance and sent me packing, politely but firmly. I heard afterwards that sometimes, after a good dinner, he made use of Fally.

So then, in despair, I went to see an elder sister of Fally's who was shut up in one of those houses, a café with dancing at night. The wretched girl's room had a dirty stone floor, its only furniture was a mahogany bed – like those of our country people – standing in a corner. On the bed, two torn and filthy mattresses. They made me feel sick. Filthy postcards and a few fair-ground ornaments on a shelf, a miserable white-wood table with bottle-marks all over it, and this sinister fat girl, her monstrous belly heaving with laughter at what I was saying. I left with gall in my heart. I can't even think about it without getting a lump in my throat, and to comfort myself a little I think: Fally must be dead. Surely, God, You must soon – very soon – have taken her away from this earth . . .

August 2. Yesterday a messed-up day if ever there was one. My bad nerves had to endure a rude assault, the arrival of these three sooth-sayers: Cocteau, Max Jacob and young Raymond Radiguet, a poet who is making a name for himself and who is only seventeen. (Max's explanation: 'My dear, infant prodigies stay seventeen until they are twenty-five.') Oh what a procession – starved-looking and dingy – led by Cocteau with his sharp, ravaged look like some vicious and anxious spinster, then shy, writhing Radiguet with shut eyes and open mouth, or vice versa, as though his skin were too tight. Max, always a bit of a carnival mask – Max had decided to live or die by every word which fell from the lips of Cocteau – of Cocteau patron of the arts, of Cocteau who puts on performances, organizes tours far from the theatres, who helps people even as he uses them as ladders.

Slovenly, incongruous and noisy, first they rumpled the rugs, smothered Georges's lavatory with tar, laid claim to our wash-basins, our soap – and to other things as well. At table it was even worse and nearly ended in tears. Cocteau – and its not as though he didn't know how to behave because he comes from a perfectly decent family of scriveners – Cocteau began without ceremony to pick at a dish of fruit standing by him, and this during the first course! I signalled to Georges who smiled and said to the indignant Fatoum 'Take away that dish', which she did. First coldness.

At the centre of my table there was a rich and magnificent vase of dahlias, yellow, red and orange. 'I can't see Max because of the flowers' – 'I can't see Jean because of the flowers' – 'Well, what of it? You don't have to see each other' – 'Yes, we do' – 'Yes we do' – 'Too bad, there's no solution' – 'Take away the flowers' – 'Liane, they must go...' and Cocteau reached out for them. Outraged, I rose threateningly to my feet and said sharply: 'Listen, I am going and you can have my place, then you can give what orders you like.' Second coldness. Cocteau let go of the vase. Max was green, I was disagreeable, Georges was embarrassed and Radiguet was scared.

My food was exquisite and they did it honour. Thanks to its succulence, tongues were loosened; but I didn't take part, grumbling to myself that I'd worn myself out preparing this meal for such a lowdown bunch of clowns.

Afterwards, the reek of tobacco, and abandon. The gentlemen threw their ash on the ground, their fag-ends into the fireplace, their matches on the carpet, rumpled the cushions, knocked my books about, rummaged through our papers, etc. What a session! I took the line of clamping a smile – the professional smile of a dancer – over my indignation. The day dragged. I made them take a walk in the park; I took them to visit a neighbouring estate, I gave them the traditional chocolate and cakes at four o'clock. They left at seven o'clock. Not one witty or amusing word or thought.

Though Max did read three or four childlike and charming pages from his next book, and sang us some of his old songs. Cocteau, who has to hold the centre of the stage, didn't care for that.

They went away at last, leaving my poor house a pigsty, my spirits depressed, my mind full of bitterness. Never again! Never more than one writer at a time! How much I prefer Auric the silent, who knows so marvellously how to express all the sounds which inhabit him. Obviously there is a choice to be made; and made it shall be.

August 13. Salomon brought me some photos of Diane de Poitiers, on whom he is working. He thinks they are like me, that I have the same fine forehead and regularity of feature. I daren't really believe him. My arms are thinner, though very well shaped, my hands exactly the same (fingers with 'stomachs'). As for breasts, let's not talk about them: hers are pure marvels. Mine are placed in the same way, very wide apart, but less firm, little and – downy, as they say. Like her, I dress in black and white. She has an enigmatic, teasing smile, subtle and engaging. Mine can't be quite so charming.

. . . .

August 21. Our trunks are locked, full to bursting [for the journey to Roscoff where they would spend the summer holidays]. We plan to cut down and take almost nothing, but they fill up as though by magic. Everything is *settled*, as the English say, our couchettes are booked. We are paying 65 francs today for what cost 12 four years ago.

Roscoff – Clos-Marie, August 22 to September 21

August 22. Arrived safely. Absolutely exhausted.

My Clos, my little Clos-Marie, which I nicknamed 'little house that's not so simple' (see *Yvée Jourdan*). Dear little unpretentious, welcoming house which everyone loves, our refuge from the heat of the summer, from the approach of the enemy and from the Gothas when they were bombing Paris. I never return to it without a pang, and memories come pouring in. I bought it in 1903, the year my pearls were stolen, after that great disillusionment. I did it up as best I could for later, for my mother. And my mother is gone, and 'later' has come. I am writing in bed, the window on my left is open. I can see the sky, the sea, and the top of my hedge of tamarisk and privet. This morning the air is soft and salty.

August 23. Everything unpacked. I know all the local news. I am still writing in bed. The old lady is taking a rest.

August 24. It is raining – November weather. Yesterday we did the rounds of the village and said hello to all our friends.

When we appeared at the hotel Madame Talabardon recoiled in horror with staring eyes. She couldn't utter a sound. I thought she had been taken ill. 'Oh, if you only knew, if you only knew!' she babbled. 'Only yesterday they told us the Prince was dead, and it gave me such a turn to see him there!'

It seems that there has in fact been a rumour that Georges was dead. The fishermen in our part of the village looked quite amazed when he appeared on the jetty. I don't like it.

I went to the end of the jetty and dipped my feet and my gout into the cold and salty sea. They soon became supple and burning hot. I am in need of this cure, and I shall follow it assiduously.

Georges is happy, cheerful and good-humoured. He is mad about this part of the world and my rustic domain. We go to sleep lulled by the waves. Few, if any, other sounds.

. . . .

September 12. The sun is brilliant, bright and warm. The sea is calm and blue. One threat in my sky: Max Jacob, in Quimper visiting his mother, is going to come and 'say hello', or so he writes. Now – I know that he will stay here as long as he is able. Now – he is not livable-with. He will eat all the plump part of a fish, empty the cream jug without thinking of those who have not yet had any, take half a cheese, the best part of a cake, almost all the jam, scrape the bottom of the sauce-boat, cynically refuse potatoes, ask for coffee every day and sweeten it with three lumps of sugar. Such a guest is a real disaster, disorganizing his hosts' larder with an unfailing touch even while he tells them in a childish voice 'How you do spoil me! In Paris I often go without dinner after lunching on a pickled herring and a hunk of bread.' One smiles; one tells the maid: 'Don't put the butter on the table, serve it in a little shell for each person; make the desserts in separate ramekins, like in a restaurant; put the fish or roast in front of me, and I will do the serving.' One becomes thoroughly ratty, one mumbles and grumbles. At last the guest takes his leave and one says 'Ouf!'

Max goes to six o'clock mass every morning, waking everyone up. He upsets the serving of breakfast. He leans with all his weight on frail white-lacquered chairs as he puts on his dirty espadrilles. He broke a bidet worth ten louis without using it, and I have seen him lying in his filthy clothes and muddy shoes on a precious bedspread of white silk damask. Every one of this boy's loutish gestures irritates me like a fly buzzing perpetually round my head.

September 14. I am down with influenza. I am furious. Max Jacob says he will be here on Wednesday at the latest, for a whole day. God must have inspired him! The spare room is ready: I have had the bidet and the damask bedspread put away. . . . .

September 17. Too ill yesterday to write a word. Max Jacob turned up beaming, well dressed, his hands full of Breton cakes and pancakes. It made it easier to welcome him warmly.

Kindly he took pity on me and was really accommodating, delighted to be back in the little Clos which gave him shelter for two months in the time of the machine-guns.

We chatted; he's a charming gossip, although rather destructive. He came from Quimper; everything went well between him and his family. Once fame has started to shine on someone, and money starts to clink in his pockets, even if one isn't going to profit by it, it does smooth out difficulties and soften asperities.........

Max found Georges marvellous, fatter, tanned, happy. As for me, I have almost no strength left and I am depressed and discouraged. I was so well! I flouted the cold and the wind, l went for long walks, I wrote, I read, I watched, I cooked, I did my embroidery and I tidied my cupboards. I was greedy and eager, choleric and alert, coquettish in my way, ironic, witty – alive, in fact. Now I'm pale, drawn, grumpy and melancholy; it hurts whenever I move.

I no longer care for people or my shelves, food fills me with disgust. As soon as I take the least drug my own nature, which is reaction itself, cancels itself and ceases to react. It seems as though something must be nourishing my illness – the bread, perhaps? It is horribly heavy and badly baked. It is quite impossible to get a good result with this appalling flour made, they say, of all kinds of war remains. They also say that this year's harvest is bad. A cheerful outlook!

I think Max and Georges despise me a little because I bought a complete set of Victor Hugo. Max gave me a sly look when he asked 'Is he a writer you like?' Today people speak of him scornfully – when they speak of him at all.

September 19. I asked Max Jacob: 'Do you often tell lies?' He answered: 'I don't often lie, but when I'm telling a story I almost always exaggerate.'

Sunday weather, singing our Lord's praises. The sea dazzling under the sun. Max celebrated Ember Day with vigil and fasting. He read edifying books. Bohemian artist that he is, with no precise rule of conduct, he finds a great deal of moral support in religion. A pity that it doesn't happen to be his own. A renegade always seems like an intruder, a sort of parasite, and race is always there.

A charming note from Salomon commiserating with my sorrows

and scolding Flossie who is still tucked away at Samois with 'someone'. Mystery and discretion. It enrages Salomon who loves our Flossie more than he admits – perhaps more than he realizes.

. . . .

Saint-Germain – October 7 to December 29

Liane's influenza lingered for almost a month after her return to Saint-Germain, and her diary entries were consequently scrappy.

. . . .

October 26. Very cold, winter is in a hurry. I saw the Roumanian princess again, she made eyes at Georges who didn't think her shoes any better than mine.
[*Liane had passed 'la Bibesco' in the street the day before, and had been embarrassed because she herself was wearing comfortable shoes while the other princess's were elegant.*]
Salomon left me a friendly review of *Chéri* by Jean de Pierrefeu. Salomon was hoping to embarrass me. 'No one has more genius than Colette.' See, Liane! 'Her precise and supple language adheres to the object (horrors!) and evokes the emotion (oh!)', then this long passage: 'The humanists of the Renaissance, culture's most admirable craftsmen, would have excluded this equivocal and fatiguing art of Colette's from the realm of that art which aims at elevating the soul and refreshing the mind. Quite apart from the fact that they would soon have grown weary of the strange, vulgar and uninteresting settings which appear to please Colette. It is time that she changed her characters; she has too much genius, surely, to persist in degrading it.' There! What did I say! I feel quite flattered at sharing the opinion of 'the humanists of the Renaissance'. Thank you, dear Salomon! . . . .
Marianne [de La Jaille] has been nagging at me to lend her my long pearl necklace. She is planning a little effect to be made with it! 'Cousin, show me your pearls. You don't wear them enough, it's bad for them. Oh how pretty this long one is, how I love it! I'll wear it for you if you like. Oh cousin! Look, it needs rethreading, let me take it to the jeweller.' I burst out laughing and so did she. 'Go on, child, take it: 406 pearls. Get it restrung, wear it, I entrust it to you for the rest of your stay.' She was enraptured. We began

to count the pearls. Marianne found 416, Chochotte 408, Bouchor 420, Georges 417! It's always like that. Margot made it 407. A little society pastime.

November 3. I am feeling better. The cold is intense and Georges condemns me to the fireside. I go on crochetting my little dresses and reading Sainte-Beuve. He mentions Madame de Duras and depicts her in these terms: 'She had an extraordinary gift for adapting herself to each event, each person, and doing it naturally, without effort or calculation.' How totally I can see myself in that! I adapt, I assimilate. For example . . . . With Georges, with Max Jacob, Bouchor and one or two others I spring upwards, I fly, I soar, I really do display a sparkling wit at times, while with cousin Marianne I go to pieces, shrivel up and become as dull as can be. Salomon – with him it's the great pleasure of listening and learning, then some detail crops up, an argument, I rediscover myself, I become excited and I tell him cheekily, as though to get my own back: 'Dear Salomon, what a lot I could teach *you*!' In the presence of my silly, overbearing mother-in-law with her loud voice I go silent and hold myself in to the point of migraine. When she leaves I burst out, Georges and I go off like a cannon (he feels the same as I do and shares my irritation). If Mariette ever dissects and judges me, she must certainly think that I'm a great fool. Her buzzing eclipses one's personality: it's not possible to argue and it's idle to attempt a conversation. Actress . . . am I not always just an actress performing a role dictated by other people and the turns of events! It is before You and You alone, o my God, that I am able to find my true self.

. . . .

November 19. Spent yesterday in Paris. Went in the metro for the first time. It's convenient, amusing, cheap, but people are glued up against each other, breathe in each others faces and travel underground.

November 24. Intensely cold. Salomon arrived while we were at lunch. Treacherous creature! He brought me Colette's short stories, *les Vrilles de la vigne*, and they really are very good. I come into one of them, the last, dedicated to Renée Vivien. It happens at Monte Carlo. This is what Colette says: 'Frail, delicious, supported, almost carried by young H and the no less young G, Mademoiselle L de P went by. She was smiling the lovely smile of a happy young mother leaning on her two big sons . . .' Behold – the claws hidden in the velvet paw! Colette is obsessed by the question of age. If you play little Claudine long enough you lose your sense of reality, you refuse to age, you fight desperately against wrinkles and grey hairs. And now comes: 'Less frail but no less beautiful is Madame CO (Caroline Otero), who is not playing today and whose brow wears a halo of melancholy . . . Alas, she says to her anxious admirers, it is because tomorrow I shall begin my twenty-ninth year . . .' There you are, any recognized beauty has to endure a scratch from the cat Colette. When I used to see the Willys, Moreno told me: 'Beware, my Lianon, Colette is vicious, cruel, jealous, she will envy your beauty, your features, your house, your pearls, your friends.' Young H – that was August Heriot (Louvre department store) whose mistress she became a few months later. She tried to make him marry her. The disappointment inspired her to write *The Vagabond*. Now, the 'no less young G' has become my husband, and it has lasted – no thanks to Colette! How she cried it from the roof-tops that it couldn't last, that G was marrying me for my money, that he would ruin me and abandon me to a poverty-stricken old age, doomed to the deepest despair. Luckily she has not proved much of a prophet – so far. When, two and a half years later, I married Georges, Colette's hatred expressed itself even more wickedly. The papers *Rire*, *Sourire* and *Fantasio* published ugly, vulgar articles striking at my dear little husband the better to hit me, all signed with meaningless pseudonyms. Some of our friends were moved to make a little investigation and they easily discovered the author: Willy – inspired and urged on by Colette. I did not hold it against Willy! God keep me from holding it against Colette!

To come back to Salomon, the beloved scholar came cheerfully into our icy dining-room on the stroke of half-past-twelve, asked for our news, then brought the *les Vrilles de la vigne* out of his pocket. The book was open and folded back at the fatal page. Pointing to this page 219 he asked me in a very interested voice who was the gambling woman referred to by Colette further down: 'Madame de la R . . . would that be Madame de la Redorte?' – 'Yes, it was her,' I answered stupidly. Now Madame de la R was given her scraping by the claws just after Otero. Salomon's pointing finger obscured her name and left clearly visible the passage in which I am mentioned . . . I understood. What a subtle fellow you are, my Salomon! What an amusing way of doing it, how kind after all, and how discreet! You thought: 'These lines contain the whole secret of

Liane's dislike of Colette. I am going to rub her nose in them to show her that I'm in the know.' It is even possible that Flossie may have tipped him off. No, my friend; these lines are the result of hatred, not a cause, and the hatred is Colette's not Liane's. Salomon, o Salomon, you ought not to stir up all this mud. I hope this malicious act will be the end of the matter between us for good and all. Go on admiring your Colette, chevalier of the Legion of Honour, and stop dinning it into my ears. As for me, I'm incorruptible!

November 28. Yesterday Salomon came to see us for a moment. I tell him a thousand things I wouldn't say to any other man. Confidence is complete. O Salomon, stay as you are but be a little less quarrelsome. Yesterday he spoke about my perfect (!) beauty and my prickly character. What cheek! Though it's possible, after all, because I do know that I am extraordinarily sensitive.

. . . .

December 11. I stayed in bed with a terrible headache. I thought about Fatoum who has still not written. That little savage taught us to expect a magnificent indifference. So then I said to myself: one does not love one's parents. One never loves them enough. Look at me, I detested them, my judgment of them was ferocious. Think how I despised them for being old, poor, simple and having principles! I took everything as my due. Proudly I accepted every one of their sacrifices. I disdained their advice. Going away to the convent put the finishing touch to my indifference. When I came back, a child no longer, I kept all my kindness as well as my smiles for the young men who gravitated towards us. Yet I saw Papa wearing worn-out shoes and in all the sixteen years of my life in that house I knew him to possess only one single overcoat and only one single dressing-gown. I saw my mother going out furtively very early in the morning carrying parcels of precious family things to sell at the second-hand shop so that she could keep our little daily round going. I saw her coming back with empty hands, discouraged, silent and resigned. I was ashamed of my parents' threadbare, darned clothes, I was disgusted by my father's tobacco, I was irritated by my mother's prayers in church. I never shared any of my thoughts with them, I disliked kissing them. When I was seven I wanted to leave them, I escaped and ran off to ask for a job at Bazola's circus. Later, I dared to reply to some inquisitive fool who was interviewing me: 'My mother was a laundress who sold me when I was twelve.' My parents, did you have to die before you could find your place in your little daughter's heart?

There were moments when I threw myself furiously on my mother in floods of tears, all love and adoration. I hugged her frantically, overwhelming her with incoherent endearments. For her, those moments made all the others bearable! I used to sulk and pretend to be ill or to have a headache in order to claim their attention. I would refuse to eat in order to worry them, to make them pay more attention to me than to the others. And my lies . . . and all the ugly secrets and mysteries of my greedy and incomprehensible little soul, sensitive and stubborn. I was madly headstrong and never gave way. And my face was the face of an angel, sweet, candid, smiling, regular. Childhood is a state of the most appalling unconscious cruelty.

December 14. I am terribly disillusioned about Salomon. Yet another idol who has hurled himself off his pedestal. Georges is gloating and I have a sort of pain.

. . . .

December 22. I have written a hai-ku in honour of Nathalie-Flossie, whom I also used to call Moon-Beam. I am sending her a picture of a little woman in a short frock smelling flowers in the moonlight; and because our mutual longing to see each other is not stronger than the times, places and circumstances which keep us apart, here is my work:

> O brilliant moon
> We see each other better
> From afar. . . .

Then come our Christmas wishes. 'She will raise an eyebrow', says Georges.

. . . .

December 25. Christmas! A warm Christmas, sweet and melancholy. Yesterday evening a knock on the door: it was Father Christmas in the shape of Rose dressed in a flowing white nightie, a white bonnet on her head and a long white cotton beard on her face. Marie followed, bearing the presents, subject of so much mystery and concealment. Georges gave me a ravishing black velvet dress, my two childhood cakes which had arrived from Lorient just in time, a box of splendiferous ecclesiastical purple writing paper, a pound of Jousset's delicious marzipan. I gave him, in addition to his shoe-presents, one thousand Camel cigarettes, three pairs of braces, a pound of marrons, a pound of pralines and – a litre of cod's liver oil! We laughed, smoked and nibbled, and everyone was happy.

The turkey arrived yesterday at midday, and is superb. We have stuffed it and truffled it. I have been sent fifteen kilos of green coffee from Haiti. Georges has written me a beautiful – and rather literary – Christmas and love letter.

December 26. I woke up rather unwell. I had a lot to do in the house, I wanted to go and hear at least a little mass. When I got back I shod myself in silk and robed myself in silver – a sumptuous dress from Lanvin – saw Rouveyre, the first guest to arrive, then suddenly my head began to swim and I only just had time to go and fall on my bed. When I came back to life I found – surprise, surprise – my dear Steinilber, very upset at my absence, and Max Jacob who had brought a box of Pihan chocolates bigger than himself ('all pralines, the ones you like best'). Auric, good brave little Auric had come too, even though he hadn't been to bed the night before. At about three o'clock I managed to get up, ate a little breast of turkey, and I kept going until the evening. Lunch had been men only, theories and discussions, almost arguments, but clean plates. In spite of his sorrow at my absence, Georges guzzled so much that he couldn't eat any tea, or any dinner either. We went down to the drawing-room, the stove was alight, the house was warm and good. Max, with a soft-pedalled accompaniment from Auric, entertained us with a rather incoherent but funny and charming little Christmas improvisation: the Virgin pregnant . . . and looking like me . . .

. . . .

1921

Saint-Germain – Pavillon de Noailles, January 1 to June 20

January 1. I had a long, clever, closely-written letter from Salomon yesterday, enclosing a copy of the impressions he recorded when we first met. Why does he send me that? I don't know. He says that I was lying down, not well, in black velvet and grey satin (my colours are sober and my dresses simple). He writes: 'She was wearing a necklace of enormous pearls and a ring of black enamel set with huge diamonds!' Well, why not? One ring and a necklace isn't much, not for the second floor of the Majestic! I'm no academic, I am Lianon the dancer at the Folies-Bergère, billed during a European tour in 1898 as 'Liane de Pougy wearing jewels worth a million'.

Salomon had got Flossie to introduce him to a chastened, suffering, unhappy little princess, wearing a black dress, one ring and her string of pearls, and he has to start criticizing! It's really too mean! He adds: 'That apart, she was irreproachable.' Thanks very much, you booby! For heaven's sake, if I never brought out my pearls they'd say my husband had eaten them!

Yesterday the goose arrived from Bourges in a huge basket, together with a fat chestnut cake in a mould and some delicious little coconut kisses. I quivered with delight as I unpacked it all. And my family's parcel was accompanied by another one, from Paris; a wonderful box of Boissier chocolates, with the good wishes of – Henry Bernstein! Well I never, what has come over him?

. . . .

January 3. Rain, Sunday calm. Humanity stops its bustle, a feeling of peace descends on everyone. I went to mass – yesterday, too. The choir was hung with red banners fringed with gold, the flag of France was hung over the altar with the heart of Jesus embroidered in gold on the white band. Three glittering priests were officiating surrounded by children dressed in red and white muslin, and young priests wearing violet. All this red and gold and all these sparkling candles inspired the irreverent thought: sugar candy! But I listened to the organ, very beautiful and penetrating, and I lifted up my heart to You, oh Lord. My quivering, purified heart dares ask You for nothing, it submits, for itself and for those who belong to it, it does no more than make simple vows of courage and resignation. When one summons the courage to see what God is to us, the Infinite and All-Powerful, one can only submit to His will, do what is right and love Him in His creation and His creatures. It is in Him that we will all find ourselves.

January 5. Visit from Salomon, but I gave orders to say that we were in Paris. I want to help him space out his visits, so that it's not all on his side. He brought me *Madame de Caylus* and *La Grande Mademoiselle*.

January 9. Salomon came yesterday. I was in bed, nursing my migraine. Georges received him. Childish rhyme composed in his honour: 'Deserving a smack – how he does annoy – neither girl nor boy – Salomon Reinach.' My idol has fallen and is broken, now I trample it.

. . . .

January 21. Charming surprise! My Flossie came to see me, after letting me know by telephone. She was dressed jauntily – Amazon style, what else! in a dark wool dress lightened by a green-embroidered white waistcoat. A caped coat over her shoulders, a plain felt hat on her blonde hair. With her brisk style, her implacable smile, her tenderness towards me, her instinctively caressing little hands, she looked very young and very happy. I plunged into this renewed contact. We spoke about Salomon. She made gentle fun of him, so indignation diminished. She stayed with me for a good hour. She has invited us to attend her Fridays, 'I'll have my Chinese music all over again for you, and you must bring Auric.'

January 23. Visit from Balthy, all in black, her ear-rings jet balls, her aigrette colossal, her eyes sharp, her laugh boisterous, calling up other laughs. She told me about her travels, New York, Los Angeles, etc, and swore that she had written from everywhere. Louise lies, but she does it so nicely! We talked antiques, works of art, theatre, fashions, cost of living. She is thin and her wrinkles have gone, her skin has become smooth. I suspect her of going to America to have her skin stretched and tightened, the way they do it over there. The shape of her mouth has changed a little, she no longer does her hair in the same way, no doubt because of the little white lines of the scars. She absolutely insisted that we should lunch with her on Saturday at Pépé's. I said yes. I can refuse nothing to my Louise when she fixes her black eyes on me and asks me for something in her vibrant, musical voice. Pépé is a Spanish grandee, José de La Pena de Guzman, etc – he has six whole lines of it! The luck of the draw landed him at Doucet's as a designer. He lives on the rue de la Ville-l'Evêque in a very big, very beautiful house belonging to Jacques Doucet. He lives alone with the most fragile of stomachs, sad, gloomy, immoral too, so they say. He is handsome, clever, distinguished and really too elegant! I used to know his wife, a former beauty, fat, rheumaticky, mottled, died in a lunatic asylum.

I was great friends with Pépé in those distant days when he made his debut at Doucet's. I remember giving him various little presents – sort of as tips – and even a few hundred-franc gold pieces brought back from Monte Carlo. He's given it all back since then! He has showered Georges and me with presents – dresses, linen, knick-knacks, furs. He is generosity itself, to the point of being embarrassing. Louise is living with him because she couldn't find a place of her own, and he's overwhelming her with them, too. We fell out because of incompatibility of temper. I'll enjoy seeing him again. He, like us, has come through a lot.

January 24. This morning I dropped in at the house agent's to discuss my house and my apartment. They suggested for us a little block of flats built in the Empire style with an adjoining lodge, also Empire, which has little columns and a pediment. It was once the Prince of Polignac's chapel.

January 25. The little Directoire house is dancing in my head. I hardly slept all night. Yesterday we went to see it. They are asking 70,000 francs. For that I would get responsibility for the upkeep of the flats and the income from them. The ground floor is let for nine years at 2,500 a year; the first floor is let for 900 francs to a tenant of long standing (eighteen years), three more years to run. It is worth 2,000. The second floor is let for 1,300 to someone who works in the Town Hall. The third lets at 1,000 unfurnished or 1,800 furnished.

It comes to 5,700. I reckon that upkeep would amount to 3,000. I would get a rent-free house and an income of 2,700. The little lodge adjoining the flats could be made liveable. It already has chic, with a little garden full of roses and a few shade trees at the back. The kitchen is a hole: a lot would have to be done. When one is reducing one's standard of living one must accept sacrifices. If I estimate my rent at 4,000 and it will be worth that once it's been done up as I intend, I'll have an income of 6,700. I don't think the necessary work will come to more than 100,000. It looks like good business, suitable to our decrepit budget.

January 26. Flossie has sent me some verses. She was supposed to come back on Saturday, wasn't able to, and apologizes in this charming way . . . .

I still have not got the little house, we are arguing over two or three thousand francs. Shall I get it? Shall I not?

January 27. The house is mine. Here I am with tenants, expenses, and rent coming in. I have paid a deposit of 17,500 and have deposited 50,000 with the lawyer, Maître Grebau. The former chapel of the Prince de Polignac is mine: I shall keep the repairs to the minimum and move in very gradually: I'm on my way down the slippery slope of poverty. I enter into possession on April 1, when work can start. What worries! But simplicity will be my foundation stone. Bit by bit I will become accustomed to the idea of leaving this large and expensive house, of living on little, of becoming content with even less. Each piece of furniture which goes will tear away a part of myself. Polignac will take the place of Noailles and when the modest little lodge is ready, so pretty and well-dressed, opening its little arms to me as wide as they'll go, I will let myself fall into them with a gentle resignation.

February 6. We have been to see old Pépé and sprightly Louise! The house is well heated and still richly furnished. It contains some fine collections: very valuable prints, Chinese blue and white. Pépé loves to rummage and accumulate. We were received with open arms, lunch was good, footman impeccable and well set-up butler.

In January my mother-in-law sent six thousand francs to her son, who is reduced to strict necessities. Good, we are glad, we are using the money. Immediately afterwards she wrote: 'It would be very helpful if you took out a subscription for me to *le Temps* for nine months and to *la Revue des deux-mondes* for a year.' A hundred and fifty francs to shell out! And a hundred and fifty francs is no joke to the poor boy.

. . . .

February 10. Yesterday a day of migraine, but I still went to see the plumber and the joiner at my new acquisition. The little lodge will be very nice once it has been done up, but the doing up will be expensive: the whole staircase to be demolished and rebuilt in a different place, simply to make the kitchen bigger; a bathroom to be fitted in; and a thousand other details.

February 13. Salomon talks in a letter about the first novel I published, *l'Insaisissable*. Another piece of treachery. I dislike this very banal book, I have told him as much and said: 'Never mention it to me!' Is it forgetfulness, tactlessness, or yet another little bit of spitefulness? Into the waste-paper basket! Into oblivion! . . . .

February 27. We found Pépé having trouble with his stomach, condemned to yogurt and to having an x-ray on Monday. Balthy had pains in her shoulder and back; she forced herself to be cheerful and keep the conversation lively. A good lunch: boiled eggs, macaroni au gratin, mullet with mushrooms and truffles, warm custard moulds, which I abhor! They should be made the day before, they ought to wait and cool in their moulds, I have principles about it! Catulle Mendès used to say to me: 'Tapioca is a beggar which must be made to wait and thicken gently on the side of the stove. A soufflé, on the other hand, is a great lord on whom *we* have to wait patiently before welcoming him with admiration when he finally comes to the table in all his opulence.'

. . . .

The next three months were tiring and rather dull: bad weather, uncertain health, continued irritation with Salomon Reinach. On May 22 Liane records that an American has bought Noailles for 550,000 francs. On June 20 she hears that her brother Pierre, who has been ill with cancer for some time, is dead.

At the beginning of July they moved into rooms in Saint-Germain. The Pavillon de Gramont seems to have been a school for young English ladies which didn't usually accept men but was willing to make an exception for Georges. Presumably the idea was that they should mark time here until

Madame Pierre Chassaigne

Anne-Marie Chassaigne, who was to become Liane de Pougy

Emilienne d'Alençon

La Belle Otero

Louise Balthy

Valtesse de La Bigne

Liane de Pougy

Marc Pourpe

Georges Ghika, la Lolotte and Liane de Pougy

The living-room at Clos-Marie, Roscoff

Manon Thiébaut

Mimy Franchetti

Nathalie Barney

Salomon Reinach

Jean Lorrain

Prince and Princess Georges Ghika

their new little house was ready; but as it turns out, they never do move into the little house and Liane gives no explanation for this in her diary.

Saint-Germain – Pavillon de Gramont, July 1 to December 21

July 1. It's over, here we are rid of that ill-omened and oppressive house. I have been unable to write, ill and overwhelmed. We are all right here: quiet, airy, good wholesome simple food, friendly people. Flossie has been to see me with André Germain, she harmonious, he stronger. Salomon came and pedantized. Georges is thin and drawn, absolutely tired out.

July 2. My birthday. There's a gastric affliction going the rounds and Georges and I spent all last night paying our tribute to it. Now we are both in bed on a liquid diet.

They are very unhappy at Bourges [where her brother had just died] and want to hear from me every day. I do not want it to become a habit. What would be the good? I know what they probably feel about me. I may have forgiven the insults I received in the past from my sister-in-law, but I have not forgotten them.

It's nice to be ill together, to look after each other. To think that one can even contrive to manufacture pathetic little pleasures out of such a condition! 'Show me your tongue, how is mine? Goodness, it's medicine time again, let's have a tisane.'

Mademoiselle Hélou is something between a doe and a mouse. She is enchanting with her children who seem to love her and obey her without being afraid of her. Very little noise. I don't think we could have been luckier.

July 3. What an upheaval in our existence this house-moving is! I feel all scattered about in innumerable packing-cases and in the rough hands of the removal men – so scattered that I'll never be able to collect myself again.

Carpentier has been beaten by Dempsey, quite unable to return the blows he received. I'm ashamed, I don't like losers. Long live Dempsey! I'm quite taken by this thug. Rather beastly of me!

July 5. Salomon Reinach has – good heavens! – sent me some chocolates! Going through some papers I found a photo of Jean

Lorrain in summer clothes. It was in that get-up that he used to stare boldly at handsome young men and be amazed to find them 'sensitive to the power of the eye'. Poor Jean . . . basically sensitive and tender, flaunter of vices, valet to fame, intoxicated with the theatre and literature, heart of a child. Poor dear charming Jean, seeking after anything that might be described as a sensation of happiness. This photo is hugely like him.

I am no longer cross with Carpentier. He's all right really, and it was brave of him to take on that mountain. Poor fellow, he broke a thumb on it.

. . . .

July 23. Georges was thirty-seven years old this morning. We did what we could. The day was lovely and very hot, the lunch good: all his favourite things, melon, radishes, sweet pimentos, lobster, roast chicken stuffed with foie gras, lettuce hearts with hard-boiled eggs, chocolate ice, a chocolate cake from Bourges made by my sister-in-law, peaches, almonds, cherries, coffee, sauternes from our own cellar. Mademoiselle Hélou sent up beautiful red roses and a pretty basket of pale pink carnations for the table.

. . . .

September 9. Tomorrow an old lady and her daughter are going to come to stay here. These people knew me in Marseilles thirty years ago, when I lived in the rue du Dragon on the third floor of a building which had a girls' boarding-school on the ground floor. These ladies have told Mademoiselle Hélou all about it, saying that I was so young, so lovely, so alone! I used to play with the school-girls when I got the chance. It was from there that I escaped over the social barriers. My name became a scandal, I am still remembered. I hadn't a penny to help me leave my husband, but Grandmother Olympe had left me a rosewood piano. I considered it my property and wanted to sell it. Someone told me that a young man who lived in the same street was looking for one, so I went to see him. He received me, gazed at me, admired me, came to look at the piano and bought it without bargaining for four hundred francs, cash down. It was in the evening. An hour later I had left for Paris, for my dream, for fame and for filth – for my tumultuous destiny. Yes . . . but next morning, when the candid young man came to collect his piano he met with opposition, first from its owner, then from all the family. In spite of my receipt which was made out perfectly correctly, the young man never got his piano and may have felt that he paid dearly for the pleasure of my acquaintance! The one and only swindle of my existence, and quite involuntary at that. My husband was at Toulon and came to see me every week. When he arrived he found the nest empty and the bird flown. It was a very well-furnished nest. He sold everything on his own account to pay debts which we had incurred together: family mementoes, portraits – Maman at six months old in Grandmother Olympe's lap, with Uncle Gustave standing beside her . . . I have always regretted that picture, which had a damaged corner and could have had no value for anyone but me.

Rain and wind . . . . I am embroidering a blind for Polignac, a beautiful white blind with a Directoire vase appliqué in the middle.

. . . .

October 10. Salomon, after going round and round it, tells me: 'Flossie plans to visit you on Monday, with a charming friend who wants to make your acquaintance because she admires your books so much.' – '?' – 'Now, I shall be coming to fetch them, though I shall be too busy to come down with them.' – '?' – 'I want to ask you something.' – '?' – 'Don't be nasty to me in front of Madame R'. I roared with laughter. 'All right – but you are preaching hypocrisy, you know.'

And then my Natty arrived with Madame R – and she is absolutely charming!

She has ravishing white hair, a gold snake round her waist, a hat made of blue birds, a red coat, a black dress, silk stockings embroidered in royal blue, a swollen ankle, wit, a magnificent pearl necklace, sky blue eyes. She remembered meeting me in Switzerland, reading and loving *l'Insaisissable*, seeing me when I was ill at Oberthurs, my son's death. In short, she had followed my career. It is time that we knew each other. She took tea and congratulated me on being me. Flossie was putty-coloured from head to foot, complexion, teeth and hair included, and delicious and affectionate. I called Salomon 'maître' and 'Monsieur Reinach', and he was pleased with me.

I love seeing Flossie again, listening to her, watching her make her way through the world of her choice – easily the most charming of worlds. And she enjoys returning to me from time to time. To some extent I am her creation. Although she is younger than I am, she was my exquisite teacher and opened horizons to me.

My little house is coming along. It is taking shape. The contractors' bills are taking shape, too. Oh the brigands, the cheats, the shameless monsters!

October 11. I opened the *Imitation of Christ* this morning and chanced on a meditation on death. I read it attentively. It is sad and true. God led me to this passage, to counterbalance words spoken yesterday by Madame R, intended for my encouragement: 'One mustn't think about dying, one should keep going, keep one's mind busy, keep on the move: it's the only way to live. My father was still busily making plans at the age of eighty, so death crept up on him without upsetting him much.' I think that at my age one becomes more thoughtful and that it's no bad thing to get into the habit of thinking of death as a long rest.

. . . .

October 29. On Thursday Salomon brought Flossie down, then left. We were alone together by my fireside for a good part of the afternoon. Dear Nathalie, so much grace and so much sweetness! So much kindness and charm! Nothing lofty was said, we just gossiped and exchanged opinions, and that was enough for the two of us, so happy at being together.

Georges tried to explain to Nathalie Einstein's theories, which everyone is talking about at the moment. He explains very well. We listened with concentration: Nathalie looked like a good and conscientious schoolgirl. As for me, I didn't understand a thing. I am furious at my mind's limitations. Nathalie got out of it with a smile and one of her pleasantly ambiguous remarks. We talked about my polar-bear rug, now hers. She said to me: 'He knew all your joys and sorrows.' I began to laugh: 'And some pretty comic moments, too.' – 'Tell one of the comic moments!' – 'Do I dare? All right. Once I was courted assiduously by a young, rich and silly Bonapartist. He heaped me with presents and money. He was always ready to obey my least – and most capricious – whim. He won over my maid, and one day, urged by her, I did an about turn and decided "So much devotion deserves a reward . . ." I thought of my bear. Getting into a sumptuous and very transparent negligée, I lay down on it. He came in, I opened my arms to him. Astonished, unprepared, he stammered – he gazed at me, unable to believe his luck – he bent over me . . . and pop! An enormous, a stupefying detonation rent the air, its origin only too obvious. I burst out laughing at the sight of my deflated lover looking over his own shoulder as though he were trying to see who had done this frightful thing. Then I was siezed with anger. "Get out of here! Get out at once! Open that door and disappear!" Oh, the excuses I had to endure, but I was unyielding and cruel. From then on I accepted all his gifts without feeling the least obligation, and as soon as I could I got rid of him. The dear old white bear saved me, that time.' Flossie laughed with all her heart and enjoyed the story so much that she made me promise to write it down here; which I have done because I can refuse her nothing.*

October 30. Salomon brought me a volume of old *Vie Parisiennes*, 1870–72. Very amusing. I told him the following little story.

One day in 1892 or 1893, old Meilhac came to ask me to be so good as to honour with my presence a performance of *Manon* (or it may have been *Carmen*) which was being given at the Opéra-Comique on the following day. I accepted. 'You must make yourself beautiful, beautiful. You must wear your tiara, masses of jewels, a lowcut dress.' – 'All right.' – 'You must arrive before the curtain goes up.' – 'We'll see.' – 'No, no you mustn't disturb the performance.' – 'I won't make a promise that I might not be able to keep.' – 'But baby! For me you can do this!' – 'I will if I can.' He left, satisfied with my promise, then back he came again: 'Bring some friends, you must have an entourage, I'll give you the stage box on the left.' – 'Good, I'll bring Marie de Lannoy and Blanche d'Arvilly.' – 'Yes, here's two thousand francs, buy whatever's necessary, wear your white cloak with the gold embroidery and the ermine lining, be elegant, be entirely Pougy in fact, and above all, above all, be punctual.' – 'All right.' – 'If you do as I tell you, there'll be a surprise.'

Next day, all flags flying, Marie de Lannoy noble and auburn in sombre jet-embroidered satins, Blanche d'Arvilly, dark and exuberant in sumptuous sables, flashing with diamonds, and me – oh me! A dream of diaphanous whiteness, enveloped in supple ermine, my dress white satin covered in pearls, we made our entrance into that beautiful box exactly a quarter of an hour before the curtain was due to go up. The theatre was almost full. The usherettes were obsequious. Nonchalantly I took my seat in the front of the box,

* Natalie Barney's biographer, George Wickes, reports that the polar bear was still on the floor of Natalie's bedroom at 20 rue Jacob even after she, as a very old woman, had gone to live at the Hotel Meurice where she died at the age of 96, in 1972.

haughtily I twiddled my ring-laden fingers. My companions surrounded me. Suddenly, as though at a signal, the whole house was on its feet and turned towards me, greeting me. Amused, I gave a gracious smile. The orchestra broke into patriotic music. Tumult. Carried away by the surge of emotion I rose to my feet, then sat down again. The house applauded. I had no idea what it was all about, although it seemed to me natural enough that people should pay homage to my youth and beauty. Blanche and Marie, serious and very beautiful, went along gracefully with what was happening. I whispered to them: 'It's some trick of Meilhac's. He promised me a surprise, we mustn't lose our heads.' Then the door burst open and in came Meilhac, rubbing his hands and speechless with delight. I motioned him to a seat and said: 'That was a very nice reception! I hope you're pleased with me? I think I played my part very well considering that I wasn't warned.' He was suffocating. At last he pulled himself together a bit and said: 'Oh baby! We're expecting the Queen of Sweden – in the box opposite – they thought you were her, it's too killing for words.' So all four of us collapsed into peals of laughter. And in fact the box opposite mine was occupied by a lanky, sad-looking woman, rather badly dressed, surrounded by quite an entourage. Her entrance had been ruined, no one noticed it. It was me, little Liane de Pougy, to whom the crowd had paid its homage – and the orchestra too, because it was the Swedish national anthem that they had played. I was flabbergasted and delighted, rather proud, too – and so were my friends. The enraptured Meilhac told the story to everyone, heaped us with presents and compliments, and announced far and wide: 'Homage to beauty! *Vox populi, vox dei*! How beautiful is our Liane! That is how people expect a queen to look, and she has proved it.' I should add that the noble lady and her courtiers opposite spent the whole of the rest of the evening examining and admiring the frail, luminous creature, its short curls crowned with jewels, which had been the cause of this 'historical' misunderstanding.

November 7. Yesterday, Sunday, we were expecting Bouchor and Max Jacob turned up instead, quite out of the blue. He spent the night here, in the best room. We found him very much himself, not at all sanctified by his sojourn in the presbytery. He is full of venom and bitterness, scornful and disparaging. He is bitter and anxious, tormented, difficult to understand. He is going back to Saint-Benoît because the life he leads there is conducive to work and meditation.

But what does he meditate? I get the impression that the evil spirits which possess him are hard to dislodge. He is spiteful about the curé, who seems to have used his authority to chastise Max's scandal-mongering. He seems to be more interested in the formal practices of religion than he is in his own development and his inner life. He must find life difficult. He is in a dilemma: either stay in Paris to protect his position – and lose his soul; or live in solitude in order to approach God – and lose his reputation. Memories are so short in the Parisian caravanserai!

. . . .

November 27. I was feeling better and rejoicing at it, and now it's all collapsed and my ailments have renewed the attack. I try to behave as though there were nothing wrong with me. I rush off to Polignac to unpack and arrange things. It will be finished by the end of December. Had a long letter from my dear Rochegrosse. He speaks of Christ with a fervour which makes me envious. He misunderstood me when I complained that for me Christ doesn't exist, I didn't mean – oh no, indeed, far from it – that Christ in Himself doesn't exist, but that I don't see Him: a screen shuts in front of my eyes. I know what must be behind it, but I am unable to open it, to see, to touch. And that is what makes me the poorest of the poor.

My Flossie came on Thursday accompanied by little Clauzel, more faded and colourless than ever. Salomon arrived before they did and told me: 'The Baroness Clauzel is wearing a superb bison coat.' I was imagining her clad in a shaggy car-rug and what it turned out to be was a ravishingly light and supple mink! Dear old learned one! [Salomon's mistake came from the similarity between the words *bison* and *vison*, which is French for mink.] The night moth seemed shrewish. I prefer my Flossie peaceful and satisfied, calm, gentle and serene. Flossie has managed to find us two rooms and two dressing-rooms at the Palais d'Orsay with demi-pension at seventy-four francs a day. It's all arranged.

I have been working at Polignac, unpacking household utensils and books. In an English novel which I was given when I was in London in 1901 I found some of Nathalie's letters, impassioned, tender and full of devotion. Her passion has been scattered to the four winds but her tenderness is still there, and so is her devotion. Among these letters, two and a half pages from Pauline. They will make a present for Salomon. No doubt he will bequeath them to posterity, fully annotated, according to his habit. I don't think I could possibly give a greater pleasure to Monseiur Reinach, in love with a ghost. Pauline's letter is rather spiteful. Our relationship was never a very fond one: Flossie preferred me and I never made much of Pauline. In that world it's either adoration or hate.

December 21. Just had a visit from Flossie and the Duchesse de Clermont-Tonnerre. They were on their way back from Robert de Montesquiou's funeral which took place at Versailles. Plenty of visiting these days: Madame de La Béraudière has bought my lovely eighteenth century pastel. Lady M, who lives here at the Hôtel de Croisille, has asked us to tea. She is a Shakespearian being imbued with a thousand dramatic essences. She married a rather half-witted young Lord who, she says, did not consummate the marriage and dumped her here. She runs madly back and forth to Paris, raging and scheming, in order to recapture a gaga husband who is not in the least interested. A little Jew from the City came on the scene in the role of secretary to her father-in-law and has completely set this rich and noble family by the ears. When the old lord died he left him as much of his fortune as he could. Not satisfied with that, the young man seduced the widow and the imbecile son. He has declared war on the young rebel wife. It is a depressing story. I used to know that young man, rather a good-looking boy with a head of silky blond hair like Absalom's, blue eyes, an innocent expression, tenacious, intelligent and – I am very much afraid – quite without scruples. About twenty-years-ago Jacques, the maître d'hôtel at the Carlton in London, came up to me at lunch one day and said: 'Oh Madame Liane de Pougy, you could win me a horse! Mr – has promised that he will give me the horse he rides in Hyde Park every morning if I introduce him to you. It is such a beautiful horse, worth two hundred or two hundred and fifty pounds!' – 'Jacques – bring the young man over to my table at once!' Five minutes later the boy was sitting beside me, I was tweaking his beautiful hair and ordering him to send the horse round to Jacques at once, which he did. In those days he was still wet behind the ears, but he had a bold and optimistic view of the future.

Madame de Clermont-Tonnerre, née Gramont, told me that young Lady M is demented and quite dangerous; in their circle they call her 'Little Madame Landrue'. I shall disengage myself gradually – I don't like crazy people.

Flossie was affectionate. We drank tea, gossipped and talked about the Duc de Gramont, *le bel Agénor*, Madame de Clermont-Tonnerre's father. He was married three times and his wives were a Wagram, a Rothschild and a ravishing Italian beauty forty-five years younger than himself.

1922

Saint-Germain – Pavillon de Gramont

January 1. I am reading the *Imitation* and find it full of beauties. For example, this sentence about Jesus and the inner man: 'He often visits the inner man and his conversation is sweet, the comfort he offers is exquisite, his peace is inexhaustible, his nearness passes comprehension.' O Jesus, reveal Yourself to me this year! If only this veil between You and me would lift! I do so long to understand and feel Your love for me, and to reciprocate with passion.

Paris !!! – Palais d'Orsay

January 4. Here we are, and I am missing Saint-Germain! Here we are, and Georges exults! The Palais d'Orsay, huge and chic, offers us the shelter of two ravishing rooms on the fourth floor. It is warm, our little bathrooms are light and airy.........

The King of Roumania has finally abolished all titles: we are no longer princes! Or at least from now on we will only be addressed as such when abroad, as a matter of courtesy. Old families like ours, which have more or less fallen to the distaff side, have no choice but to accept it.

January 6. I can't resist the pleasure of quoting the pretty turn of phrase used by Duchess Elisabeth de Clermont-Tonnerre when she was giving her opinion about me: 'Where I expected to find no more than a whiff of scent, I found fresh air.'

Saint-Germain – Pavillon de Gramont, January 27 to February 9

January 27. It is a long time since I wrote. Naturally life in Paris was charming and eventful. Every evening fatigue threw me onto my bed, quite overcome. There was nothing for it but to pack our bags and return to the inhospitable fold provided by the Hélou ladies.

I stayed for Flossie's Friday. Madame Fabre-Luce was there, prepossessing and blooming and determined not to leave my side. Duchess Elisabeth arrived later, forced her way through the crowd, smiling from afar, with her hand outstretched, declaring: 'It's for your sake that I'm here.' Auric was there, and Madame Claude Farrère, alias Roggers, with whom I have had a coldness. The other ladies' friendliness infected her and she had quite a long and amiable conversation with me, very nearly confiding in me. Salomon appeared for a moment, kissed the tips of my fingers and slipped away, André Rouveyre joined us, then André Germain. Pierre Drieu La Rochelle was introduced to us: he is very agreeable and could claim successes in other lines beside poetry. Jean de Gourmont was there, shy and nice. We outstayed the crowd and had dinner with Flossie. It was eight years since I had dined out. I survived this debauchery very well, only to renew it on the Sunday evening at the Duchess's, a ravishing little Directoire house on the rue Raynouard, modernized with the most perfect taste. After dinner mattresses covered with velvet and cushions were spread on the floor of a little Chinese room, intimate and warm, and I was persuaded to lie down. Flossie, whose eye trouble was making her feverish, came and lay beside me and the Duchess sat close to us and quizzed us gaily.

January 28. The day after our dinner party Duchess Elizabeth left for Austria to look for platinum and jewels which, it seems, can be bought there very cheaply and on which we can make a good profit. The Duchess pooh-poohs the current rumours about epidemics in Austria.

Eating out all over the place like this is very funny. Our friends were determined to put on a good show for us, and at the moment the most expensive thing is chicken. So we could be sure that every meal would include the appearance of a beautiful roast chicken. Georges and I couldn't catch each others eye without laughing; we really went off it. Finally, when I got an invitation I said: 'I must warn you, I'm not allowed chicken.' – 'How very odd,' people said. 'Chicken – the white meat, anyway – isn't usually forbidden.' Then I would tell my story and everyone would laugh.

On Wednesday, lunch with Balthy. Louise was very gay, she had been dancing until three in the morning. At present she is collecting blue and white from China and Persia. She has blinds made of ostrich feathers and cushions made of fur. I caught her in bed, having herself daubed with oil of turpentine by her masseuse as she reclined on pink crêpe de chine sheets! Nathalie came with Romaine Brooks to pick me up; they wanted to see her close to, and seemed disappointed. Romaine was sporting the Legion of Honour. Nathalie took me to Madeleine Vionnet, the great dressmaker of the moment. A plain dress of black crêpe de chine, with no embroidery or decoration: 2,600 francs! 'What would its sale price be?' – '1,600 francs.' Nathalie was able to wangle it and got it for 1,000 francs. But that's still dear, for a reduction.

Then Flossie took us on to Madame R, who was giving a tea party in my honour. It was big, grand, cold and comfortable. I'm enormously fond of Madame R . . . but my Flossie! What a matchless creature she is, what a rare wit! She has it and she inspires it. When someone said that her house was very dusty she answered: 'But dust is pretty, it's furniture's face powder.' We saw her little old mother, frisky, alert, sparkly. Georges is mad about her. An incredible youthfulness runs in her veins, shines in her eyes, curls her white hair and vibrates the feather on her hat. Long ago, in our wild young days, she disapproved of my relationship with her daughter. I can hardly blame her. We didn't stir up the past, pressed each others hands and paid each other compliments.

The next day, lunch at the Rouveyres, then on to see the Countess de La Béraudière who was expecting us. Masses of wonderful things: Raeburn, Lawrence, even Greco – but everything liberally covered with . . . face powder!

January 31. I must have done with this visit to Paris, which is beginning to fade from my mind. At Flossie's brilliant party we were introduced to the old Marchioness of Anglesey, a dowager so beautiful that even at over eighty she draws all eyes. A lady wearing a coat lined with jaguar, who looked perfectly capable of having killed and skinned the animal herself, was bent on enflaming me with her conversation, her compliments and her burning looks. Flossie was ravishing in a white crêpe dress and a turquoise blue

Spanish shawl embroidered in white, her hair making a turban of gold. She was leaving for Saint-Moritz that very evening.

February 2. Duchess Elisabeth is a sensual, greedy, lovable child who uses all the gifts with which she is endowed to the top of her bent. When she laughs she stamps her feet as though she couldn't contain herself. Her hair springs up as though it were impossible to control it. She eats as though she were starving. No doubt she is a voracious lover. She has the most delicious thoughts: she ought to have them published. I have been told that she has shed bitter tears over Nathalie, but nowadays they have a very close and tender friendship.

February 9. .... I have read some of the *Almanach*, given me by its kind author the Duchess of Clerment-Tonnerre. It is a jewel of a book, sensual, enlightened, even erudite, and above all full of poetry. One learns delightful things from it: that quails are highly immoral and will marry anyone, the best seasons for eating this, that and the other. She despises radishes, extols the poultry of La Flèche and the strawberries of Plougastel. She quotes Nathalie Clifford Barney, Renée Vivien and others. It is written with carefully polished wit. Even apart from her blue blood, this duchess is quite someone and I feel more and more flattered by her good opinion of me: 'Aha! Princess Georges Ghika, the most charming of letter-writers and perhaps of women!'

Saint-Germain – Hotel de l' Aigle d'or, February 19 to April 16

February 19. At last we have escaped from those atrocious Hélous! We are not too badly off here, in the rue du Vieil-Abreuvoir. At first sight it is dreary and banal like any little provincial hotel, but our room on the first floor overlooking a tree-filled courtyard is handsome, with large windows and tall Directoire doors. It is light, quiet, large, warm, with a dressing-room and two good brass beds. The bathroom works, the people are clean, friendly northerners, and they charge less than those stupid people who treated us so badly.

In *l'Intran* they describe, without giving my name, a charming Roumanian princess, celebrated by Jean Lorrain, who is writing her Memoirs to be bequeathed to the National Library for publication in a hundred years' time. 'But who knows,' they add, 'whether the National Library will accept them?' I remain unmoved.

. . . .

March 4. Henry Bataille died the day before yesterday at six o'clock in the evening, in two minutes: a stroke. He was writing, he felt ill, he called Yvonne, got up and went out onto the stairs saying 'I'm suffocating – get me ether!', fell down and was lifeless for ever. Yvonne is in tears and his great family, the theatre, is stunned. We are all striken. It took place at Malmaison – it seems that he bought that house among the treetops just to die in it. Georges went there yesterday evening. He saw him. He was beautiful and looked as though he were asleep, the expression of his mouth so ironic and intelligent. Bataille was more than a friend. Whenever we were up to it we met with so much pleasure and affection, we wanted to know everything, we commiserated, we appreciated, we liked each other so much. In twenty-eight years he only had two mistresses that I knew of: Berthe Bady, who died less than a year ago, then Yvonne de Bray. Georges found her yesterday collapsed beside his bed, pressed against him, her face all swollen, unable to cry any more – it's frightful.

. . . .

March 11. An impudent and charming note from that little flatterer, Clauzel. She offers me the corners of her mouth – which are indeed extremely pretty, childlike and mischievous. She offers that, as though it were a pot of blue hyacinths, at my age! I am a bit tough with her; I don't really like her all that much.

I have been exercising all my felinity in playing with Salomon. I was kind, approving, unguarded. He was jubilant. I showed him the scar on my right thigh from my dreadful car accident. He was hesitant and disturbed – it's said that the only nakedness he has ever seen is that of statues.

March 20. On Saturday we were deposited in Paris at 27 rue de Ville-d'Evêque by a cheerful Salomon who was on his way to see General Lyautey. We found Pépé very weak, very pale and ultra-chic, sitting in an arm-chair with a pillow at his back, a black and white fur rug lined with violet over his knees, a shirt of fine linen with pretty pleated cuffs falling over his narrow wrists, a black velvet dressing-gown lined with violet, and a filmy white Shetland shawl over his shoulders. Splendid and touching! It was his saint's day and his drawing-room was full of flowers. We added ours, wall-flowers in two little Dresden china pots, very old and much sought-after by connoisseurs. The Baronne de l'Epée was there, very attentive; she takes a lot of care of Pépé and seems to be part of the household. He lunched in his arm-chair, near the table. Pépé had an operation for hernia in his own house. Now he is free of business, can sit in the sun all day, and is planning, much encouraged by me, to drive out next Sunday and drink his chicken soup in my Polignac cupboard. At about three o'clock my Flossie arrived. We lay down to rest in the overwhelming scent of flowers. She took me in her arms and caressingly . . . we were both equally stupefied by tender-ness. The Countess de La Béraudière looked in for a moment to throw a charm on our voluptuous stupor with her caressing, slightly purring voice. Yvonne de Bray inherits the Château at Vivières, the property at Malmaison, the royalties from Bataille's four best plays, all the furniture in the flat on the Bois, and whatever liquid assets Bataille left. His other royalties go to his nephews and nieces. He made his will only two months ago.

March 21. Saw Yvonne de Bray; attempted to produce some sort of stupid and useless comfort. Her mother was there, and some men of business.

> Time's patina
> On precious things
> And broken hearts –
> Time's patina
> Heals and erodes
> In equal parts.*

She was pale and tall in black wool; no make-up. I stayed with her a good two hours. We must see each other again.

. . . .

April 5. Visit from Max Jacob yesterday. From time to time he has to leave his monastery at Saint-Benoît-sur-Loire and come to Paris to look after tiresome but essential money-matters. He agreed with his publishers to get three hundred francs a month on the one hand, five hundred on the other. Then he had to share what he was writing

---

* This is my wife's, unexpected and charming. Georges G. Ghika.

between them. This annoyed them and he stopped getting anything because each of them wanted to monopolize him. So – poverty, scruples, schemes. Max says that when he's in Paris he is a great sinner, so he makes his confession at the Sacré-Coeur before he goes back to Saint-Benoît because there he has to confess to the curé and since he lives with him he would be embarrassed........:.

. . . .

April 14. I have been to confession. I told Monsieur le curé my big sin: 'I took pleasure in receiving over-emphatic signs of affection from a woman friend, and in front of my husband who wasn't at all angry about it, he laughed.' The dear curé looked quite embarrassed and told me: 'If you feel that it was wrong, you must not do it again.' I gave him a few more details in case he should think that it was worse than it was. He is a good and worthy curé. He is aware of the efforts I make and doesn't keep me on too tight a rein. The Laglenne sisters are urging me to take communion. I want this communion, I *am* seeking Jesus. One thing's for sure, at my first communion I was not seeking anything at all, in those days I was a heedless, greedy little beast, a hot-blooded young animal chafing at the bit, laughing at Hell, pausing at neither the Passion nor the Cross, glimpsing death only to cock a snook at it. I used to steal apples, strawberries, copy books and bars of chocolate, and then get myself caught by generously distributing my booty. I wouldn't have taken anything from another child, only from the community. I would have sold my soul for a beautiful box of coloured writing-paper with my initials on it in silver or gold. I learnt my lessons during church services, I recited La Fontaine's fables at prayers, I wrote impassioned letters to my best friends and I snipped bits off the shawls of my favourite nuns and preserved them between the pages of books. Now that I have been through every kind of suffering, have measured the infamy of human beings and the cruelty of fate, the insecurity of every living thing, God has become necessary to me. I want Him, I need Him, I seek Him, I call on Him, I pray to Him. Perhaps holy communion will speed my efforts towards success?

April 15. Madame R writes to say that her husband's health has improved. I like that woman a lot. She gives the impression of wanting to break out, but well-established habits are difficult to break: her chignon has no intention of being let down! Her voice has a decisive little ring, crisp and high, quite unsuggestive of voluptuousness. She's like someone in a theatre, sitting in a box. Yes, that's it, she has never had any role to play but that of spectator, and time is passing – and she would so much have liked to join the dance. Pretty bird in a cage, watching the world which it has never known.

April 16. Easter Sunday: sun and rain, the weather sad and cold. The hotel packed with noisy people.

I took communion this morning – I prayed to the best of my ability, I accomplished my religion's rites coldly and precisely. It is only in bed that I can pray properly, in darkness and silence, specially when the window is open. Then I feel God. As soon as it's a question of Jesus made man in order to save our souls, I might be trying to awaken a lifeless body. Nothing in me quivers, nothing responds, nothing speaks, nothing moves me. I will not despair. God has come down so low, I mean so far from Himself, in order to look for me.

Roscoff – Clos-Marie, July 4 to November 29

July 4. Two days ago I was fifty. I don't feel at all old. We arrived here on June 22; have spring-cleaned the house from top to bottom. Georges is enraptured, although we have had nothing but wind, cold and rain.

July 5. Our life in Pépé's house was nothing but joy, pleasures, parties and feasting. Everyone was so happy to see us, they danced attendance, they spoilt us. Pépé went off to work at Doucet's and was delighted to find us there, often with a crowd, when he came home. The servants were perfect, our first reception magnificent, the buffet (shared between us) sumptuous. Madame R was there, so animated, so joyful that she quite forgot her revived husband's mutterings. Nathalie came, the Countess Clauzel, Madame de Lubersac, the Countess de La Béraudière, the most famous actresses: Marcelle Lender, Germaine Gallois, Cora Lapercie, Amélie Dieterle, Madeleine Lambert, Vollerin, my dear Vollerin, devoted and sentimental though now he is quite swallowed up in Sacha Guitry's fame, being his secretary and his soul. In short, there were seventy of us, all having a lovely time watching, gossiping, flattering, tippling. Pépé received the guests in the big drawing-room, helped by the Baronness de l'Epée, and they were brought through to me in the little red drawing-room next to the dining-room where the monstrous buffet was spread. Robert de Rothschild made an appearance. We had three musicians: Auric, Poulenc and Eric Satie. They played some of their works. That was when Georges and I made the acquaintance of Francis Poulenc; Max Jacob has talked about him so often and was always on the point of bringing him to see us. Well, he is charming! I was wearing my black georgette peplum by Madeleine Vionnet, something quite unique, admirable, it works so perfectly that one can't describe it. Even Pépé, in spite of professional jealousy, had to bow down before this masterpiece.

What pearls there were! Madame Marthe Besnut, Prince Coloradi-Mansfeld's (?) fiancée, was wearing three millions' worth. Pépé was so enchanted that next day he gave me a beautiful grey wolf – the fashionable fur at the moment – and a very chic bracelet made of a circlet of onyx.

The next day we visited our neighbour Jean Cocteau, who was laid up all winter with a painful neuritis. He was preparing to leave for the Midi.

July 7. I have sent Pépé a beautiful lobster. He spoilt me terribly. The cook used to come and take orders from me. Our guests and his mingled to their hearts' delight. Nathalie came to Pépé, Pépé went to Nathalie. Her set is really select, their morals easy-going and their intellects unsparing. Lucie Delarue-Mardrus comes to sing poems while Armand de Polignac and de Chabannes play her own music as accompaniment. Auric and Poulenc come to play their new works. Chana Orloff, Madame de La Nux exhibit at Nathalie's: Orloff wood carvings, de La Nux boldly executed drawings, lightly coloured. She did a portrait of me for Nathalie, a very beautiful synthesis, the head tilted a little back, breasts bare, eyelids weary over a feverishly brilliant gaze. I sat for it at Flossie's house one thundery day in the poor light of a bedroom made even darker by a tree outside the open window.

We had five or six lunches at Nathalie's, plus her tea parties and her Fridays. Madame R took us for drives in the Bois, to Bagatelles among the roses, to the Cascade for tea under the trees. Once she took us all the way to Saint-Germain, back home, where I gave her a pot-luck tea. We kept meeting here and there, to our mutual pleasure; at two or three tea parties at the Countess de La Béraudière's, and another day at the Duchess Elisabeth's house. Madame R made me a present of a ravishing little silver-grey velvet handbag with a Chinese frame from Doucet's, where she took us one afternoon to see the models. There I was welcomed by Jacques Doucet, my former supplier, all shrivelled up and very changed. Pepito, enchanted, gave me four beautiful dresses and a cape – on the sole condition that I went to be photographed, which was done by Manuel and by Baron Rhebinder, Jacqueline de Pourtalès's husband – and then a superb wrapper in mauve crêpe de chine in which I could perfectly well dine, or even appear at a formal tea party. He gave me a beautiful sable muff which used to belong to his wife, who was very fond of me. We did everything we could to spoil him, too, and to make his life pleasant and happy. It was rather tiring for us to lead a double life like that, seeing his friends as well as ours, and then Georges was ill . . .

July 8. . . . very ill with amoebic dysentry which started suddenly, the day before our second reception. There was a wild and noisy Brazilian orchestra and eighty pleasant, happy and indifferent people to smile at. The doctor, called in at once, ordered bed, but Georges insisted on getting up and spending a short time in the tumult, which complicated his illness. He is still feeling the effects.

If it hadn't been for this tormenting worry, our second party would have been splendid. A buffet worthy simultaneously of Gargantua and of Brillat-Savarin. Madame R triumphant, Nathalie infatuated. As for Madrazzo, he was mad about the negroes and couldn't tear himself away from them, surrounded by Poulenc, Darius Milhaud and Georges Auric – not to mention Paul Morand, man of the year.

July 9. There has been a violent gale blowing in from the sea all night, the waves are breaking very high, the rain is falling in sheets. I do tapestry, write, read . . . .

When we were in Paris we went to the theatre only three times, to matinées. Once to see Sacha Guitry . . . . I said to Sacha: 'You must have a child to carry on the brilliant line of Guitrys.' Sacha sprang to his feet: 'Princess, your wishes are orders, I will see to it at once,' and he left the dressing-room. I blinked, and there he was coming back in again with a beautiful tiny pink baby in his arms – how we laughed! It was the child of Yvonne Printemps's dresser. We had taken young Poulenc with us, thrilled to meet the famous Sacha. Papa Guitry made his appearance while we were there. He is terrific! An old man in a class of his own, who looks as though he had descended from Olympus in order to wipe a nation out or to load it with blessings. He dominates. Old as he is, masses of women are still in love with him. When he came in Sacha raised his head, got up, took one step backwards, stretched out his arms and threw himself towards the immobile old man in order to embrace him. Next the blonde Yvonne advanced lightly on tiptoe and reached up to the sacred cheek with her little pointed muzzle. Then me: 'I'm not going to be left out . . .' and there I was in Lucien's arms. Finally we tore ourselves apart. And that, no doubt, will be that for several years.

July 10. Still dreary and wet, the tourists are postponing their arrival. If this goes on it will be very hard on the locals.

To continue the story of our stay in Paris. We went to Sarah Bernhardt's theatre. They were doing *Régine Armand* by her son-in-law, Verneuil. During the first act the principal female part is taken by young Simone Fréveilles: a ravishing creature with charming regular features, long, slim, graceful and not at all bad. In the second act Sarah appears, seated in an actress's dressing-room. It's as though she were in her own. She looks much older, a shadow of herself, and she begins to speak in an undertone: the golden voice hardly carries at all. (It was a beautiful Sunday in May and the theatre was almost empty, no doubt Sarah was saving herself.) She shows nothing but her proud and beautiful profile, so clear-cut and regular (people used to say mine resembled it), her make-up is skilful, light, smooth, telling, unique. She knows better than anyone else how to use drapery, her gestures are marvellous, full of restraint, grace and style. At a given moment little Fréveilles has to approach her and take up a dialogue. Well, she simply ceases to exist beside Sarah! Sarah wins, and wins hands down, in spite of illness, age, the falling away of her voice, and a set of false teeth which threaten to follow suit and which is continually being brought to order between the measured syllables by a neat and clever flick of the tongue. Poor admirable Sarah! She will die on the stage like an old soldier at his post. One can only applaud and envy her.

July 11. This is what Sarah said to the person who told her that Réjane was dead: 'Réjane dead? It will be Granier's turn now.'

Today I want to talk about my conquests. Rediscovered Nathalie comes to coax and caress me, and murmur 'My first love, and my last.' I see her bending over to enfold me, and it seems that I have never left her arms. Inconstant Nathalie, so faithful, in spite of her infidelities. She celebrates my body down to the waist. That is all that I allow myself to grant. The rest belongs to Georges and no one else in the world can touch it. The rest would make the sin too big; and anyway that rest is so accustomed to Georges that it throbs for no one but him.

In second place comes Thérèse Diehl of the beaky nose, the wicked eye, the sensual mouth, very chic, candid as a child, unaffected, impudent, artful, simultaneously boring and attractive. She amused me; her skin is resilient. She is a good healthy Basque. She goes to mass every Sunday and doesn't at all allow her disorderly life to disturb her relationship with God. She shares a mad apartment with her brother Carl, a charming and well set-up invert who gets on very well with her and runs the family factory. Thérèse pursues happiness in pleasure, she drinks hard, talks too much, is a bad hostess, pays out generously, but lacks flair. Her head is charming when she tips it back. We went no further than kisses on the mouth. Then I went to dinner with her. There her furniture and her guests enlightened me: I was bored to death. I wrote her very charmingly, truly my letter was a song: 'Forgive me for having loved you because I can no longer tell you that I do.' That is a splendid sentence and always works. I have used it a good deal in my time.

It was then that poor Dora turned up. I had to pretend that I'd gone away. The telephone rang day and night. Pépé would answer: 'The princess is in Saint-Germain for a few days.' She loathed Nathalie and would never consent to meet us there. She did, however, bring her orchestra to the Countess de La Béraudière's. Funny little woman; she told me she was forty, because in an attempt to put her off I had advanced my fiftieth birthday. God! when a woman gets something into her head, how hard it is to get it out again!

My other conquest was Madame Bonin, heavy and hot. We met at Nathalie's and sat hand in hand during the whole two hours of that tea party. Another time I invited her to Pépé's house. I was alone. She arrived trembling and panting, fell on my bed and wanted to offer me everything. I drew her attention to the barrier raised by my principles across the bodies of women, just a little below their hearts and their breasts. She tore off her clothes to bare the latter, neither beautiful nor ugly, too big and a bit squeezed together. The top part of her arms was ravishing. She is a woman for men, designed to serve them, amuse them and then, very soon, to bore them. I took it into my head to offer her something to eat and dragged her into the dining-room where she devoured a bowl of cherries, reproaching me the while for getting her 'into such a state'.

July 12. Nothing amuses me this morning. Still, I would like to talk about my third conquest. At my request I met the daughter of an old friend of mine at Flossie's house. Betsy has her mother's superb fair hair, fashionably cut, a long face, a clear complexion and soft, roving eyes. She gives the impression of tempered steel, an indomitable character. She has her wits about her. At our second meeting, which took place at Pépé's house on a day when I was in bed, she threw herself into my arms, tremulous with passion. Astonished, I held her and began to stroke her hair. She offered me her lips. What could I do but kiss them? I did so with the utmost tenderness and with a touch of alarm, since the vivid impression made by Madame Bonin was still with me. Betsy was gentle and tender, she knew how the situation should be handled. She was a little bit lost for a day or two.

They were copying my dresses in Paris. We had dug out a poor little lady in reduced circumstances who was working on commission for a couturier. She could do a georgette dress embroidered pretty well all over for two hundred francs. Since we were going out a great deal, and in a very fashionable circle, I had to renovate my wardrobe a little and I ordered three: black embroidered with silver, grey the same, and white embroidered with dull white beads. These little slips of dresses had a mad success. All my friends wanted them, several of them at a time.

July 13. My photos have come from Manuel. The old girl doesn't look too bad now that she's fifty, wearing a lace dress in a couturier's advertisement!

I met Nathalie's sister again. Dear Laura seems frustrated and hard. One feels that she is hatching dark plots under her silence. When she speaks, the sentence falls – into emptiness! She looks down with disdain on her sister and her sister's friends, on her husband, on plates, glasses and desserts. I thought it would be nice to remind her how charming I once found her offer to save me from the life I was living by giving me her dowry. She shot me a glance heavy with unspoken thoughts and couldn't bring herself to answer. Her husband thought fit to say: 'How lucky Liane didn't accept. I had no idea that Laura could be so imprudent.'

July 14. We are having the doors and shutters of our little Clos repainted. I am giving it a summer dress in the hope that it will be welcoming Nathalie and the Duchess.

As soon as I arrived in Paris Yvonne de Bray came to see me at Pépé's, draped in a sort of toga of black veiling, very impressive. 'It's the costume I wore in Henry's last play. He saw me dressed like this, it was his idea. I can't bear to wear anything else.' Rather theatrical, no doubt, but very graceful. She took me to Saint-Honoré-d'Eylau and swept through the church and then through the sacristy as though she were in her own house. She walked fast, carrying a key, looking neither to right nor left and without uttering a word, as though she were accomplishing some rite. There was something moving in her loneliness and rapidity. She went down some steps into the crypt, stopped at a little door, opened it: there, by the flower-covered coffin on which I piously placed a bunch of Parma violets, she burst into tears. Two candles were burning at the head of the coffin which was raised on a dais. I took her in my arms and mingled my tears with hers. I have not seen her since then. She is busy – and it will do her good – with Henry's bequests, his plays, his memorial, his posthumous reputation.

. . . .

July 20. . . . . Rochegrosse has sent me Giovanni Papini's *Story of Christ*, which is much discussed at present. It's in the form of short chapters each devoted to one of the facts of Jesus's life. It is easy to read, written very poetically and very accurately. I can read it with enthusiasm, soak myself in it, take in every detail – and the Gospels leave me unmoved, or almost so. I am still too thickly enveloped in flesh – and yet I really detest this tired, painful flesh. I despise it. Flesh ought to be alive and beautiful, firm, vibrant, animated. All that is over as far as I'm concerned. I hear a voice saying: 'Surely you don't want, after playing fast and loose with the flesh as you did in the days of your beauty – surely you don't want to turn to the divine consoler just at the moment when the ability to do wrong is leaving you?' Yes indeed, that is exactly what I want. And anyway, my crimes were not all that bad! Always so many arguments cancelling each other out, and me in the middle of it all with a sick body and an anxious soul. So then I fly to my beloved, tender, merciful Saint Anne! And suddenly everything lights up, I feel my strength renewed, I become resigned, I begin to hope. Saint Anne, do not abandon me, you are all I have! And through you I will find the rest.

July 21. This morning the painters finished dressing up the Petit-Clos. It was the least we could do for Gladness (the Duchess) and Harmony (Nathalie). Now we can face them without blushing.

July 29. The end of the world has been announced for the last days of August. Seventy volcanos are going to erupt, all at the same time. I wonder what I would do if I really believed that the end of the world was at hand? I would go to Flossie's house in Paris, be there between Georges and my darling, wearing my prettiest dress and my pearls. I would ask Auric to play the piano – or perhaps driving along a road in a car with those two, eyes fixed on the last landscape the earth's crust would ever offer us? Or there's church, of course – organ music, lights, the ardent prayers of the faithful, the exhortations from the pulpit. There would be danger of panic there; one can pray elsewhere. Alone in my bed and in Georges's arms? Rather frivolous ways of preparing to meet God!

August 4. Rain, grey sky. Everything looks dark and dreary in my eyes. Summer refuses to start. Even my roses – they are rotting before they open.

Letter from Max Jacob. Crafty – this is how he does it: 'Jacques Emile Blanche (painter and writer) is waiting for me in Normandy, the Lazarus family has asked me to Hacqueville, the Daudets want me in their country house – but, my dears, it is you I choose!' Thanks a lot! We are not going to answer. If he turns up we will accept him as a gift (!) from God, Whose will it is that His creatures should be put to the test.

. . . .

August 20. The Duchess and Nathalie arrived at about midnight, exhausted but so charming! They had wanted to see Mont Saint Michel, call on Seignobos at Paimpol and heaven knows what else! They are still asleep as I write. How I hope the sun will come out to shine on our joy and this celebration of friendship.

August 21. Charming day with my charming friends. The regatta didn't disturb us, siestas, rest, good food and conversation. Afterwards I took them onto the jetty to show them my cliff kingdom and the twinkling evening lights of my village, which is all of Roscoff. The duchess is a delicious being, interested in everything; and how she does love life! How well she knows the art of living fully and beautifully!

They like the Petit-Clos. Nathalie is the connector, the bringer of order, she is redolent of an art which everyone ought to command and which she, with her smiling, silent grace, bestows on all of us. The Duchess played the flute. She is pure Watteau. She has brought some pretty clothes: pearl grey costumes, a pleated skirt, a duffel jacket, a little felt hat worn over one ear, black and gold pyjamas. I asked her: 'Duchess, tell me the first thing you can remember from your childhood.' – 'Aha,' she said, 'I've thought about that already, for my memoirs. I was two and a half. I had lost my mother so I was being brought up in England by my doting grandmother. She imagined that it was her duty to send me on a visit to my father, who was a brilliant cavalry officer, stationed at Melun at the time. When I got there I was stunned: he was the first person in the world who hadn't prostrated himself before me! Then he took me into a garden where there was a plum tree which he shook violently, bringing down a hail of plums on my little head and hurting me much more than he amused me.'

August 22. Yesterday I took them to see the beautiful cathedral at Saint-Pol, then to Penzé where we explored the mysterious alleys which I love so much. We greeted the tower of Berthe Bigfoot in passing and stopped at the illustrious calvary of Saint-Thégonnec. They bathed in the sea with Georges. The Duchess has a lovely swimming costume of violet wool. Undressed she is superb – dresses thicken her and spoil her shape. She soothed our siesta with the silvery accents of her flute. It was soft, pastoral, plaintive. She really does have tremendous style, always, in every one of her gestures, in her every attitude. Nathalie was sulking yesterday. It was obvious, so the Duchess made herself attentive.

After dinner we went up to my room. Georges and the Duchess smoked. I got into bed. Flossie came and lay down beside me . . . I committed the delicious sin of abandoning myself to her caressing hands while the Duchess and Georges went on talking literature with the utmost gravity. Nathalie and I were laughing like children at nothing and everything and it was infectious. The little Garat girl had come for the drive with us and was tired and happy, embarrassed at seeing us in each other's arms; she didn't know where to look, so then we teased her and she began to laugh with us. Goodnights were said. The Duchess came to sit on my bed for a moment. She was disturbed. She kissed the back of my neck, then my mouth.

August 23. Day follows day, fine, happy, golden within and without. Our friends are beautiful, cheerful, healthy, delicious and pleased with everything, all quite naturally, without effort or strain. At Santec we walked barefoot in the sea and the warm, soft sand. We drove back by the Isle of Sieck and by Saint-Pol, past the Danielou estate with the famous fig tree which spreads over six hundred square metres and is supported on ninety stone pillars. Our friends exclaimed: 'But it's a marvel! People go all the way to India to see giant baobabs or to Africa in order to rave about enormous rubber trees, and this beats the lot!' When we got home they went swimming, with Georges. Wrapped in her white towelling robe, the Duchess is as attractive as ever. No one else has such a majestic walk. For breakfast I give them toast, warm brioches, milk bread with raisins in it, tea, the freshest butter and our famous Plougastel strawberry jam, served on Quimper china. They make short work of it. We never stop laughing, we understand each other, we blend and mingle. In the evenings . . . the plot thickens. The Duchess came to lie on my bed and Nathalie snuggled between us. Caresses, loving kisses. It was charming – perhaps a little nerve-racking. Camille kept her head turned away so that she should see nothing. Georges read poetry aloud. Nathalie remembered something Marguerite Moreno said when she was staying with friends in the country, on a rainy day. Someone had asked 'What shall we do?' In her melodious, beautifully modulated voice Marguerite let fall the one word: 'Fornicate.'

I love my friends. Surely, dear Lord, it can't be a great sin? It is You who sent them to me all open-hearted, it's You who made them so sweetly fond and sensual, it's You who make them lean over me with such tenderness – surely it is?

'The Duchess is flighty,' says Nathalie. 'Elegantly, indolently flighty.' What else should Gladness be? No doubt the tenderness displayed by Harmony is more penetrating. As for me, I am Abandon: joyful, strung-up, with – this morning – a headache, a back-ache and my head in a whirl. But still a haze of happiness covers everything brought to me recently by my friendship with these charming beings. It is, in fact, an exquisite occasion in which we are all delighting in our true affection for each other. The sin would be if there were dishonesty or trickery in it, if there were an ulterior motive – snobbery or gross sensuality – or if decisive gestures had been made. Whereas these delicate, tentative caresses, like inhaling the perfume of a flower . . . ?

August 31. Read in the papers that at the celebrations at Caen Emilienne d'Alençon went up in an aeroplane piloted by an 'impresario'. When they were landing they ran into a tree, the machine blew up, the impresario was killed on the spot and Emilienne has been taken to hospital in Livarot with serious injuries. But what an idea, to get up to anything so dangerous, and at her age – which is the same as mine!

A card from my Flossie, another – exquisite – from Madame R and one from Salomon who has already heard about the radiant visitation I received. So he's grimacing and flattering and hinting. I am going to answer him without saying a word about it.

September 1. Such a charming note from my dear little Duchess. In my answer I am doing as she asked and describing one of our days in full. What a charming thought!

September 7. Everything the Duchess does is so charming – she has sent Georges a delightful poem celebrating our excursions in my beloved Brittany. It is very modern, and to tell the truth I'm a bit baffled by this kind of complicated thing which has to be read almost like a puzzle.

September 9. I am reading the letters of Madame de Maintenon. How that woman did love to give advice! She was only a school-mistress, but what a school-mistress! She seems willingly to have sacrificed herself and all the joys of a woman's life for the sake of directing and commanding. She never stopped beating time for other people to dance to. There is something very unattractive about this woman getting what she wanted by reason, patience and self-effacement. I prefer the actress who dances her way into the arms of a prince.

September 10. Cocteau has sent us a brochure which is entirely about himself. It's the fashion. They open their stomachs and say 'Look what I've got inside me!' The spectacle is neither clean nor pretty!

September 11. Madame de Maintenon asks the Abbé Gobelin for Saint Teresa's *Meditations on the Father*. It is my own bedside reading. It is very well designed for every day of the week, and I find it most helpful.

September 15. I am very kind, my kindness is measureless, but it doesn't last. It suddenly switches away from people, rejects them and turns towards others. And for those I have rejected, I feel nothing but indifference. I try to love Jesus. It is my constant effort, my daily prayer; and I cannot achieve it. Effort and reason have nothing to do with love. But perhaps this effort is in itself love? I don't see Jesus. I don't like the victims of persecution. It's like this: my reason wants to adore Jesus and my instincts jib. I lay my free will at the feet of my dear Saint Anne; I wait the divine love which must regenerate me, I accept non-love as punishment. Giovanni Papini's life of Christ, which I read every evening, is very beautiful; I read it, alas, as a pagan.

October 27. Georges becomes more and more disagreeable, hostile. He shows no consideration for the balance of my poor nerves, achieved with such difficulty. He no longer bothers about the harmony of our existence. To me this seems stupid, destructive. It is such misery to live like this after having chosen each other, as we did. I am losing my vivacity, my energy, my youthfulness of heart; in a word, I am being ill-used and that makes me bad-tempered and unhappy. I hate this man; I have taken a real dislike to him.

October 28. I think Georges is making efforts to mollify me. They are not very happy ones – they lack conviction. His mind is no longer capable of conceiving anything but outward forms. Perhaps he no longer loves me? Perhaps it is simply the necessary bonds of habit which link him to me? At the beginning of the war I hated him so much that I wanted him – in spite of his bad health – to join up. Our misfortunes and my grief had a hard time bringing us together. Travel? I would be dragging him behind me wherever I went. That's why journeys no longer tempt me. Wherever it goes that soft, evil paw treads, crushes, destroys. There isn't a landscape or an attempt at escape which hasn't been ruined for me. All my troubles come from that, from him.

October 29. I have had such a lovely letter from Nathalie. We love each other deeply; she has always given me so much pleasure intellectually. Our souls understand each other and mingle so tenderly; our bodies' gestures are dictated by the movements of our souls. There is no ugliness there, no brutality, no dirtiness. I love to lie down beside her, be in her arms, fall asleep lulled by the thoughts she breathes in short, sweet phrases. My Nathalie is a gift from heaven! Georges is stagnant, swampy, without strength, unwholesome; Nathalie's a luminous and subtle ray of light which gilds everything it touches.

November 18. Received this delicious letter from the no less delicious R. 'It is still quite delightful to go to Doucet's, and to Callot's too; but where are the sultans for whose sake one would wish to wear all this finery? Leave these temples of elegance and all one sees is appalling human nature under a foggy sky . . .' Madame Strauss is in mourning for her son. I shan't repeat here all her determined nastiness towards me: Princess Georges Ghika forgives the enemies of Liane de Pougy.

Naturally I had a dream about Madame Strauss, meeting her at the races, her youth and beauty restored. I also had other dreams, distinctly Freudian. I shall have to abandon myself to conjugal caresses this evening for my health's sake, and out of habit – and from love too, in spite of everything.

. . . .

November 21. Death of Marcel Proust. We have known forever that he was delicate, and became used to seeing him surviving in spite of it. His death has taken us by surprise. It has impressed and saddened us. He really did have talent, a strange talent: a sick man's rarified talent which weighed and pondered everything; an elegant talent, above muscular materialism; rather a mannered talent, a bit snobbish, but large, in spite of being diminished by the sick-room. When the Duchess was here this summer she had a letter from Proust who called her Emilie, although her name is Elisabeth; we laughed a lot about it. Perhaps he hoped for an answer putting him right? He was clever, loved titled and highly placed people. He was teasing and disdainful, vain and proud of his real importance. With all that, not tremendously sympathetic. His work is beautiful; no mystification there. It is short. He was approaching forty when he gave it to the public, just at the start of the war, and success came to him straight away. Last year he was given the Prix Goncourt.

. . . .

November 29. I've received a photograph of the portrait Madame de La Nux did of me last summer, at Nathalie's house. Georges is crazy about it, he gazes at it, cooes over it, smiles at it, is dreaming up an ebony frame for it, or one of black lacquer. I like my eyelids in it, little half-melons, and my arms and my breasts. It was summer, or rather the very hottest days of spring, and I posed nude to the waist on Flossie's downy bed, buried by her in the softest cushions. I remember that Madame R took me by surprise like that. I seemed unmoved, but really I was embarrassed. The clever little artist, dark, with huge black eyes, had such pretty gestures. From time to time we exchanged a thought or two, or Nathalie, lying in her dressing-room next door, threw in a sentence. We and our two husbands had lunched with her. What, in fact, were our two husbands doing? Pierre de La Nux had gone racing; Georges was resting in the big round drawing-room on the first floor, smoking and burrowing about among Nathalie's scattered books and papers. He looked in from time to time, friendly and happy; I could feel that he liked the atmosphere and my pose.

1923

∾∾∾∾∾∾∾∾∾∾∾∾∾∾∾∾∾∾∾∾∾∾∾∾∾∾∾∾∾∾∾∾∾∾

Nice – Langham Hotel, March 18 to April 16

March 18. No blue notebook for three months! For three months I led a dissipated, self-diminishing life without meditation.

I took New Year presents for all my friends, my intimate friends, to Pépé's house. Trunks unpacked, things put away; Pépé apparently happy, we too, smiling servants. We are going to have such a good time, give parties, go to them, eat, drink and be merry . . . Yes indeed! Saturday the 6th was the chosen date, five hundred invitations were sent out. Man proposes, God disposes . . . To be continued tomorrow.

March 20. I left matters at my arrival at Pépé's house, full of joyful promise. On New Year's Day we gave a large and splendid lunch. It was very gay. Pépé was just back from Germany feeling much better because of a strict diet, but not cured: and Pépé wanted to taste everything. We had endless trouble persuading him to stick to his noodles, his roast pheasant (Robert de Rothschild had sent me three) and his boiled potatoes. All day long there was a procession of his friends and our friends bringing good wishes, flowers, sweetmeats, kisses. I can still see Pépé coming over to me and saying in triumph: 'I've been eating the lot and it's wonderful, I haven't had the slightest pain' – whereupon he plunged into the chocolates and marrons glacés. On the second we lunched with Nathalie, the Duchess and Rouveyre, feeling rather anxious because Pépé had been smitten with a terrible stomach ache during the night. We went home early. We found Pépé in bed, pale, feverish, and groaning, his secretary at his side. He absolutely did not want us to call a doctor. I argued, I begged, I implored and at last he allowed me to telephone Jean-Charles Roux. Yes, but – J-C Roux was in Germany at a conference. Pépé continued to groan, I thought of Gaston Lyon. He came at once, palpated Pépé and ordered absolute rest, the strictest fast and bags of ice on the stomach. On the morning of the third I found Pépé up, green in the face, contorted, howling, insisting that he was going to the office. Georges and I forced him back into bed and the doctor came back: 'Keep absolutely still, not even a drop of water. I'll come back this evening.' I sent Georges off to lunch at the Rouveyres with Nathalie and the Duchess, and I stayed in. Pépé's howls redoubled, his face was haggard, his skin was waxy and he was frantic for a glass of milk. I prevented this until the doctor arrived at five o'clock. 'Keep absolutely still, not even a drop of water, I'll come back tomorrow morning,' and off he went . . . or rather, off he was going, because I caught him on his way downstairs and said crisply: 'Doctor, you simply cannot leave my patient like this. He is very ill indeed, his temperature is rising. It is essential that you come back this evening to check on him, keep him calm, prevent him drinking – and you must bring another doctor.' He gave me a look and said: 'Well, if you want to know the truth it's not another doctor I need, it's a surgeon. I was going to tell you tomorrow morning.' Something made me say forcefully: 'No doctor, not tomorrow morning. Now, this evening – and quickly.'

Half an hour later he brought us that great strapping Professor Le Senne, whom he'd had the luck to meet. After a careful examination Le Senne came into my room, shut the door and said: 'He'll be dead by tomorrow if I don't operate at once.' I pulled myself together. 'Very well, doctor; I'll take responsibility as though he were my husband. Operate on our friend quickly, don't let him die.' I was not proud. Le Senne went on: 'It's a dangerous operation, I'll see to everything. It will have to be done upstairs, I daren't risk bringing him down on a stretcher.' I went through three hours of atrocious anxiety. It was nine o'clock. I'd had no dinner and didn't want any. Meanwhile Georges bustled about watching over everything and making sure that everything would be ready. The Celer agency sent round six men and two women to turn the sitting-room upstairs into an operating theatre. It was really extraordinary to watch the speed and completeness of the transformation. Jacques Doucet came round. Georges told him the exact truth and he comforted and consoled Pépé by pretending to know that it was appendicitis. He offered to stay with us all night, and remembering his seventy-one-years I was tremendously grateful. The operation began at ten o'clock.

In the middle of it my room was plunged into darkness; the lights had fused. 'Oh my God!' I screamed, 'Pépé's up there with his stomach open!' Absolute panic. Georges flew out and came back beaming; the upstairs fuses had not gone. I was so stunned, so overcome, that I had not been able to pray.

It was all over by eleven. Pépé, carried back to bed by the benevolent giant Le Senne, woke up with no pain. The doctors told us: 'The gall bladder had swollen to the size of an aubergine and was on the point of bursting. We have excised what we had to, and have inserted drains; he is still in danger, great danger. We cannot promise anything. Till tomorrow!'

I am abbreviating. It really was marvellous, progress was so rapid. Pépé was up by the end of the week, eating chicken on the fourth day, playing up with his nurses, grumbling about his servants, wanting to know everything that was going on, listening to every sound in his house and becoming so intimate with us that it was soon perfectly insupportable. We wanted to leave. 'Don't forsake me! Don't make me unhappy!' So we stayed, pleased to have saved him and glad to see something of our friends. But day by day Pépé became more didactic, more demanding, even tyrannical, quite grossly rude. He no longer restrained himself at all. We had become things to him, slaves. We didn't belong to ourselves any more. He gave orders. His tone was sharp and peremptory. I understood Balthy.

The day after the operation, when the doctors were still forbidding visitors, Pépé whispered softly: 'Liane, if Louise comes, let her give me a kiss.' So at about eleven o'clock we went round to fetch Louise with Nathalie (who was almost as worried for us as she was for him). Balthy already knew all about it and nothing would shake her, she did not want to come. 'Shit!' she said. 'It's his wickedness that poisoned him. You're not getting me there.' – 'My darling Louise, he's dying.' – 'Shit!' – 'My darling Louise, he's asking for you.' – 'Shit!' – 'My darling Louise, he does love you underneath it all.' – 'Shit!' Nathalie added her urgings to mine. Finally Louise let us shove her, drag her, shut her into the car, carry her off. She was saying 'Shit!' all the way to the house. She went upstairs; Pépé saw her, opened his arms to her, they kissed. Then Louise made a silent and dignified exit from the room, gave me a look, murmured a last 'Shit!' – and departed, never to return. Faced with Pépé's behaviour to us, I understood, sadly I understood, and I wrote to tell her so. What a delightful holiday! What charming gratitude!

I saw Sorel again, splendid and sprightly, condescending and gracious, attended by her faithful Ségur. She had us to lunch one fine morning when the Seine was rippling like blue *moiré*, in her beautiful marble dining-room on the marble table which cost – so Pepito said – a hundred thousand francs. This table was covered with a pink cloth glimmering through gold gauze, strewn with multi-coloured tulips and fragrant mimosa among which were scattered peaches, pears, grapes and bananas. Célimène's lovely hands wandered about this flowery meadow, distributing fruit hither and thither. Everyone produced what was best in him or her. Sorel smiled, Ségur contemplated her – but without forgetting to do honour to the exquisite viands. Cécile's whole purpose is to dazzle and charm and it's done so nicely, so sincerely, that it works. Her apartment on the Quai Voltaire is grandiose, rich and in faultless taste. Everything is carefully chosen to provide a frame for a beauty composed wholly of artificial elements who is able, carefully and deliberately, to impose her own terms. Sorel brought me some beautiful roses to Pépé's house. I sent her a bottle of 'Liane', the toilet water sold by Delettrez with my picture on the label and a few approving words which I put together for him. Little Ségur is crazy about it. He wants to marry her; she resists. Will she ever do it? Backstage gossip has it that Guillaume de Ségur's mother is vastly rich and is against the marriage; so Sorel refuses and keeps him captive by love alone while she waits for the mother – who might conceivably dare to disinherit such a charming daughter-in-law! – to die. The little fellow is very well-off, and no fool. Sometimes when they are on tour he is given a part in a play beside his beloved. He has a good time, looks after the lighting, organizes visitors, has a hand in arranging tours, rehearsals, fittings, photographs, posters. We had a good laugh together. He knows how to enjoy life. He knows how to eat.........

March 22. .... Nathalie is miffed. She promised that she would come here with the Duchess at the end of March, and now she looks like going back on her promise. Having been offended, I wanted to offend in my turn. I wrote a very poetic letter to the Duchess suggesting that she should come with Mademoiselle Lefranc. Whereupon my Nathalie was stirred to wrath and wrote me a stern letter accusing me of not being pure gold. Nathalie is becoming cantankerous; it must be the change of life; she bristles at the least thing, her voice goes arrogant and pompous. I had a taste of it on December 27th or

28th; it passed, obviously, but it happened. For four days I flinched away from her as though she were a red hot poker. I called her 'Extra-dry, for the American market' and for a time withdrew the sweet name of Harmony. She was penitent and found charming ways of making up. I do like Nathalie, but she scares me and being scared does *not* suit me.

The Duchess was exquisite from beginning to end of our stay in Paris. She came to cheer us up every day, telephoned every morning, gave a lovely luncheon for me, then a tea party with the famous Ricardo Vines who played me marvels by Granados and Albeniz and insisted that I should sit by him as he played. The Duchess took us – Georges and me – to the Vieux Colombier theatre to see *le Carosse du saint-sacrement*, the most delightful comedy in twenty years, and so well acted.

March 24. A Spanish writer who is much discussed at the moment, Ramon Gomez de la Serna, has said in one of his books that women's breasts are incapable of sensation! How could anyone have the pitiful impudence to be so far from the truth as that man! Breasts – my own and almost all those I have known – the little points of breasts live a life of the most intense passion. What an idiot! Nathalie has put him right in a charming article under the signature 'The Amazon'. How can anyone publish and spread such nonsense? The man must be a brute.

March 27. Thérèse Diehl was with me almost all day yesterday. She was biddable and adorable; towards evening she seemed sad and languid. She's the same kind of person as Bernstein; like him, she can sometimes be carried away by her own play-acting. That reminds me of a funny story about Bernstein and Missia Edwards (now Madame Sert, née Godeski) when she was repudiated by Edwards because of pretty Lantelme and wanted to engineer a little scandal to her own advantage, in order to excite her husband and recapture him. Attracted by Henry's record, she picked on him. I had run away for the sixth time and had gone into hiding – very boring it was, too – in the depths of a little hotel in Passy. Henry knew where I was, came to bang on the door, implore, threaten. He tried to bribe the gardener to throw a sack over my head, tie me up and hand me over. Then it occurred to him that the trail laid by Missia might provide an agreeable diversion, so he went off to find her in Baden-Baden. The first evening Missia betook herself with precautions and abandon to Henry's rooms, complete with all her nocturnal gear including her pillow. Henry looked askance at all this and said to himself: 'This is going to be tough – the whole night, for heaven's sake!' He loved his comforts and could have cried at this depressing sight. Two more nights followed – the same thing all over again. In despair he began to shower me with emissaries, letters, telegrams, 'Come to me, Liane, my only love, the only sensible woman in the world, come to your Henry who is dying for love of you.' I was tickled by all this so I went to Baden. Henry drove to intercept me a few stations before. He threw himself on me, looking frantic, caught me up in his arms and carried me to his car. Pale, in tears, he babbled: 'Don't speak . . . don't speak . . . this is too strong, too beautiful for words.' At the hotel I found a most sumptuous suite. It was intoxicating. Missia and Henry had parted in a very ill-humour with each other. When they saw each other again they were cross and distant. Missia wanted her revenge and involved her first husband, the Jew Natanson, to this end. He picked a quarrel with Bernstein at the Authors' Society, and Henry flew into a passion and took it up. Oh that duel! What a performance my great actor made of it! Everyone round me was sworn to keep it from me, but an indiscretion – cunningly devised between Bernstein and Vanderein – took place by telephone; I pretended that I didn't understand. Lucien Guitry pretended that he'd made a mistake about the time and rang to ask the result: I got rid of him by simulating being cut off. When Henry left me he gave me long, speaking looks, his kisses were manly and reticent; I played the innocent. As soon as he had left I received a vast sheaf of roses complete with a letter on black-edged writing paper – a sort of testament of love meant for posterity and to drive me frantic. I roared with laughter. Marguerite Moreno was with me, she began to tell me about her love affair with Catulle Mendès and time passed cheerfully. Someone brought me the telephone, I heard a grave, gentle voice: 'My Lianon . . .' – 'Oh, so it's you. Aren't you dead?' – 'Oh Liane, how can you speak to me like that, at this moment?' – 'Frankness is suitable for any moment.' – 'Lianon, I'm coming round, I'm wounded.' – 'Are you? Where? In the tongue?' – 'Oh Liane, my knuckles are grazed. Did you get the roses?' – 'Of course. The ceremony was complete, except for the finale.'

March 28. Sarah Bernhardt is dead, the golden voice is silent. We almost believed – or wished – her to be immortal. Oh Sarah!

What a magical being, what a revelation to my candid sixteen-year-old self – that *Tosca* I was taken to by Armand Pourpe during our honeymoon! ....

April 7. Lord Carnarvon, the archeologist, is dead. He was my love when I was eighteen. It was here at Nice, at the Restaurant Français, that I first saw him. He was twenty-five. I thought he was so fine, so distinguished, so thoroughbred, so chic that I adored him. Just to watch him and admire him was enough for my enthusiasm. He was introduced to me that same year at the clay-pigeon shooting at Monte Carlo. Tremendous heart-fluttering, I could have died at his feet. He left the next day! What a dear little silly I was. A few months later I saw him again in London, at Covent Garden. Lady Dudley had the measles and the key of her box was for sale according to custom, and I had bought it. Carnarvon walked in absent-mindedly during the interval: flutterings, smiles, excuses, compliments, confessions. He was vicious, an invert so they said. He loved me all the same . . . and was a delicious, agonizing lover, full of charm and cruel grace. So I became the rival of Lady de Grey – Gladys. I had the upper hand. He didn't make me very happy; he was fugitive, a traveller, always off to India, the Baltic, Scotland. I have kept a pearl in his memory, the most beautiful of all my pearls, the one valued today at a hundred thousand francs.
. . . .

Saint-Germain – Hotel de l' Aigle d'or, May 23 to 24

May 23. I lunched with the Lazaruses in Paris. After lunch Georges went to the Gare Montparnasse to prepare our journey to Roscoff, while I escaped to my dear Duchess in the rue Raynouard. She was in – and without Nathalie! The welcome she gave me was loving, joyful, tender, caressing. She was still my own Gladness. Dear, spontaneous, warm little Duchess. Her worldly duties are keeping her very busy these days, but she found time to tell me about the letters of Robert de Montesquiou and Marcel Proust, very curious letters. Montesquiou was so unkind to the gentle Marcel that it amounted to ferocity. It would be very interesting to see them. My Duchess has met Reynaldo Hahn, whom she likes very much. There were blue hydrangeas fading in her garden, and an African god commanded the entrance of the front court. She gave me some red roses. It's impossible not to love her! And how cross I am with naughty Nathalie, making me tell her lies like this, and avoid her! But I can't help it, I don't want to see Nathalie and they are always together. In the Duchess's bedroom I saw two pairs of slippers under a Louis XVI chest of drawers. I thought – the grey pair are Nathalie's, and I wanted to pull a face at them. Anyway, I showed Gladness my delight in being near her, in kissing her, in having her in my life, my thoughts, my heart. She was looking young and beautiful with a jaunty little almond-green hat, a chiffon scarf flung carelessly round her neck, a dark green satin Poiret-Egyptian dress embroidered in vivid colours. I feel quite impregnated with her tender warmth.

May 24. At about eleven o'clock I was just going out when I heard the magisterial voice of Salomon Reinach asking if we were in. He is no longer banned. I opened the door, and my little Duchess who was hiding in the alcove flew into my arms! She brought me a bouquet of purple roses and the delight of her sparkling presence. She talked to me about all kinds of things. With her everything is quick, vibrant, joyful and colourful. Salomon was rather left out but was happy to watch, analyse, calculate.

Roscoff – Clos-Marie, June 7 to December 30

June 7. At last! And for months . . . months . . . months . . . How happy we are together in our loving solitude surrounded by the endless space of the sea outside our windows, the fresh air, the simple little house. Here all is repose; wounds heal; thoughts become harmonious; bitterness sweetens. We retain only that which is charming.

June 8. It is thirteen years today since we took our love from the town hall in the rue d'Anjou to the chapel of the catechism in Saint-Philippe-du-Roule. They are cooking us turbot and chicken. The weather is magnificent and full of lovely promises because it's Saint Médard's day. It's also, and above all, the feast of the Sacred Heart.

I talked to Jesus last night. I told him: 'Jesus, I long to love

You. Perhaps Your incarnation makes me see too much of the man in You, and that puts me off. Men lack sweetness, generosity, justice and devotion.' An inner voice answered: 'What about your Georges? Isn't he sweet, generous, devoted, and so close to you?' Then I felt my heart growing tender. Oh my Saviour, help me to lift the impenetrable veil in spite of my unworthiness and my lack of merit. Come to me, Jesus, because I long for it and because I have suffered.

June 9. Salomon writes me a charming letter. He has regained his good opinion of me since he saw the Duchess kiss me. It's always a good thing to shake people up some way or another. Tacitly we have bestowed the name of 'Daughter of Louis XV' on my dear Duchess. Royal she certainly is: she commands a couldn't-care-less nonchalance, distinction, arrogance, condescension. Her fancy inclines towards me at the moment. I have become 'one of the good things of France' in her eyes.

June 16. Tolstoy wrote: 'To love is to prefer another to oneself.' Perhaps I prefer Georges to myself – sometimes; but if he preferred me to himself at the same time we would be like two polite people hovering in a doorway, doing that dance of hesitation and withdrawal. I offer Georges the best part of a cake, he offers it to me, and all three (I include the cake) get nowhere. I feel disinclined to make love; I'm unselfish and offer him my body; he knows how I feel and refuses – then what? We have to fall back on the mutual concessions which keep all successful households going.

. . . .

July 28. Max Jacob has arrived. He has been having a bad time with his family, who would only be capable of understanding his talent if he could produce decorations, a car, a chauffeur and a profusion of thousand-franc notes. He's brought a trunkful of old documents. He intends to do an enormous amount of serious work.

August 1. Max is working hard. In the evening he reads us his poems. He has written two charming ones. He tells us anecdotes. He is amusing and likes being here. He claims that Roscoff suits both his piety and his work. He goes to the 6.30 mass every morning, he takes communion, he does the stations of the Cross, he meditates, he reads holy books. 'It would be impossible to be better,' says

Camille – she herself is falling off a bit, caught up in everyday life.

August 4. Max has caught the sun badly on the top of his head and his nose. He has made a cigarette burn in one of my linen sheets. His table manners are becoming bad. As soon as you indulge Max he becomes insupportable. He is going to force me back into cold looks and chiding words.

. . . .

August 6. Max is a real fish out of water in our religion! His instincts are against us: sourness, arrogance, malice, insinuations. In spite of his masses, communions, stations of the Cross you can feel it all bubbling about in him. He fights it as best he can, he takes pains – really furious pains – to summon up his resistance, but it oozes out of his every pore. He is envious, jealous, slanderous, false, gossipy, blundering. It's a curious thing to watch. He is dirty, untidy, unwholesome, garrulous, pompous, greedy, either flattering or impertinent . . . he's inhabited by every sort of demon; his envelope contains a hundred-headed hydra. Georges is some protection against all this: pedantic, prudent, choosing his words and looking before he leaps. He can use his head. But he can still recognize the troubles with which other people are afflicted. And to those troubles he brings the most serene indulgence. He really is the pick of the bunch.

August 8. We are going for long walks. Max does not come with us. He works and meditates. . . . .

August 11. Max is in a good mood, good health and pleased with his work. He has given me a superb cake which he ordered from Quimper and I know he has a big box of pralines hidden in his cupboard for my saint's day. But his best present is his dedication of the new edition of his *Cornet à dés*.

August 14. Max has started to tell us the story of his life. We have reached 1904. First it's funny, then it's touching. He tells it with humour and irony. His early days were very hard, and that is how his life still is, in spite of his success. Max is only forty-seven but he looks sixty: no teeth or hair, a lisp, fat, short, a nervous cringing expression and a spiteful eye. But he has found God and that is the only treasure, true wealth, real magnificence.

August 15. My saint's day sung in by bells, by the wind, by the hearts surrounding me. Georges opened fire yesterday evening with a letter-poem, then Max with a huge box of chocolates and an adorable, miraculously preserved box of about 1830 with miniatures of little people under glass surrounded by delicate flowers and semi-precious stones – a little masterpiece of a knick-knack, really pretty and genuine. He had it sent secretly from his mother's antique shop in Quimper. I am spoilt, cherished, cossetted, loved, kissed, celebrated: cards from everyone and everywhere.

August 19. Max tells us about Doucet, the couturier who made a great deal of money and endowed a library for the State which bears his name and is full of very valuable manuscripts and rare editions. The manuscripts were procured at bargain prices because the Maecenas took advantage of hard-up young writers: he made them allowances – thirty francs, fifty francs, sometimes a hundred francs a month – on condition that they wrote him long letters, one, two or three, containing analyses of books by their contemporaries or of other interesting subjects.

As a couturier Doucet was only mediocre and as far as we women in the public eye were concerned his taste could add nothing to our elegance. The materials were beautiful, the dresses were well-made, but he had a hostile attitude towards the capricious movements of fashion and was determined to remain 'Doucet' through thick and thin! Poiret's enjoyable and spirited fantasies seemed to him like fancy dress. He fitted us out like good mothers of families – or at least like colonels' ladies! Basically what kept him fashionable was his address in the rue de la Paix and his enormous bills. His *vendeuses*, who were paid on their turnover, were well-spoken – and anyway we were mugs! Doucet's was a good meeting place, we could make the rounds of the neighbouring jewellers; actresses and great ladies brushed shoulders and the new rich had no need to manoeuvre their way in – they were welcomed, their chatter was smiled on indulgently, they were shown the greatest deference. It is all a bit different nowadays. Behaviour has become more natural, one goes out to dinner in a shift, one dances half naked. The ruined rich open studios and have fun designing dresses.

August 20. Yesterday Max was splendid in white linen trousers and a geranium blazer. I took him for a walk to show him off to the village as though he were a child delighting in new clothes. He spent the morning at his devotions: two masses, confession and communion. Saint Max all day. Jacob when he is naughty.

August 30. Max has seen me putting my pearls in a bowl of sea-water to freshen them. Yesterday he recited these two lines:

> 'The princess keeps migrating birds
> Imprisoned in a bowl of sea-water.'

And Georges and he went on and on and on admiring them and declaring 'That is a really enchanting poem, to anyone who can understand it.' Max then said: 'Because you like this poem so much and it was the princess's gesture which gave me this happy inspiration, I am going to give it to you. I shall write it out and it will be just for you. I undertake never to have it published.' Well really! . . . Is he making fun of us? Or is it . . . I'm quite worried and must keep an eye on him. I must put them both on a healthy diet, feed them up – I'm afraid they may be going gaga from anaemia of the brain.

September 3. Yesterday morning, Sunday, Max devoted to church. He exhales all his piety there, and what he brings back to the house is cheek, tiresome whims, boorishness. We had words at table.

. . . .

September 13. Benjamin has sent a telegram saying that he hopes to be here on Friday. Max is rather worried, he would be! He is wondering how a Jew will take his conversion; and he's also jealous at the thought of having to share our attention with another person.

I have been gardening. I have pricked out my pinks, taken some geranium cuttings and done some planting.

September 17. Benjamin has been here since the 14th. Max is sulking, suffering from held-in jealousy – and also from incontinence! His liver is playing up as a result of all this. It relieves him to be disagreeable to the point of boorishness and to exhale his rancour in remarks such as: 'It's the people I love, only the people. I'm one of them, and that's what I intend to remain!' Then – aimed at Georges, who makes a point of being absolutely polite whatever happens: 'If there's one thing I can't stand it's politeness.'

September 18. The little devil Jacob is stuck in bed under a pile of dirty old rags. The doctor has diagnosed a liver attack and a slight pulmonary congestion. So there we are! He's as tetchy as can be and lends himself very badly to the anxious care we are trying to give him. I have taken him up the vegetable soup the doctor ordered, and lemonade. Georges puts on his mustard plasters for him and has visited him a dozen times. Having friends to stay is not all pleasure!

September 19. I'm afraid that Max, seeing us bending so attentively over his couch – not that anything so dirty deserves the name! – has started to play the spoilt child. He is such a bizarre creature. He veers between being arrogant and humble, too much and too little, brash and sly. He is not without wit, but it's an ill-tempered, desperate wit which is turned odious by lack of manners, scruples and honesty. Max is certainly his own worst enemy, and he doesn't realize that he is frightfully difficult to live with.

September 20. Max is making the task really too much. Georges is becoming as weary and disconcerted by it as I am. It gives me no pleasure to see my beautiful quilted bedspread – so expensive nowadays – bundled up under Max's dirty chin unprotected by the sheet which he's managed to lose – the precious thing used as a towel, covered with pencils, open books, grubby papers, spent matches, spots of soup and lemonade. Our best course is to get him better and get rid of him. He will be furious about it, but we can't look after such a messy invalid right through the winter.

September 24. Max has gone! At last! We are disinfecting his room. He is now inspiring me with the sort of fond respect one has for dead people. I am sorry for him. He left without seeing me, mumbling vague phrases of so-called politeness. Madame Garat said goodbye to him for me, and told him I would pray for him. At those words he almost burst into tears and said: 'And I will pray for her, I do love her so.' Then a moment later he was seized by his demon: 'The truth is, you know, that I'm republican – I loathe royalty.' My old friend François asked me whether he was a bit mad. His daughter saw him in church making crosses with holy water all over his body, even on the tips of his toes. That is probably it: he is a bit mad. His chastity – if you can use that word for a negative condition – has gone to his head. I remember hearing him yelping genuine lamentations inspired by his fear of purgatory – 'Where everyone' he cried, 'will have to go for a very long time and the flames are as hot as those of hell.'

September 25. Yesterday a problem: two lovely Saint-Benoît cheeses – the same type as camembert – arrived for us, ordered by Max Jacob. He gave the order quite some time ago. My first impulse was to refuse them, but everyone contributed an opinion: don't complicate matters, don't insult the absent, they'll go bad, a pity to waste something so good, think what the poet spent on them and so on and so on. Then Benjy came in and said: 'Be *grand*, keep them.' So we kept them – and very good they are.

. . . .

October 22. Sad letter from Nathalie. She is evidently haunted by the idea of death. She says that she hopes she will have the courage to die alone, as she has lived. It's a heart-breaking remark. I tell her to think of me, older than she is, ailing and always delicate, and follow me bravely and cheerfully. Nathalie has no notion of God to support her.

October 24. I am haunted by death. I see such appalling things that words fail me. When Georges has left me, or if he dies before I do, I shall shut myself up in a convent, I shall try to find the courage to die alone, as Flossie proudly says.

. . . .

December 30. Can it be winter? It's hot, airless! I have had a present from my dear R – a marvel! A huge and sumptuous shawl in magnificent white crêpe de chine, with a big black pattern. Nothing could have given me more pleasure.

Enthusiastic letter from Max Jacob. How funny it is! After all that passed between us, here we are, possibly better friends than ever!

1924

〜〜〜〜〜〜〜〜〜〜〜〜〜〜〜〜〜〜〜〜〜〜〜〜〜〜

Roscoff – Clos-Marie, June 22 to December 25

The Ghikas went to Paris early in January – Liane briefly records the fact that she is packing for the journey and that Lewis has promised her some hats – and have now returned to Roscoff for the summer.

....

June 22. Corpus Christi: the bells are ringing, people in their Sunday best are thronging, the best hangings are being shaken out, gardens are being looted of their flowers, wayside altars are appearing in the squares; and the holy day is bathed in golden sunshine.

All the long time we were in Paris I didn't open my notebook once. I never had a minute for it, nor the energy, nor even the wish.

June 24. Missy has been here since yesterday, arriving in her beautiful red car with her chauffeur and her maid. Missy is Mathilde de Morny, daughter of the Duc de Morny, Marquise de Belboeuf, returned – since her divorce – to being Marquise de Morny once again. I have not spoken about her before because there was a coldness between us. She dresses as a man and has the ways and morals of a man. Her cigar used to give me a headache. Whereupon Missy grumbled to mutual friends: 'What a bore Liane is, with her migraines.' They repeated it. In short I let her drop, quite gently but firmly. This year Nathalie the despot said in front of me that she wanted to meet Missy so that she could introduce her to Romaine Brooks. I offered to act as intermediary. I wrote to Missy: 'Dear Father (she calls Georges her son), we never really quarrelled and we are dying to see you again. Write to me soon and tell me when it can be, open your heart and your arms to me once more.' Touched, Missy stopped being grumpy, unknitted her brows, changed directions and her mind, and came to see us the minute she arrived in Paris. We took up our friendship again with evident pleasure on both sides. But lo and behold, Romaine Brooks had gone to London and Nathalie – ungrateful, ill-bred creature! – disclaimed the whole thing and told me crisply that she wouldn't dream for a moment of receiving a woman of such ill repute who dressed as a man and had neither talent nor wit. Stunned, I told her: 'Do you consider that *you* have anything to be ashamed of as far as morals and reputation go? Missy sculpts quite as well as the Duchess. She's of good family. There's nothing to choose between you but a pair of trousers.'

I told all this to my dear R who at once began to long to meet Missy. I arranged a tea-party in our little nest at the Palais d'Orsay. In came Madame R, elegant, old-fashioned, smiling; candidly she offered an intrepid hand to the ambiguous Marquise, saying deliberately: 'Madame, when my husband was a boy he was madly in love with you. He was at Stanislas with your brothers and used to wait impatiently for Sundays in the hope of seeing you in the parlour. All the other pupils felt the same, full of admiration for your beauty.' At that Missy allowed her natural affability free rein; the two ladies had a long chat and were delighted with each other.

June 28. I saw Sacha Guitry again, and Yvonne Printemps, affectionate and full of success. I saw Jean Vollerin, a distant friend and Sacha's secretary. He asked us to dinner and we made the acquaintance of the Dolly Sisters, nice little acrobatic dancers, modern mechanical toys, funny, not pretty but made-up and dressed with enough charm and intelligence to take the place of beauty. Paris is crazy about them. They earn wads of money, bounce about the place to great effect, gamble in the casinos, dress at the great houses and buy and sell property wherever they go.

June 30. Missy decided to leave at five in the morning so as to avoid driving in the heat of the day. Sweet and contrary, she's perfectly impossible at meals. A guest to beware of! 'I can't eat eggs, or fish, or peas, or beans, or tomatoes, or veal, or pork, or cheese, or cakes, or strawberries, or apricots, or . . . or . . . or . . .' – the list is endless. Are you serving a salad? 'I eat only the ribs of the leaves' – scurry to cut out the ribs! Cauliflower? 'I eat nothing but the stalks' – quick, make a little dish of just stalks. Cucumber? 'Mine must be quite dry.' Chicken? 'Only the dark meat, please.' Rabbit? 'I dislike everything but the legs.' So this morning everyone is saying 'Ouf!' And it was supposed to be fun!

. . . .

July 3. Card from Madame Georges Menier who is the prettiest woman in Paris. Robert de Rothschild came to meet me at the first of Nathalie's Fridays. He was charmed by this amusing and ill-assorted gathering and enchanted to see me again and find me still so beautiful. So one fine Sunday he organized a luncheon at the Lebels – big industrialists somehow connected with the Meniers of Neuilly. It was dreamlike. Our photographs were taken in the garden, everything seemed intoxicating, we chatted, we smiled, we laughed, we wanted to shine with every facet. A few days later I had a telephone call from Georges Menier whose marvellous wife had just had an operation: 'My wife is allowed visitors since yesterday. She was so very sorry not to see you the other day at the Lebels' – I wonder if I dare ask you to drop in on her at the clinic?' When we went in to her room, which had been transformed into a blossoming hothouse, we saw a goddess nesting in flowers on a white cloud, in a snowy whiteness of fine cambric, entwined in yards of matchless pearls! A divine face, smiling, regular, pretty. A lovable, simple child, surrounded by four tall sons, her husband and her father-in-law. I gave her my white violets and signified my sincere admiration and my tender solicitude. She said all the right things. I had a friendly word with my old Gaston Menier, the senator, who often does helpful things for me. I like that beautiful, simple, friendly, perfect, irreproachable woman. All Paris admires her. When I talked about her to the Duchess she said: 'Oh, they say she's so lovely! But she keeps to her own kind of people, she's not a snob. It's a shame for our lot, whom she avoids so carefully.' In my opinion that's another thing in this charming woman's favour, and I am proud that she wanted me to come to her.

. . . .

July 13. When I'm thinking about this past spring I keep seeing the Cochon d'or, a restaurant at la Villette almost opposite the slaughter-house. All the snobbiest people were mad about it. One day my sultana, Madame Fabre-Luce, let fall: 'I never go anywhere, but I do, do, *do* so want to see this famous *Cochon d'or* everyone's talking about.' We went into action at once. Georges telephoned the handsome Italian *patron* and a menu was planned. The Duchess came disguised as a rake – little brown suit, hat over one ear, scarf flung carelessly round her neck – her dear little face alert and amused. Nathalie – grey – was the foreigner who is eager to see everything. As for my sultana, she was born along in her sumptuous car – after a detour to pick us up – her usual self: rich pastel finery from the rue de la Paix, pearls, rings, gleaming jewels, Cartier handbag with coral, ivory, onyx and diamonds . . . She descended from her chariot with a little amused look as though she were playing a practical joke on someone. 'Oh my God,' I thought, 'they are going to jeer at us! Whatever will happen?' I tried to shelter and surround my sultana. The *patron* conducted us to a little back room where our table was reserved. It was a Wednesday, market day. We were surrounded by huge, sweaty, red-faced men finishing their lunch, not very reassuring. They stared, but not unkindly. My friends' charm got to work. Voices became less loud. No one lit a pipe, no one spat on the floor, no one swore. It was as though we were providing them with a charming little performance. The commonest of the lot kept on winking at me. We ate like ogres. The pâté was really excellent, the chicken exquisite. As for the steak, we cried our admiration aloud. You don't know what red meat is if you haven't had it there: firm and melting, with an unbelievable flavour; you put it on your tongue and it evaporates – a marvel! We exclaimed with delight, our confidence quite restored, enchanted to be there. We felt that all those men were our brothers!

Certainly the Ritz, where we went five or six times, is good fun like a big liner packed with smart strangers; but the food there is horrible.

July 15. . . . . Georges doesn't laugh enough. When I scolded him for being sad, he answered: 'I'm not sad, just empty. I'm in pursuit of nothingness, of vacuity.' To my mind he's found it.

July 22. Max Jacob wants to come back here! And look at me – touched and softened, I tell him to come, that the Clos will open its doors to him and we will open our arms!

As for Cocteau, he's desperate to be in love! Mad with grief at Radiguet's death, he has fallen for that sweet little Garros. She's a charming creature who became drunk on literature while living with Mireille Havet. Jean, an invert in his time, is beginning to climb the slope – a real woman would have been too much to start with. Jean has celebrated her in verse as he celebrated that magnificent child

Radiguet in *le Cap de Bonne-Espérance*. May they live a virtuous and happy life together like Georges and me. Cocteau has already been madly in love with Madeleine Carlier, who was cruel to him. He expressed his suffering in a book which wasn't very good. Everything that happens to these gentlemen ends as a book.

July 27. Max arrived yesterday morning. Saint Anne's day – I think she must have sent him to me. I received him kindly and installed him comfortably, he feels at home, he was charming. We were mutually conciliating and ready to make concessions. Long may it last! He gave us a moving picture of the moral cruelties inflicted on him by the Abbé and some of the boarders at Saint-Benoît, particularly a young man called Pierre Robert who was his own protégé to start with. This young man had no money, no scruples, and a sort of commercial-travellerish cheerfulness which delighted everyone at the monastery so that he supplanted Max. He teased him endlessly, called him 'Monsieur Dumou', barged into his room whenever he felt like it, played practical jokes on him, used his paper, his pens, his books. On top of everything else, this young man of twenty-three became a lay brother at the last pilgrimage. Humiliated and tormented, Max became jealous and that's why he packed his bags and came to us. 'Being here is like Paradise after hell, my dears,' he said. He has started work already, his room upside down and his table loaded.

July 29. Max says that poems have started to flow. He read me some of them. Ho hum! I am not up to them. Here's one of them: 'Zambelli (dancer at the Opéra, past it) – elected legs – Brique Jean – go screw yourself – *Every Day.*' Georges is thunderstruck and heaps him with compliments. As for me – I say: 'Read it to me again.' Max gives a superior smile and goes on lisping away. I raise my eyebrows and try to raise myself to this intellectual level, but I always tumble down again, humiliated. Apparently it's euphonious and full of meaning.........

July 30. They have let me know that I have been granted the Military Medal in memory of my son who had the right to it because of his two citations. The address proclaimed 'Widow Pourpe'. I am absolutely *not* the Widow Pourpe, nor have I ever been, having been divorced. In law I then reverted to being Madame Chassaigne. So the Widow Pourpe is informed that she will be given the Military

Medal for her son Marc Pourpe, killed by the enemy; that if she wants the ceremony of handing over she must travel to Longvic, and that she will not be reimbursed for any expenses she incurs! If she prefers, she can have it brought to her by the commandant of her local police station. I feel shocked, bruised, wounded, ruffled and indignant. To be threatened with the police! The neighbourhood will think that they are coming to arrest me.

. . . .

August 6. Affectionate letter from Nathalie – rather affected, I think. Poor fat old Nathalie, grumpy and cantankerous. The Duchess has vanished into silence. I no longer feel that I'm the couple's 'beloved child'. They are intelligent women, sometimes charming, often amusing, very superficial. When you want to go deeper you find that these intoxicating goddesses are banal and ugly. After that you have to manoeuvre to keep a distance between you and the banality.

August 7. Salomon made me reread the Epistles of Saint Paul. I don't understand them very well. He says that if you do not believe in the law but practise the virtues demanded by the law, then you are saved. That reassures me about Georges, and about me, too. Georges practises all the most serious virtues: gentleness, kindness, patience, and generosity. Honesty too. He sets me an excellent example. He denies everything without denying anything. 'Anything is possible' he says, with discouraging assurance. Salomon says that there is nothing but death and the smoke left by fame. Max insists at the top of his voice that he has an unshakable faith in every single thing taught by the Church.

August 11. A young poet called Malraux, one of Max's friends, has stolen some statues worth a million and a half from some holy temple in Indo-China. He was arrested, tried and given three years in prison. It happened at Pnom Penh. Max is in despair; this friend was always asking him out to dinner and paying the most immense bills in the very smartest restaurants. Max says: 'He is young – twenty-three – and fired by lyricism; lyricism raises a man's soul above the kind of scruple which constricts the bourgeois soul.' It's being discussed in the papers, they want to find excuses for him but it's difficult: his case is very weak. Max wrote about it to *l'Eclair*: I'm afraid that all he really wants is to draw attention to himself.

August 17. Missy arrived yesterday and Max took her for a man without a moment's doubt. She brought a rather commonplace and boring young couple with her. A sort of daily bread, not very well baked, heavy and indigestible. Max seems to be annoyed by this disturbance to his habits and his work.

August 18. Missy's guests are Swiss; the husband edits a review called *le Magazine*. They live at Lausanne and have an intolerably ugly accent, rather Germanic. Max is going all out to please them – saying to himself, I fear, that perhaps through them and their magazine he'll be able one day to reach the laggardly, gaping Swiss. He holds forth on literature, takes them for walks and flatters them. I dread the brick he's always on the edge of dropping.

. . . .

October 4. Here I am with a bad attack of gout in my right big toe. Georges made me smear the sick toe with glycerine and cover it with cotton wool, and the pain disappeared completely in five minutes. Uncle Max [Missy liked to be called Uncle Max] is on to a good thing there; I have just been writing her an unsolicited testimonial. Uncle Max has heaps of good recipes. There's one for polishing fingernails, another for copper, and one for building movable library steps. Tanks, she insists, were her invention. She is much drawn to the cinema.

The other day she caused a great sensation in my room. I was in the dressing-room with Georges when suddenly we heard the dear 'old boy's' high-pitched monotonous voice announcing: 'Children, I have a confession to make.' She's broken something in her bedroom, I thought. 'Go ahead,' I called. 'Well, listen: twice in my life I have slept with men . . .' Hearing that, and imagining it, was so comic that we burst out laughing. She went on: 'One of them was my cousin Alexis Orloff. He said he would kill himself if I resisted, so – well, I didn't resist, but I refused any repetition. The second and last was Lord Yume [sic]. He was a very good-looking boy and he adored me, he wanted to marry me. He wore me down, so at last I said "Let's try," and I was his mistress for ten days. Then I'd had enough so I refused his proposal.'

. . . .

December 25. Christmas! All the shoes left in my big granite fireplace were collected this morning by their owners. It was fun to have all these curious, greedy, cheerful, delighted, surprised people jostling round my bed.

We ate the truffle yesterday. Exquisite! I had bought a little brown casserole with a tight-fitting lid. When I lifted the lid we were intoxicated by a dizzyingly heady aroma. It smelt of richness, warmth, celebration, elegance, the triumph of gluttony! I had stewed this precious thing from Orangini for two hours over a low heat, shut tightly in with slices of ham, fillet of beef, some good white wine, a vegetable stock and rashers of bacon. My Georges ate it slowly, gravely, silently – and went on thanking me for it all day. There's nothing more sincere than the gratitude of a satisfied palate!

1925

〜〜〜〜〜〜〜〜〜〜〜〜〜〜〜〜〜〜〜〜〜〜〜〜〜

Paris – Palais d'Orsay, January 28 to March 22

January 28. Paris, softened by sweet and premature spring weather!
We are back in our two comfortable and pretty rooms which a cheerful sun has been illuminating all day. Everything unpacked and put
away. I alerted only my furrier and Margot de La Bigne. The
furrier has delivered everything and Margot has called in to give me
a kiss. What a lovely girl, fresh, stylish, dazzling rosy complexion,
the look of an archangel at the gates of heaven! Her skirt was very
short and revealed her right leg, imperious and agile.

Georges seems very happy to be back in Paris. I shall make an
effort to be a good and agreeable woman of the world, smiling, futile,
indulgent, charitable, cordial. I have made up my mind – but I still
feel wild.

February 4. Very tired by life in Paris, the constricted horizon, the
thin air, the useless words .... When I was at a matinée at
the Vaudeville .... Madame R sought me out. I was beautiful
and sedate, in black. That afternoon I made a conquest of a charming
little actress, Mademoiselle de Guise, who is working at the Palais-
Royal theatre. At my age! I was astounded by it. Since this morning
I have had – we, Georges and I, have had an apartment on the
fourth floor at 64 rue Saussure. Simple house, vulgar street,
pleasant little 'flat' which will do as a pied-à-terre.

. . . .

February 13. Day spent with Nathalie. Georges left me with her this
morning, then went to see his mother. Exquisite lunch with an
affectionate, friendly Amazon, siesta, visit to an exhibition of Chana
Orloff's sculpture about which I have nothing to say. Nathalie was
very decent when she came to see our little hovel. She said: 'Don't

spend too much on it. If we can find you something better you can sell it.' But I don't feel like moving house yet again. When you have not got what you like, then you must like what you have. I shall try to like my living-room. Went to Poiret – such a disappointment! Enormous premises, rich and tasteless. The struggle to be unusual has ended by making it impossible. It's like a sweetshop: green, pink, mauve, red. Poiret has a tartan motor-car. He is superb, fat, round, taut, a majestic buddha: black trousers with a thousand stripes and a white frieze frock-coat – very smart.

March 2. Yesterday I played the sultana. I draped my bed in the finest cambric and the rarest lace, I put on a tunic of violet crêpe de chine and a tiara of lace and pearls, and I received visits. I was shaken by a stubborn cough and it was agony when everyone did what they thought was their friendly duty and forced me to talk.

March 27. I have been unable to write during the mad days when my Thérèse was staying here in apartment 327. Yes, mad days . . . an enormous room, an immense divan, fur rugs, cushions, two beautiful and loving women dressed in gleaming satins, covered with pearls, and sparkling jewellery, surrounded by a constantly renewed crowd of elegant, laughing, inquisitive women; friends, a piano. Georges Le Baillif played – he's an excellent musician. Twenty-three-year-old Pierre Meyer, gifted with money, beauty, youth and a very beautiful voice, sang for us. Our mouths mingled. Georges, my grave and happy Georges, sitting opposite me, faint glimmers of light from neighbouring rooms; cheerful tea parties, improvised dinners, flowers, caresses. Quick, a drive to Versailles for some fresh air, or to the Bois, or to Longchamp, or to a fitting – and the endless, exhausting ringing of the telephone.

Challes-les-Eaux – Château de Trivier, August 20 to September 28

Almost five months have gone by since my last lines. Paris life: stupid, muddled existence, self-made occupations and duties, fatigue, uneasiness, laziness. One avoids thinking, it's a victory of the material.

Now I'm staying with Lucienne Rouveyre in an enormous old

château, comfortable, peaceful and well-kept. How many years has it been waiting here for us! Nathalie, who arrived before we did, left last night. Excessively hard-working as usual, she has managed to cram into eighteen days first a cure for her rheumatism at Aix, then one for her throat at Challes, then the preparation with André Rouveyre of a volume of a hundred letters which she received from her great adorer, Rémy de Gourmont. André helped her organize them, and illustrated them and the book's cover with his lovely woodcuts.

August 20. We spent four days at Honfleur with the Duchess: four charming, happy days, an island of calm in the exhaustion of our house-moving. We have stripped the de Polignac lodge of all our belongings and stuffed them into the living-room at 64 rue Saussure. It has become a charming spot, comfortable, cheerful, light and sunny. We like it very much – and would like it better if it stood in some other neighbourhood. Its own neighbourhood is within our means, makes life as dictated by the Roumanian exchange easier, and demands pots of geraniums on our windowsills.

The Duchess's house at Honfleur is a little eighteenth century lodge which used to belong to Admiral Hamelin. It's shabby, pleasant, a lawn in front and a shrubbery surrounding, big rooms with old woodwork which creaks of an evening. There's a view over the estuary and Lucie Delarue-Mardrus as neighbour. And neighbourly she is. The Duchess invited her to dinner; she brought her poems and began to read them as soon as the meal was over. In return we visited her at her place, the 'Pavillon de la Reine'. It's very pretty, a dream . . . one big room where the poetess works, the lavatory shut into a big cupboard, to the left a sort of little dining-room, shining with cleanliness. Flowers everywhere, and sweets of every kind. At present Lucie Delarue-Mardrus is painting misty-looking but brightly coloured flowers – after Odilon Redon according to Georges. She frames them in black, and here and there on the glass which covers them she places a spot of colour. It's amusing and original. She hangs them on the doors, which is unexpected. When I was admiring her taste and artistry she offered me one of them, and did it so sweetly that I kissed her. Afterwards I sent her a lot of sweets from Paris. She was very nice to us, to me. She told us that her little house was built for Marie Antoinette when she had to spend two nights near Honfleur........

Balthy's death! My Louise is no more, and treated me so badly during her last days that our friendship had already perished. I have not felt it a great deal – I reproach myself for that – and I am praying for her. I am really not sure what she had against me. When we met anywhere she would leave, she would walk past me in the Bois without greeting me. I don't go on loving people for long when they don't love me. She made fun of the modesty of my new apartment. I went to see Yvonne de Bray one day at Malmaison and she greeted me with brutal sarcasm: 'Liane, what's this nonsense about living in a lodging-house in the rue Saussure?' I looked at her in astonishment, and then I understood: Balthy had been leaving as we arrived.

She left a great deal of money for her sisters to share out in a friendly way without a will. She had suffered – she had cancer for several years. Sharp and proud, she defied the illness and took great care to conceal it. The blonde and attractive Béatrice Yturbe saw to it that her life was splendid. Her house was beautiful, her taste was sure, her relationships were stylish. She was openly scornful of my modest ways and resented the fact that my sober existence at Georges's side had saved me from her kind of life. She died on the crest of the wave, loved, spoilt, having just signed an engagement for the winter at the Apollo, which meant a great deal to her. She was in bed for two days, without suspecting that it was the end. Since her death, I met Pépé at Thérèse Diehl's. He threw himself weeping into my arms, weeping for his Louise who was never a bit nice to him. He loved her deeply, it was painful to see his grief. So now we have made it up, but I don't feel enthusiasm and Georges feels even less.

Lucien Guitry is dead. Sacha's grief really hurt me, the shock on Yvonne Printemps pretty face was striking. And then Lucien himself – he was magnificent, white, calm, imposing. I went to his funeral with Georges – it was there that I saw Balthy for the last time. She did not look at me. Her turn was coming, so near. I also saw Max Maurey and his wife Yvonne de Buffon. It awoke no feeling in me. Those are the people who are really dead, as far as I am concerned.

Poor Lucien Guitry was a tremendous eater, greedy, gluttonous. One evening after the theatre he had a supper of a hundred snails, twelve hard-boiled eggs, several slices of mutton, cheese, fruit and several glasses of beer. The next day he was laid up, very ill. He never got out of bed again. He died three weeks later. It seems that he often ate such suppers, for pleasure as well as to show off. 'There's nothing wrong with my appetite,' he used to say, laughing.

I had just got to Honfleur when Lewis telephoned me about Balthy's death. I had heard nothing. I was overcome and telephoned her sister Justine, a twitchy, bony little old woman of seventy-one. 'Justine, it's Liane, I'm appalled. Is there anything I can do to help?' – 'Yes,' replied Justine crisply, 'there is something you can do to help. You can send me some chocolates.' I almost dropped the telephone. I ordered 'la Marquise de Sevigné' to send her a bag of chocolates and enclosed a card with our condolences. That's Basques for you, a race apart!

· ·

September 2. One day we were lunching at the Ritz with Balthy and some friends when the Maharajah of Kapurthala went by without recognizing me. He wanted to carry me off to India in 1893. We were the same age. Rather annoyed, I said to the maître d'hotel: 'It's sad to grow old, Olivier. There's Kapurthala sitting opposite me and gazing at me, without remembering that once he wanted to marry me.' Olivier went over and whispered in his ear. Kapurthala got up and came over to greet me; I introduced my husband to him, he apologized and pretended that he had recognized me but hadn't dared to show it, then invited us to lunch at his pretty house on the Bois de Boulogne. It was charming, a lunch for twenty with two of his sons, some Egyptian princes, Turkish ministers, American mothers and daughters, etc. Perfect service, good meal, comfortable house. Nothing beautiful. I was on his Highness's right; we talked about our young days. He showed us his house. Two or three fine tiger-skins filled me with admiration and longing, which I expressed when we were drinking coffee alone with him on a little terrace overlooking the flower-garden. Two days later he sent me – a photograph of himself in a gold and silver frame! He is a childish sovereign, well-behaved and serious, more the slave of his ministers and the teachings of his religion than he is of the English. When we were walking along the well-raked paths of his little garden he said to me: 'The English don't like it if I come to France too often.' He has cut off the pigtail which used to crown his head when I first knew him, and has adopted European clothes. His accent is common, without charm or originality; he made me think of Ahmed who used to be our footman. He has vulgar tastes. Yet he is called on by the grandest and smartest people and his receptions are crowded. It will be a long time before Paris loses its taste for the exotic!

. . . .

September 7. I was telling Lucienne how, when the Tsar scolded the Grand Duke Constantine for using coarse language at table in front of the Tsarina, the children and the servants, the Grand Duke began clamouring for 'ches'. Baffled, everyone wondered what he wanted. What he wanted was *pea*ches! The Tsar saw red and Uncle Cogny had to leave the room . . . So, were those happy times? Not for me, flotsam stranded in Holy Russia, misled, seeking my true way. It seems to me nowadays that I wasn't truly myself; that only after Georges had entered my life did I rediscover my true self. I remember one day in Italy, at a circus somewhere, I was looking at myself very deeply in a little mirror. I did not recognize myself. Inside myself I asked: 'Is that you, is that really you, Marie?' I was there with some good-time people. I felt that at that precise moment I was denying myself and that my whole background was denying me. But I also felt a strong force pushing me forward. So I began to smile and chatter and fill myself with the belief that all was well, that I was having a lovely time, that I was destined for the most brilliant adventures, that neither Heaven nor the devil existed. There is nothing you can do against that force!

September 15. We have been told that silk will become very expensive this winter, so it's only prudent to lay in a stock. I have ruined myself: white crêpe de chine, black crêpe de chine, white and black satin-backed crêpe, white damask, cyclamen crêpe de chine. Let silk go up, I have nothing to fear. I have enough to dress well for two years.

September 21. Nasty little bits of gossip arrive from Paris. They are saying that I am kept by Madame R . . . That is the most dreadful lie. Georges and I don't deserve that! No one's life could be more proper than ours; it's almost saintly, people don't believe it because it's so very unusual.

When the engagement between Stanislas de La Rochefoucauld and the Roumanian artiste Alice Cocéa was announced, they said Cupid was paying back on France the trick played on Roumania by Georges Ghika when he married Liane de Pougy. All I can say is may they be as happy as we are, as tenderly close to each other in sorrow as well as in joy.

September 28. I'm reading some fine poems by Essenin in *le Figaro littéraire*. They bring that crazy Isadora Duncan to mind.

She wanted to 'procreate', if not with gods, at least with the most famous men of the age, the most intelligent in the world. About fifteen years ago she focused the full strength of her desire on the poet Henry Bataille. Yes – but Bataille was living with Berthe Bady! Fanatic that she was, she set about indoctrinating Bady: 'But darling, you must understand – no love or sentimentality, it's just the act I want, nothing more. Think of it, a child born to ME, by HIM – what a miracle! What a heritage to bequeath to humanity!' Bady was amused and agreed – having, anyway, an increasing reason not to be jealous. They agreed to meet in a beautiful Neuilly villa where Isadora happened to be staying. Disconcerted, weak and delicate, the highly strung, ironic Bataille took rather a long time to get going . . . Bady was called in. Bataille was beginning to rise to all this assembled good will when the party was interrupted by the sound of a key in the door: the arrival of a rich American who was supposed to be far away. Poor Bataille was shoved out onto the back stairs, clutching his clothes in his arms.

Came the war, Isadora made for Russia and set her heart on Essenin: a very free Russian-style marriage. She brought him to Paris. Nathalie captured the couple for one of her Fridays. Essenin recited his poems in Russian – she laughed when she told me about it because no one could understand a word but they all raved. From time to time he intoned 'Lou-pa-nar, sy-phi-lis'. Madame R gave them a lift home in her car. Two such irresistible forces could hardly meet without a thunderous din resulting in battles, struggles, separation. . . . .

September 28. 'If I go down into myself and question my nature, what, o God, do I find? A mind full of uncertainty, always ready to go astray; inconstant affections; an inexplicable mixture of hopes and of vain fears; vicious inclinations; a mass of innumerable desires which agitate me and torment me without cease; sometimes a fugitive joy; usually a deep weariness; some sort of instinct for heaven and also for all the passions of the earth; a weak will which simultaneously wants and does not want; great pride in great poverty. Behold in this my condition as sin has formed it, and within myself I feel that I am powerless to raise a nature fallen so low.' I read this in my *Imitation* and I am sadly aware that it could be applied to me. There is some comfort in feeling that I am not the only one of my kind!

Paris – October 18 to December 2

October 18. At last! Here we are in our own home where we have been for eighteen days, having arrived at about midnight of September 30. No maid; in the hands of our concierge who is taking great trouble to see that we lack for nothing. The nest is charming! Now that it's transformed it gives the impression of being half of a quarter of a wing of a château. We still lack shutters and a maid. The fine white linen blinds embroidered with sayings which Nathalie gave me have been hung, delicate and transparent like my opaline glass – which I am beginning to go off. The stair-carpet is down; the lift functions; the telephone works. Everything is clean, light, blue, red, white and gold. Our shelves are beautifully tidy. In fact everything is fine except for the flu, which torments us both.

. . . .

November 21. . . . . *Le Figaro littéraire* has devoted an issue to Courteline. I was much taken by an unpublished fragment of Boubouroche which someone found by chance in a café blotter: 'I am a bad adviser in matters of love because my way of understanding and practising love is rather special. No one in the world has loved more than I have; I have spent my life at it. When this little accident befalls me I play my part stoutly and I let things happen without doing anything to speed them up, *seeing that there is more delight in wanting a woman than in getting her, that a woman's power lies wholly in the desire you feel for her and that the intoxication of possession is always inferior to the dream one had of it.*' I underline the part which I feel and understand as a way of showing the opinion I share. The fever drops, the thing is seen for what it is and beauty is rare in this world . . .

. . . .

November 27. Lunch at Betsy Gautrat's with Nathalie. Archie had to leave very early, called to the Palais. We went to lie down on a big velvet divan in a Chinese room. The light was draped. Georges was on a low seat, smoking. Oh! such tender playfulness, such playful tenderness . . .

. . . .

1926

〜〜〜〜〜〜〜〜〜〜〜〜〜〜〜〜〜〜〜〜〜〜〜〜〜〜

Paris, February 24. On Mardi Gras I had fifty-two people to a party!
The day before I was feeling deathly. I was looking so ill that when
I saw myself in a mirror I nearly fainted. My neighbour downstairs
took pity on me and prepared a divan so that I could go down there
for a rest if I collapsed. Well, on the day itself, in spite of my anxiety
I stood up to it, I summoned up a cheerful greeting for my cheerful
guests, I handed round innumerable pancakes, I talked to some, I
introduced others, and from then on I have been going from strength
to strength.

Pepito lent us marvellous Persian costumes: cloaks and head-
dresses. Mine was bright red embroidered with gold, tall silver and
gold hat embroidered and re-embroidered with emerald drops.
Georges's was bright green braided with gold and sashed with
violet, with a surcoat of deep pink fringed with gold. The Duchess
came as Confucius: spectacles, mustaches, little pigtail, magnificent
antique Chinese robe. Nathalie was a conquering hero – Attila,
perhaps? – complete with embroideries and a sharp weapon,
threatening and gruff, with a panther-skin slung nonchalantly over
her glittering rags and a primitive little hat, rather Chinese. Madame
Lucas was a Tunisian woman and relieved my tottering frailty of
some of my tasks as hostess. Madame Beamish de Foras made a
mysterious masked entrance in peasant costume with a basket on her
arm containing two live ducks – her butler came in the car with
her to take them back to the farmyard at Croizy. Betsy Gautrat was a
Russian in pearl-embroidered red and a long veil hanging down
behind, very beautiful. .... Margot, delicious in Nattier blue
of about 1830, her mass of hair dressed à la Lawrence, mittens on
her beautiful white hands. Madame Blanchon looked burly as an
Apache in red and black; her friend Madame Renaud-Badet as his

fancy girl in the same colours. They had prepared a little number with a leading dancing-master and performed twice, to tremendous applause, like two angels from the slums. Pepito came as a convalescent in a cyclamen dressing-gown of crackling silk, wearing odd stockings and slippers and a shirt with a pleated jabot . . . .

In fact it was a very successful party and everyone was thoroughly comfortable in our little living-room-turned-buffet – where the traditional pancakes made their mark, as well.

Saint-Germain-en-Laye – March 2 to March 24

March 2. Salomon Reinach left us here yesterday, in this nice little family pension, well within our means.

Our reconciliation with Max Jacob took place the day before yesterday: it was nice, and seemed to be sincere. The Duchess and Nathalie came to lunch and were charming to him. Nathalie made a conquest of him, looking after him at table, listening to him, strewing the precious pearls of her wit before him all the time. Max felt happy and celebrated, behaved well and we shall see him again.

March 24 . . . . They look after us well in this simple little place, it costs twenty-five francs a day, and the guests are an odd mixture. We are Roumanian; then there's a young Turkish woman who is recovering from anaemia. She is pretty and very young, not yet twenty: Georges has nicknamed her 'Albertine Imprisoned'. Then there's a really exquisite girl, my new little friend, Manon Thiébaut: an artist, trying to earn her living making woodcuts and drawings, and by illustrating pious books. She has wit, talent, easy manners, charm, wonderful eyes, beautiful tousled hair worn bobbed, a pale skin and an enchanting fragility which she has come here to cure. She shuts herself up to read and work and has hardly any appetite. She has been suffering badly from neurasthenia and is hardly over it yet. There is sympathy between us, we read the same books. I think we will see more of each other.

I have seen Lady M again, in bed just as she was when I left, under fine cambric loaded with fabulous embroidery and marvellous lace, a sheet worth seventeen thousand francs! When I raved about it she said she possessed them by the dozen!

I also saw my dear curé, Abbé Duchemin. He visited me here and yesterday I made my confession. So here I am, all tidied up. I like confessing to him. He's so good and gentle, so indulgent!

Paris – March 30 to May 14

March 30. .... Should I give thanks to heaven? Certainly it heaps me with physical ailments, but I think it has sent me a treasure, a friend: Marcelle Thiébaut, so full of kindness, wit, tact and courage. I love her already; she seems drawn to me. She has smiled on me, I have kissed her. She has had several affectionate impulses; I have had that of inviting her to spend the summer with us at Clos-Marie. She dreams of Roscoff, and we think of it greedily. These pages will reveal what comes of it . . .

. . . .

April 21. Letter from my dear Frédéric de Madrazzo who had invited us to visit him with the Tiny One. The Tiny One is Mademoiselle Marcelle Thiébaut, also known as Manon. As far as I'm concerned she is my Tiny One.

Tiny One wanted to paint on glass, and it's not easy. Joujou (Frédéric) has done it and at my request he was going to show her the technique; and Joujou picked that day to be somewhere quite else!

. . . .

Roscoff – Clos-Marie, June 2 to November 3

June 2. Tiny One arrived yesterday evening in torrential rain. Luckily an omnibus which plies to and from the station brought her up to the house, together with Georges who had gone to pick her up. Tiny One is enchanted with what she saw of Brittany out of the window of the train, with her arrival in Roscoff, with the Clos, with the drawing-room, with the bedrooms, etc. She went to sleep peacefully after a nice little supper which she ate sitting on my bed.

At about five in the morning the elements broke loose, the wind began to blow so violently that it shook our beds and the whole house, the rain became fierce enough to break windows, the sea roared. Towards six o'clock I ventured into her bedroom, wanting to reassure her – and woke up poor Tiny One who was sleeping soundly and who said at once: 'Oh how good it is to be here, what a marvellous storm!' Then she jumped out of bed and went to open her shutters, knocking over her letter-rack, her books, an ashtray – crying out 'How beautiful! How beautiful!'

Her little head must contain the most powerful forces, for her arrival to have put the elements in such a rage! Today we are far from the 'pearly sea-shell'; it's more like a copper kettle boiling over. Houses have been flooded, roads are under water, the wind is blowing skirts and umbrellas inside out.

Tiny One is here with her beautiful eyes and her friendship. It's a joy sent us from Heaven.

June 4. I have flu. One can't help exposing oneself to draughts while tidying, and my age makes me ultra-susceptible.

Tiny One continues to smile on everything. Her happy looks are our thanks. She has made a conquest of the whole household and the neighbours too. She understands how to look at our great landscape, how to feel things, how to appreciate the delights of comfort. She is unimaginably small, but beautifully built. I fuss over her and she allows it. Everything is going very well. She reads a lot. So do I. I have just read *Morvagine* by Blaise Cendrars. It's hellish! Today's taste for gloomy writing. People like horrors, they relish them. Cendrars has a powerful talent; he emerges splendidly out of the slough in which Aragon wallows so grossly. They made such a to-do over Zola's realism! These people leave it behind by miles. Even Cendrars's evident and moving talent can't make me like this kind of thing. Against my beloved landscape's infinity and in this fresh air the animality displayed in these squalid and deplorable offerings doesn't work.

June 8. The anniversary of our marriage. Sixteen years – and the bond has become closer. We have been kneaded and blended into one.

Yesterday Georges went to Saint-Pol to find me thousands of treats and collect – at last! – the fifteen thousand francs his mother has been promising since April. As soon as he left me I was racked by the most frightful anxiety; my nerves were on edge, I kept having the most gloomy presentiments. We went to meet him, darling Tiny One, Camille and I, and as soon as I saw him in the middle of the road my balance was restored. Thank you, God! I believe we are closer to each other than twins. Sixteen years! The dear sweet work of sixteen years! Even the rages which rumbled inside me and afterwards threw me panting into his arms, pinning us cruelly together; even the little secret tricks each of us had practised out of pity for the other's weakness or sensibility: all these miseries of human existence, all this space shared in the same atmosphere, the same pleasures, the same desires, the same tears in face of the same hopes, all of this lit by the most luminous sincerity. Yes, we really are embodied in each other. I offer thanks yet again, o God, for all the frail yet genuine happiness which this morning I can feel behind my dejection and which is swelling my heart with tenderness. I submit myself to these sweet familiar pleasures which bring me nearer to God and distance me from the world, because to some extent that is the consequence of our long days of solitude. Georges my husband, my love, my all, I bless you.

June 9. Yesterday passed pleasantly, except that I felt vaguely uneasy all the time. Rain, stormy weather, tiredness. I have let my diet slip: lobster, chicken, chocolate soufflé and champagne have all made their appearance on our table.

I have had a friendly letter from Cécile Sorel, now Comtesse de Ségur. It arrived aptly for our sixteenth wedding anniversary. I had congratulated her on exchanging her queenly crown for that of a countess, all for love. Guillaume de Ségur has been her lover for years and years. He is at least twenty years younger than she is. She hesitated; when we last met I gave her encouragement by our example, so she says in her letter. May Heaven protect them and preserve them in a state of grace!

We went round to our nice little Boignaus to hear Reynaldo Hahn on the gramophone. I was disappointed. I didn't recognize his lovely, arresting voice, warm and slightly husky. Perhaps its rhythms and easiness were there, but the machine's hard metallic resonance suppressed the charm and musicality and added touches of vulgarity. A wonderful invention all the same, but still a long way from perfection.

. . . .

June 16. Yesterday Tiny One went in to Saint-Pol with Camille. They saw everything and did masses of shopping for me. They came home on foot in pouring rain, enchanted by it. Tiny One thinks the whole country is superb and Saint-Pol is beautiful, with a great deal of character. Tiny One knows how to see and how to feel. Her soul is as ready to see and understand as are her magnificent eyes.........

June 18. Sorted my old papers and family bits and pieces. At home at rue Saussure I have a few old portraits: Grandfather Lopez, his wife née de Montessuy, her mother Madame de Montessuy née d'Arey, Madame d'Arey née de Ruys and Madame de Ruys née Embito. There's a paper concerning the last after she had become the wife of Hyppolyte Thomas Marie d'Arey, affirming that in the terrible year 1793 (the second year of the Republic) she had not emigrated and had paid her patriotic contributions, etc. That paper can have been no joke and must have frightened the good woman and made her get rid of her title by marrying a little magistrate from Rennes, Monsieur Delacour, whom Maman could remember from her early childhood. Leafing through these papers I noticed that during the years of the revolution this former Mademoiselle de Ruys who had married a d'Arey wrote her name as one word: Delacour. Soon afterwards she retrieved her 'de' – de Lacour; and later still she made three words of it: de la Cour! ....

These, my old family papers, are my title deed to possession of my Brittany, and also of a few fine feelings, principles and prejudices. I inherit the utmost frankness from all these proud Bretons, and I have the faults which go with it.........

June 20. The weather is trying to be fine; can it bring it off? They are saying that it's the waves transmitted from the TSF which have caused all this rain.

My little Thiébaut is charming, her mind is so open, so broad, so subtle. And such pretty manners into the bargain. She is gentle and authoritative at the same time. She is perfectly well-bred. Every day she thanks us for having her. She works away at her little wood- or lino-cuts, her painting and drawing, for three or four hours every day. She has quite a few orders, and they are repeating. Her work is good, clear, witty, enjoyable.

June 22. Letter from Max Jacob. I think he wants to come here in July. And I think turning a deaf ear is the best thing to do. I am neither strong nor patient. Max's presence is a gruelling test which I always fail sooner or later.

. . . .

June 27. The local people arranged a pilgrimage to Lourdes. All Brittany went on it. The sister of my cook, Marie, took part. She prayed for me and asked that what I wished for should be accomplished. She came back yesterday, and no later than that same evening I had a telegram from an agency saying: 'Have found firm purchaser who sees solicitor tomorrow, drop all negotiations.' A little miracle! Coincidence, a sceptic would say, but I prefer to believe in miracles. Is not every person's existence a miracle in itself?

. . . .

July 4. Georges loves Tiny One! Tiny One loves Georges! Crack, it has happened! Is it worse than cancer?

Georges admitted it this morning, then Tiny One was summoned and came in very white.

I have been saying to myself for a long time that something was bound to happen. Georges is so much younger than I am, he has given me eighteen years of happiness . . . I must think! It's a very banal situation, after all. I don't want to make a grand tragedy of it, and anyway love carries the day. If it is a true love it will bend us to its laws. If it's a passing fancy it will pass. Yes, but . . . my nature is a difficult one. I don't yet know how I'm going to react and how I'll behave to them or to myself. Tiny One is adorable, well-bred, very intelligent, has lovely eyes, a young body. She has neither health nor money! Perhaps she is a bit of a schemer? Georges is hooked, but he insists that he adores me and can't do without me. My great, splendid, complete, pure happiness is over.

July 5. I am going to put this notebook away for a while. Georges has left me. He went away with Mademoiselle Thiébaut yesterday morning and here I am quite alone with the ocean and my disaster. I have not yet shed a single tear. Eighteen years of magnificent happiness have brought me to a quite atrocious resignation.

July 10. My god-daughter Margot de La Bigne has come. I leave with her for Paris on Wednesday the 14th, to start another life. To make use of my life! That is all I ask.

Liane put her journal aside for three months after her husband left her. When she returned to Roscoff in September she took it up again, starting by summarizing the events which followed his departure.

September 23. After a great deal of coming and going, packing and unpacking, here I am back at Clos-Marie. Here I am back with Camille and with a friend called Mimy Franchetti, an adorable young Italian who was brought to me by Nathalie and has been my consolation.

October 8. I thought I would die . . . I was unable to sleep, I was taking far too many drugs in order to get two or three hours of sleep a night. Here I have rediscovered everything, peace and natural sleep. Basically it has all been a deliverance.

Ought I to describe it all? Why not?

On July 4, curtains drawn on the appalling day that was about to start, I heard footsteps in my bedroom. I opened my eyes and could just make out my husband's silhouette in the duskiness, standing by my bed. Only half awake I said: 'Georges? Is that you?' – 'Yes, my darling. Have you slept well?' He got into bed with me, took me in his arms, covered me with kisses and said in a rather strangled voice: 'Listen, I've got a confession to make.' Accustomed as I was to him as the being from whom all sweetness came, I imagined some clumsiness; yes, the only thought to enter my head was that he had broken one of my ornaments, a piece of opaline perhaps. I smiled and said 'Confess!' Then he began mumbling that he couldn't do without me, that he adored me, that he would kill himself an hour after I died, but that he couldn't do without Tiny One. I didn't want to understand. I stammered: 'But Tiny One is here, you have got her.' – 'No,' he said, 'but I shall have her. I've got to. I've never deceived you, I want to tell you everything. Yesterday evening we kissed for the first time, we told each other of our love. The child loves me as I love her. I'm a bit old for her, but she doesn't mind. If you agree, nothing need change. The three of us can live together. I can't be happy with you and without her, or with her and without you.' My whole body began to tremble. I said to him: 'But you are murdering me. It's appalling, get out of my bed.' He hugged me tighter. 'But I adore you. You'll see, you'll have two people to adore you instead of just one. We'll cherish you, we'll take care of you, we'll make you so happy. She's mad about you – she'll obey you, you will always be the mistress, the queen. She will take second place, she will submit to you. I have told her all that and she has accepted it. Everything will go on as it is now except that I will go to her at night. No one will know anything about it, not even the maids or Madame Garat.' I prayed to God, with open hands I said to Him: 'Let Your will be done, oh God! Make me say what You want me to say. Help me, Saint Anne! This is the worst blow fate could give me. Don't let me cry like a fool, don't let me faint, but I wouldn't mind dying. Protect me!' Georges went on: 'You'll see, we'll be gay and happy. In Paris she can sleep in my bedroom and I can have the little divan in the dressing-room. During the day it can go in your big cupboard.' – 'Get up,' I said, because I didn't want him to feel me trembling. 'I have got to think. I have got to go away and think without hate or anger or torment. I shall go away with Camille for a week, somewhere far away from here, from you two, and then I shall tell you what we are going to do.' – 'If you leave,' he said, getting up at last, 'if you leave I shall hate her. I'm going to bring her in. She is waiting. Neither of us has slept all night.'

October 9. Then Manon came in, pale and trembling, trying to look me in the face. She threw herself into my arms as though to kiss me. I pushed her away gently and said: 'Do you love my husband?' She cried out: 'I love you both! I'll do what you say. I'll kill myself if I must.' I replied: 'That's beside the point. I see now that you're both mad, I'm the only grown-up here. I am going to think this over, somewhere far away from you. I shall leave.' Then Georges began again: 'If you leave I shall hate her.' This annoyed the girl, who sat down opposite my bed and said. 'No, I'm the one who will leave.' I made up my mind: 'Yes, Mademoiselle, that in fact is the best thing you can do. It is better that I should be the one to stay in my own family house. Go, I accept that you go. Madame Garat will fetch your trunk down. Go to your room.' Georges, furious: 'If you drive her away, I will follow her.' Me, calmed by the decision made and the completeness of the renunciation: 'I am not driving her. Mademoiselle Thiébaut says herself that she would like to leave, I accept. As for you, YOU HAVE GONE ALREADY!'

They brought me up my breakfast. Making a great effort, I ate it, then I gave the cook her orders. I got up and dressed. Rigid and tense, I simply tried to get through the activities of every day. Then I went into Mademoiselle Thiébaut's bedroom where the trunk was not yet packed. Her expression had changed. She had lost her child-like look and seemed ill-natured, older, formidable, evidently on the defensive. Yet for her this was the moment of triumph.

Georges was packing her small case. Having filled it he was bringing her things which she put into the trunk as I watched. I said: 'Don't keep my husband up too late. Don't make him drink or smoke; he is delicate, he needs a lot of looking after – and so do you.' Then I said: 'It's quite natural, if he loves you he'll have to follow you. You would have a frightful life with me. You have to consider my temperament: I am not dissolute, and then I have a violent nature. I would probably make your life quite impossible. Where will you go?' Georges – yellow, rattled, incoherent – muttered something about Brest or Morlaix. I advised; 'Paris would be better, it's the easiest place to hide in. Or why not Roumania? Life would be easier for you there.' Georges's eyes were pinpoints. He seemed to be suppressing a frightful rage. In all the eighteen years of our life together I never saw him look like that, but it's only like that that I see him now. I have lost the memory of all his other faces.

I saw that they wanted to gain time, so I said: 'I'm going, I'll go out and leave you alone. Georges, give me all the keys and put labels on them to help me in all the chores which I shall now have to do by myself. Give me my passport and my resident's permit. Go to the lawyer here and get me a power of attorney so that I can sell the two houses in Saint-Germain without you (we were well advanced in serious negotiations about them). When you are in Paris go to my lawyer, Maître Collet. Tell him everything and ask him to look after me. From now on you must write to me at his address, only to that address and only about business.' He said with difficulty: 'I have got sixty-five English pounds of yours. I'll get them for you.' I refused; 'Keep them! You are going away with a woman, you will need money.' He accepted and I went downstairs calling out: 'Goodbye! Be happy, if you are able to build your happiness on my distress!'

They left. The girl said to Camille: 'The worst of it all is that now the Princess will never believe how much I love her. Because I do love her.' – 'What do you mean?' said Madame Garat. 'She won't doubt it for a moment. Look how well you are proving it!'

October 11. At the age of eighteen I had a husband and a child. At that age I ran away from it all, driven by a fatal destiny.

Up to the age of eighteen: family, principles, routine and gentleness. From eighteen to thirty-six (another eighteen years) I lived in turmoil and among passions – every kind – either experienced or endured. I learnt to know the world, a sad distinction. At thirty-six I met Georges. And now, after another eighteen years, my life is renewed. Now I am alone and free, purified by that long period of duty, tenderness and trust. Alone and free: proud words, let them be my rule and my message. Alone, I will draw nearer to You, oh my God. There lies my longing and my will.

And yet . . . close by, under my roof, just opposite my bedroom door, there sleeps the most beautiful, the most ardent, the most seductive of women. Is it one more test? Is it consolation?

October 12. We have cleaned out the cistern, we have checked the roof. The garden has been tidied up. All the rites governing life are going smoothly, both within me and around me. More smoothly than before, yes, more easily, more gracefully and naturally than when he was here. Georges is a hostile person, clumsy and ill-natured. Stupid and without principles. One has to face it, he was a brute! I knew it, but I believed he was loyal, bound and attached to me with the full force of his evil nature.

The day after he left – it was a compensation from Heaven – every trace of my rheumatism suddenly vanished; every pain in my body fled away. Nervous shock, said the surprised doctors. I felt refreshed and rejuvenated and everyone said as much, both here and there: 'You are looking so young and beautiful' – I, who thought I would die!

October 14. I shall write to my husband through my lawyer, suggesting that he asks for a divorce. 'The Princess cannot do it except by the formality of making a confession, but she can submit to it and it would relieve her of a difficult situation which, although it was brought about by you, can hardly be agreeable to you either. The Princess is constantly in need of signatures and authorizations which still have to be given by you. For example, on the eve of her journey abroad last summer she almost failed to be granted a visa, lacking your permission. She was forced to renounce the opportunity to make a film, which would have given her an interesting and profitable occupation, for the reason that she did not want to depend on your consent.'

How much more freely I would breathe! How much less heavy

my burden would become! I am constantly afraid of what my assassin may do; even, and especially, that he may come back.

October 16. This morning we are driving to Morlaix to spend the day, Camille, Mimy and I – because I have a little Mimy in my life.

Mimy followed me, led by friendship, drawn by my grief. She followed me, ardent, passionate, true and beautiful – oh, so beautiful! Mimy never leaves me by day or by night. She is here with her fervent and splendid soul, her fierce Italian love.

My husband is in correspondence with Maître Collet, to whom he writes false and insinuating things such as: 'Do everything you possibly can, dear Maître, to help my wife, of whom I never stop thinking with immense grief.' Then: 'If my wife considers our separation to be final – something which I am unable to believe (!) – I ask that she send me all the letters I received from her, which are in a casket together with all her photographs.' – And then this: 'You hold my will, which is in my wife's favour. It will remain so. Be good enough to attach this letter to it in confirmation.'

Nathalie Barney flew to my side as soon as she heard of my arrival at Margot's little flat at 91 boulevard Malesherbes. She knew Eugène Thiébaut, a former diplomat at Washington, who was Manon's uncle. Nathalie brought him to see me. He showed me a letter dated July 6 in which Manon asked him to let her family know of her 'departure with Prince Ghika for abroad, and for many long years.' She had no doubts about it, but she did add that she was very sorry for the distress which she was about to cause her family, and for ruining Princess Ghika's life. At bottom the Thiébauts are divided between shame and the wish to see their Manon become Princess Georges Ghika as soon as possible. As for the Ghikas, they must certainly be satisfied at our separation, but worried about what that idiot Georges is getting up to now! At twenty he wanted to kill himself for Ventura (of the Comédie-Française); at twenty-six he married Liane de Pougy! Now, at forty-two, he lets himself be abducted by a little schemer. All this is likely to cost money, and Georges has none. I have my little income; while he was with me he fell into neither debt nor folly.

October 17. By dint of putting rouge on my cheeks and listening when they tell me I am beautiful and rejuvenated, shall I end by forgetting the burden laid on my heart by life?

October 18. I have Mimy. It happened like this: during the summer Nathalie wrote me a line saying that she was in love, madly in love with a woman, and that this love outstripped all her other loves by a long way. Rather vexed, I answered: 'The best in your life was me! Me! Me!'

As soon as I arrived in Paris, in Margot's charming little flat, I called Nathalie who came to me, affectionate and approving: 'You have done the right thing, Liane, I am so glad. You must keep it up . . .' She held me in her arms, listened, advised, sent flowers, took me to the Duchess's, showed me the sweetest and most compassionate tenderness. My friends rallied round, adorable to me and indignant at Prince Ghika, saying: 'It's abominable! How could he fall so low! You were his whole truth. He will be sorry – but don't ever take him back! He was such a bore; he got on everyone's nerves; he diminished you.' I heard endless versions of this. In short I was made much of, comforted, smothered in flowers, almost celebrated. Jean Cocteau came, very shocked, to pour out calming words, floods of healing poetry with which to express my agony. As he will also come, I hope, to sing my deliverance.

October 19. My little Margot offered me a room and a bathroom in her new apartment at 15 rue Verniquet, and it was a life-raft. I accepted with affection and enthusiasm. Camille had a little mattress in the bathroom. She never left me, my faithful newfoundland, devoted, alert, rather crusty, a little bit mangy, but mine come what may with all her loyalty and love.

And Nathalie was there. I – who am so scared of her thunder and also so afraid of doing her the least harm because through it all I love her deeply – this is what I did or rather had done to me, because nothing was started by me except a loyal and determined struggle in which I was defeated because Mimy, my Mimy is here, she's asleep in the room next to mine as I write these words and I shall soon be going in to kiss her awake.

Nathalie, sitting by my bed one day: 'Liane, the one I love is waiting outside. You are so beautiful, you have been so great, so admirable, may I bring her in to see you for a moment so that she can contemplate you, so that you can see her?' – 'Yes,' I said without much interest. 'Bring her in, go and fetch her.' And in she came, tall, slender, white as a magnolia flower, her enchanting gestures so graceful, small, rare, precise, fiery eyes, an almost unreal fineness. She bent over me, over my cruel suffering.

Nathalie smiled. It was Nathalie herself who prepared her own fate.

We talked. I told my pitiful story for Mimy. She didn't say a great deal. Nathalie wanted them both to carry me off to the country. I refused, overcome by weariness. They left me. But did they really leave me? Two minutes later a bunch of fresh roses was brought in which they had left for me at once, before going right away.

October 20. They came back. It was in the middle of the night. I awoke to hear Nathalie's voice calling me. Camille went to open the door. It was her, then Mimy with a violinist friend of theirs, Pola (who was a pupil of Sarasate). It was like a lovely dream. Nathalie on one side, stroking and caressing me; Mimy on the other, her lips on mine; Pola playing for us in the next room . . .

They came back – often. They made much of me, they took me out, they dressed my wounds. Mimy and I loved each other. Her presence was my heaven of joy and forgetfulness.

Nathalie became jealous. Nathalie loves in her own way. She wants her friends to be happy up to a certain point. She is dissolute; she adores directing love's revels, leading them on, halting them, starting them up again. What she loves is bodies, and reactions. We ran through the whole gamut – but Mimy loved me and I found her adorable.

October 21. Before I left for Deauville with Margot and Camille I decided to end things, avoid goodbyes, behave as though I were indifferent.

I arrived at the Normandy and I had not yet taken off my hat when I saw Mimy's maid pop up in front of me with a note from Mimy telling me that she was there, loving me and waiting for me. I stamped my foot in a moment of rage at my courage being wasted like that; then, with my heart leaping, I followed Suzanne and fell straight into the arms of Mimy: a tired Mimy, a Mimy in bed, a Mimy who loved me and wanted me and pursued me.

October 22. In joyful gratitude for this fresh dawn which illuminates my awakening, I want to record here my forgiveness: I forgive Georges, and Manon. They have gone right away, they are dead to me. They have suffered their fate – the fate they chose and which they deserve. This morning, oh Destiny, I accept you with the utmost submission. I forgive. And you, my Heaven-sent love to whom I open my arms, will make me forget.

October 23. Clos-Marie is no longer mine: I have just leased it for eighteen years to my Mimy, to the adorable woman who has shown me that I can still be loved – oh joy! – and still love – oh happiness! She is beautiful and vital, fervent, subtle and fine, amusing and gay. She brings together every one of Heaven's gifts. She is charm itself. She laughs, and everything around her becomes joyful. She walks, and the dance of her graceful body dazzles those who watch. She speaks: her voice is serious and soft, arresting, a little husky. She sings: one is conquered to the very depths of one's being by the warm, velvety, harmonious, enveloping timbre. She is tall – the tiniest bit taller than I – fine boned. She has the prettiest gestures. She is white, her eyes gleam, a greenish hazel, her eyelashes throw shadows, her eyebrows are delicate. Tiny blue veins are visible under the transparancy of the skin on her face and neck, on her body too. She has the most ravishing legs in the whole world, long, with amazingly delicate joints.

October 25. Mimy's love is ardent, impassioned, whole, jealous. Love in the Italian style! It sings, it shouts, it howls in keeping with her beauty, her gestures, her fiery glance. Mimy is a creature of excess.

We stay in bed late of a morning; we have breakfast; we tease; we laugh; we kiss. We open our letters. She gives me an Italian lesson: verbs, vocabulary, dictation, translation. We have a very good time. She sings me the blues, which I adore, or else Italian songs, in her deep, vibrant voice. We separate, then meet again on the little rock-beach. Mimy hunts for pebbles. She loves stones and discovers marvellous ones with bright colours and unusual shapes. We trim the shrubs in the garden. We go into the town. Everyone loves my Mimy, everyone smiles at her and gives her flowers. We take heaps and heaps of photographs. We come home again and Mimy plays the gramophone. She opens a book: D'Annunzio's poems or the stories of Mark Twain. I read too. Time passes so quickly. Everyone is amazed by my cheerful face, suddenly so much younger. They all say to me: 'Your expression has changed. Monsieur le Prince never used to laugh, you used to look as though you were bored.' It was true, yet I thought I possessed a marvellous treasure!

Sometimes we have quarrels: Mimy has already accumulated so many memories! Me too. We tell each other – and that's a mistake. The one who is listening suffers and becomes angry.

October 26. Comœdia have asked me how much I would want for my memoirs. I've turned them down.

October 27. I have written to Eugène Thiébaut, Manon's uncle. He answered that his niece had spent the whole summer with my husband's mother.

By the same post I had a letter from the lawyer warning me that my husband had given him a new address in Switzerland and that no doubt he would be coming to Paris, which would simplify the divorce. I am thinking of Moro-Giafferi for my advocate. I shall need the best!

To return to Mimy and her determined amorous pursuit. When I got back from Deauville I tried to escape yet again. I refused to sleep with her. That was when I accepted an invitation to spend two days with Madame R at her château. There again Mimy turned up, arriving with Nathalie at eleven o'clock in the evening simply in order to see me, kiss me and tell me: 'We are at Barbizon, we will sleep there and tomorrow we will come for you and drive you back to Paris.'

The next day I saw Nathalie who overwhelmed me with reproaches to start with, then cradled me in tenderness. Mimy took me out to dinner in Montparnasse. We came home, and all veils were rent asunder. We abandoned ourselves without remorse and without restraint to the delirium of our love. Days went by in sweetness and tumult.

We packed our bags for Venice, Margot, Camille and I. Lolo (Margot's friend Monsieur Lopez) and his family went on ahead. I had trouble with my passport and was almost stuck for lack of my husband's authorization, but finally my lawyer managed to get the necessary visa and stamps.

I departed, leaving my Mimy breathless and Nathalie full of hope. So there I was in Venice. My room at the Grand Hotel – a pretty double bedroom on the corner of the Grand Canal, with an enchanting bathroom – was perfumed with carnations. I stayed six days. Mimy was impatient, hatching plans, hunting for her passport which Nathalie had pinched and hidden. We went back and forth between the Lido and the Grand Hotel. I met friends: handsome little Pierre Meyer (son of the proprietor of 'Old England') and his lot. There was much talk about the Lido and sun-bathing. Pierre had a cabin on the famous beach. It was because he invited me that we were there every day, Margot, Camille and I in pyjamas! We lunched at the little restaurant underneath the Excelsior where they accepted pyjama-clad and partly-pyjama-clad people. Camille, sitting with us at Pierre's big table, had an English neighbour who wore nothing but his pyjama tops, giving his naked thighs a look at the summer weather which caused his red hairs to stand on end in astonishment.

I met Bernstein, who came to offer me compassionate condolences; Guillot de Saix who did a drawing of my profile which appeared in *Comœdia*; Baroness de Meyer, the Lioness of the Lido; Kapurthala; de Meyer's friend the Prince of Prussia. I said to Pierre 'You mustn't introduce me to the Prince of Prussia. I don't mind that he's a pederast, but I can't forget that my son was killed in the war.' – 'Oh Liane,' said Pierre, 'the war's gone quite out of fashion, we don't think about it any more.'

The days went by very cheerfully with this crazy group of young inverts, all quite unrestrained in their behaviour, displaying their vice with the greatest nonchalance. When I got back to the hotel I would feel rather disgusted. My life felt empty of meaning, stupid, hectic. In the daytime we laughed a lot at the thought of my husband's expression if he could see the three of us dressed in his finest pyjamas!

October 28. The Lido was madly crowded; cabins became drawing-rooms, arranged like the most mysterious of opium dens: cushions, mattresses, divans, embroideries, scent. Skins were oiled with rare and precious substances, people walked about naked or nearly so, took the sun, the air, the water, dried themselves, smoked, drank, loved. It was relaxation, a break in the year's complications. Beautiful bodies displayed themselves proudly: our Pierre's was marvellous. It was all for the sake of tanning, that was the pretext and the excuse! At lunch the women, more coquettish, looked as though they were acting in a fairy-tale: Schéhérazade, Salomé, Salammbô – oriental ladies from rich harems. They went by in sumptuous pyjamas of silk or figured velvet, brilliantly coloured, glittering with sequins and stones. Fantasy reigned, at its wildest.

There was a big fancy-dress ball. That evening all my Lido friends came to have dinner at my hotel. I was starting bronchitis. I had a temperature, but I enjoyed my little party all the same.

October 29. The whole happy – and depraved – band came up to my room to make themselves up before leaving for the ball. The handsomest, as always, was Pierre Meyer dressed as a Scot in a delicious little kilt, with his bare bronze legs, his cheerful boyish face and his great height. One couple (!) went as pierrots with pink roses in their mouths. Antoine, the hairdresser, was a superb Byzantine empress followed by his heart's beloved dressed as a Chinaman. Antoine had a gilded gondola decked with lights and flowers and filled with musicians. Antoine is rich. He has the taste of the sculptor he used to be and all the audacity of the pervert he is. His gondola carried Margot and her court to the Fenice. César Mauge de Houcke was in midnight blue, a dress which was once Lady Abdy's, and was very proud that the pretty lady's shoes fitted him. Rheims was a Neapolitan in pink and white. Guillot de Saix looked much as he usually does as Alfred de Musset. Having a beard, he always adopts this easy disguise. Monsieur de la Pena collapsed under the weight of a rich and heavy costume which made him look like an exhausted old Shylock. Everyone apart from him was laughing, joking, singing, dancing. They wanted me with them and tried to drag me along. I was stoic. They were all very full of the young inheritor of the Italian crown whose presence was going to give lustre to this charity ball. They told me that Antoine made the greatest sensation. We – he and I – were honoured by *Comœdia*. Yes, they wrote as though I had been at the dance, and one of the most beautiful there. They even published a drawing of me lying on my bed, which Guillot de Saix had made during the evening. I look like a queen reclining carelessly on her litter. I said to myself: if Georges sees this in Roumania he's going to think that my efforts to take my mind off stop at nothing!

Two days later I left Venice, and hardly was I in the train before my temperature shot up. My companions didn't know what to do. I had the courage to carry on as far as Lausanne. There we left the train at dawn and I was put into the Royal Hotel. A doctor was called who diagnosed congestion in both lungs. Margot sent a telegram to my Mimy who answered at once: 'Will be in Lausanne today all love.' The darling! So Lolo, who had to be in Paris urgently, was able to continue his journey after finding a flat for me and my friends, paying for it and leaving me some money. Margot was ready to stay with me but I know how crazy she is about her Lolo and how she needs him, so I insisted absolutely that she should go with him. I was getting better. Stuffed with drugs and shattered by that frightful journey, I plunged into sleep and my body's natural defences did the rest. When Nathalie came into my room next morning, followed by Mimy, they found me so far on the road to recovery that – although Mimy dared to rejoice – Nathalie was quite cross with me for not being dead after upsetting them with such an alarming telegram.

I had to stay at Lausanne for five days. Meanwhile Nathalie sent to Paris for her car, her smooth, shiny, silent, Buick; and after entrusting Camille to the express and her own resources, Nathalie, Mimy and my almost recovered self set off.

The first stage was as far as Thonon. The Hôtel du Parc welcomed us agreeably: two nice communicating rooms, one with two beds, sharing a bathroom. That was how we lived for five days. We covered 1,500 kilometres, laughing, singing and – Mimy and I – loving. We restrained our love in order not to give too much pain to Nathalie who began to torment me with the most bitter reproaches, really absurd, and to make the most unexpected suggestions: 'Do this to her, not that; give her this and not that.' I told her: 'Nathalie, I am me. It was you who brought her to me and threw her into my arms. Instead of frivolity and naughtiness, what happened was the birth of feelings which both of us need.'

October 30. One evening we slept at Bourg. Still Mimy in the double room chosen by Nathalie and me next door in the little single room as though I were their daughter. Although we did try very hard, Mimy and I ended by joining each other. She made me laugh so much when she said plaintively: 'Since when have mothers-in-law insisted on travelling with young couples?' We were cruel in the way we let ourselves go. All day in the car we held hands, our lips met.

November 1. We left for Roscoff like two children going on holiday. Nathalie left for the South of France. She must have been furious with me.

When I and my burden came into Mimy's life she reached out to offer me help. She sensed the truth of my grief and my life. She loved me, she still loves me. It cannot last – nothing lasts. But it's so beautiful, so simple, so complete. Perhaps this morning, when my kiss wakes her, I shall feel that her love has vanished during the night . . . I am alert for anything, I clutch at nothing, I let myself drift. I pay attention only to the present, I let the minutes run through my fingers and see only the last of them. Grace is refused me. I love Mimy, but whether she stays or whether she goes my love will not be transposed. She is there and she is not there. I hold her and I can't feel her. I hold her and I see her going. I believe in her love and already I'm sacrificing it. When she tells me 'Always', it is I who want to leave as the word is uttered. When I answer 'We will never part' I feel the wish to disappear for ever, to flee without looking back. I don't really know what I want; I don't really know what I feel. If I spend an hour apart from her I truly believe that it will be for ever. Georges killed all the trust in me, even trust in myself. I say to the Lord: 'My God, it is You I love, it is You I want to serve, it is You I want to find! I do not live according to Your law, but what am I to do? I deliver myself utterly into Your hands. Tear out that which displeases You, make me what You would have me be.'

November 2. Collet wrote to Georges about divorce proceedings to be taken out against him and at the instigation, more or less, of both parties. He had revised my draft because he said my husband could not ask for a divorce on the grounds of his own errors. Prince Ghika's response stunned me! He declared that he was not envisaging divorce, that he failed to understand the difficulties created for me by my present situation, and that he acknowledged yet again all the wrong he had done me. Never shall I understand that creature. Never did I understand him. I see things straight and distinct and clear; he is obscure and tortuous.........

The idea of Georges in Paris is not a pleasant one. Meeting him would be disagreeable and useless. That little viper wrote to her uncle: 'Abroad, and for many long years.' What can have happened to make them change their minds?

November 3. Mimy has the flu but we are going ahead with our preparations to leave on Friday. I like the idea of taking action, pushing on ahead, tackling seriously this divorce which will free me completely. A sad freedom which I never foresaw, but still a deliverance! ....

I am very resolute, very calm, I shall even go to the conciliation interview. I hope I don't meet my husband there.

November 4. I have Moro-Giafferi as advocate. He is the champion of champions and he will deal with my case himself.

We are packing. Mimy is exquisite, easy and tender. Our intimacy is going to be somewhat interrupted.

Paris – November 7 to November 24

November 7. Here I am installed with my Uncle and Aunt Burguet; Mimy has gone home to 44 rue du Bac, feeling ill with a bronchial infection which she thinks has been building up for some days. Away from her and her charm I breathe better, I feel more myself. I think more freely, I live more healthily. Mimy never stops smoking, loves sauces, rich cakes, staying in bed, making scenes, reading funny magazines, running down her friends. She is fanciful, bossy, wounding, inconsistent. She is a conquest-maker. She loves me, but she indulges in a lot of little affectations which don't, in fact, conceal much. I have to say all this in order to recover my freedom of thought and action; and I am able to say it because I am clear-sighted and at present am incapable of a great love or even of a serious infatuation.

November 15. The most frightful things are going on! Georges demands that I should forgive him and says that if I don't take him back there is nothing left for him but death. So that is what the little schemer has reduced him to. I sent my answer to Madame Morel by Mimy. 'There's nothing left to hope for. I am going on with my divorce.' I see Maître Moro-Giafferi every day. I am not a good Christian but I have been brave in my renunciation, oh God, I have given myself over entirely to Your will. Come to my aid. I say today, as I did then: 'Make me say what You want me to say; make me do what You want me to do.' But . . . what a terrible confession I am going to have to make to Your representative. I dare not approach it. Help me!

November 19. Article announcing my divorce in *le Journal*. The rags have picked it up and repeated sentences out of it. The editor of *la Cigale* wants to see me. They come here to interview me. Orders are strict: they are told that I am in a nursing-home. My first application has been signed and despatched.

November 20. Maurice de Rothschild has invited us – Mimy and me – through Marthe Hollier-Larousse, to have dinner with him on Monday evening at the rue de Monceau. I long to see all his lovely things, and him too – I knew him when he was eighteen.

He was an adorable creature in those days. It seems that he has changed a great deal! That was twenty-seven or twenty-eight years ago. I was his first love. Mimy is his cousin. If he imagines that we are going to give him an evening of depravity he is much mistaken. We have made up our minds; at the first offensive word we put him sternly in his place. If he goes on, we leave.

November 23. Maurice behaved quite properly. He enlarged with pleasure and feeling on memories of our amorous youth. He showed us his house and his museum. I rediscovered the little Momo I used to know, a bit swollen and distended. Mimy was ravishing; I was all right in glittering black.

November 24. An atrocious day yesterday! Waiting at the lawyers. Waiting at the Palais de Justice. My divorce is going all right. Today I am quite shattered from the ordeal undergone by my nerves. I've still got the 'conciliation' to get through. Since Georges's legal domicile is 64 rue Saussure, we are sending the documents there. As he has left the conjugal home he won't get these documents and will probably fail to turn up, which is what we hope. Oh! please, dear God, forgive him as I do and grant me the favour of never seeing him again! I want him dead, not savagely but simply to end his suffering and his wrong-doing. All his and my responsibility I lay to the account of Manon Thiébaut, because in spite of her big innocent eyes she is tough, energetic, greedy, a monster of selfishness and cynicism, very responsible.

1927

Paris, January 1. 1926 over and done with: a year which – without doubt – I must consider one of deliverance. I welcome you with open arms, oh my destiny! Thank you for the flame which lights my hearth, for the good fire which warms me. Thank you for friends, for gifts. Thank you for what I am still able to detach from myself and give to others. Thank you for Jean Cocteau's intelligent and soothing telephone call, for Max Jacob's feeling letter, for the dear Burguets' heartfelt hospitality, for Mimy's love.

What a lot of blessings I owe you already, first day of the new year! Smiling resignation, calm, cheerfulness.

Thank you, God, for everything.

That entry is followed by two months of silence. When Liane takes up her pen again Georges is back. She does not explain how this came about. Her new name for him, 'Gilles', is evidently an attempt to convince them both that they can make a new start.

Boulouris – March 1 to April 28

March 1. My shipwreck has cast me up here, in a pretty white house standing quite close to the sea among mimosas, pines and eucalyptus. Georges Ghika has gone away. He has gone away for ever. But I have a certain little Gilles at my side, grave and sweet, affectionate and very pale, thin, sad at having hurt me so much. I do not think that Gilles can cure me of this hurt, but he might perhaps be able to help me to endure it. I have with me Camille, loving and bustling, awkward and clumsy; and I have Pauline Morel. I have a duty, an ideal. I am totally immersed in learning to know myself. I am here to straighten both of us out, to care for him, to do him good even if it means doing some harm to myself.

With him I am alone. Gilles still contains Georges Ghika, his faults, his instincts, his baseness. He gives me all of it, wrapped up in his love and remorse, and in a good deal of reserve. So the gift he makes of himself is complete! Ought I to feel sorry for myself? I let my life drift; it carried us along, separated us, brought us together again. I have left Mimy Franchetti who would have liked me to live against my inclinations, against what I firmly believe to be my truth. I am afraid of every word we pronounce, I don't speak unless I cannot avoid it. I also distrust the silences.

Gilles is shrunken, older, grinning, maniacal. We are living in the house of Jane Henriquez, the former singer reduced to this work by the cost of living – really rather hard for a nightingale! We go for walks . . .

Mimy Franchetti was dreadfully unhappy when I left her. I was unhappy. Our sensuality had its dear little habits. I tore all that up in one minute.

Gilles spent three weeks in a nursing-home at Chatenay near Paris, to rest, rediscover himself, try himself out, tidy himself up. I went to see him every day but all I saw was crime and darkness. Gilles has no gift for throwing light on things, nor any wish to do so. Our story has done nothing to illuminate him. I returned from these visits tortured, overcome, so tired . . .

My divorce was left unfinished. I stopped it for an indefinite period. If I no longer have Georges Ghika – if he has changed so much that I have had to invent Gilles – then it is true that I am not the same, either. New things have taken hold of me, have been unleashed in me. I used to be a magnificent creature, I have become a poor unhappy woman, desperately damaged, hurting all over.

March 5. Yesterday the sun gave nature and its creatures a rough shaking. Today it's rain, wind, storm over a grey sea, cruelly narrowed down. We huddle among the palm trees and mimosas surrounding this house, a nest buried in greenery. A train goes by and breaks the silence in which we live.

How I wish I could bypass this crisis in my life, this bankruptcy of my heart. Jean Cocteau met Georges Ghika and Manon Thiébaut in a Paris cinema. He told me: 'She's frightful! She's like a little monkey. One wanted to offer her a nut!' I answered: 'Her nut is my happiness.' He exclaimed: 'My love! You'll find your happiness again!' I know perfectly well, I feel very strongly, that I shall not. Besides, I am not looking for it; but I am waiting for something before I die – yes, I am waiting . . .

March 10. I am so unhappy I could die. I told Jean Bouscatel to introduce Mimy to Emilienne d'Alençon. Today Bouscatel wrote to say that he is going out with the two of them all the time. And it pierces my heart! My Mimy is going to forget me, to find consolation. She is with Emilienne; for me it's all over, over for good. I loved her so, so much . . .

Letter from Salomon Reinach. He is ill. He is wrong in supposing that the present blue notebook will be edifying and fascinating. Our life is pretty awful and I absolutely refuse to expatiate on it. I don't even want to think much about myself, I want to keep busy, devote myself to something . . . My aspirations are always lofty. Will they ever be crowned in keeping with their elevation?

March 20. Gilles and I wanted to have a little party: dinner in our room, with champagne. This morning we gave Camille the impression that we had remarried. As a matter of fact it happened on the first day. What would be the use of denying pleasure to our bodies?

Gilles tells me that I intimidate him dreadfully. No doubt his amorality is afraid of my purity – because I am all purity. And then, he loves me. He trembles before me, before the beauty he admires; he represses and restrains himself.

April 4. We spent a sweet day walking in the woods at Esterel among balsamic perfumes, under a blue sky, in the sun. Our sadness was still there, latent . . . and perhaps it has to be there. It's our point of contact, our way of communicating. Apart from exasperated embraces our sadness is now the best we have to give each other.

April 6. Gilles is tired, nervy. He is not smoking much and is not even thinking of getting drunk; watches me all the time with sorrow and affection – I daren't any longer say with love. He needs to be leaning against me, or in my arms; then his suffering diminishes and peace descends on him.

April 9. Moral collapse of Gilles: his idea – he confessed it to me – is to go out and solicit women wherever he sees them – unknown women – and do it very fast! 'Because if I have to talk to a woman for twenty minutes I stop wanting her.' He would like to bring them back to me, to go in for the most obscene and lewd games. So now what! I am going to consult my confessor and Father Sanson. I asked my dear Pinard for his advice, and according to him the calm and dignity of my household depends on soothing baths and doses of cascara. Dear God, I have no one but You!

In between times Georges tells me that he adores me, that he can't look at me without wanting to burst into tears (and there are tears in his eyes), and that he is unable to control himself any longer. He begs me to shut him up in a mad-house, or to kill him. It is complete disaster.

. . . .

April 17. I can't bear any more! He's a sort of madman, erotic and hysterical to the highest degree. He has told me that we ought to live together 'lightly'. That means – so he explains – having other women, taking me to brothels whenever he feels like it, sleeping with me every day – because he adores me . . . I am adored! I think he is really ill, his health completely undermined.

April 18. Enough of all that, time will sweep it away.

Letter from Sonia. I had sent her Vladimir Miatleff. Vladimir is a poet and a madman. I knew him in 1894 when I was playing in pantomime at St Petersburg. He ruined himself for me, just for the pleasure of looking at me.

He had married the daughter of General Richter. On his marriage night Vladimir realized that he was impotent. His wife deceived him with Prince Gagarin. Miatleff fought a duel with Gagarin – his wife was pregnant and Mia didn't want any bastards in his family. The Miatleffs belong to the highest nobility, more ancient than the Romanoffs. On the evening after his duel, honour satisfied, Miatleff, who was a guards officer, gave a big dinner for his fellow officers. They drank as they do in Russia, and towards the end they began to talk about the recent arrival of some beautiful tarts from France. Mia, who was over-excited, yelled: 'Beautiful they may be, but there isn't a whore who is better than my wife!' In a second the unfortunate, staggering Mia was surrounded by a circle of lowering comrades who thrust a large sheet of paper in front of him and said 'Sign this, resign your commission. You are no longer one of us. You have dishonoured yourself, speaking about your wife like that!' Mia signed, red to the top of his head with shame. His comrades embraced him and had to watch over him – drink with him too, I think – for several days, to prevent him from killing himself.

I turned up two years later. Mia had cheered up. He was still impotent and had become a terrible masochist. He took me to his estate at Goloubin in the region of Kursk, and heaped me with gifts.

One day he summoned a Paris jeweller, Jacques Goudstickker, so that I could choose a row of pearls and some rings. Jacques – the tempter! – spread a million and a half's worth of jewels on the table. I was recovering from a fever . . . I came into the room and stopped, dazzled. I looked at this, tried on that, and couldn't make up my mind. There were ruby and diamond tiaras, emerald necklaces, diamond chains, a parure of turquoises and diamonds, etc. Mia was pacing the room – I can see him now – with his hands behind his back. Finally I cried out: 'I simply can't make up my mind! Mia, you decide – they are all so beautiful!' Then he gave me a charming smile, looked at me with his big black eyes and said simply: 'Take the lot.' I took the lot. He was a great nobleman.

Paris – rue Saussure

May 7. Here I am back home, with Gilles. I am looking after him. He has seen Vinchon who says we must take care of the body in order to reach the mind, and has prescribed to that end. Doctor Paul Emile Levy, on the other hand, claims that we must heal the mind in order to reach the body. Professor Sicard has declared that my husband could have no better doctor than me and that his idea of living beside me as calmly as possible will be the best thing in the world – for *him*!

After their return to Paris Liane put aside her blue notebooks; from then on she never wrote while they were in Paris, only when she was away – which was quite often. Except for a few pages in May 1928 there was to be silence for sixteen months. When she began to write again it was to record an event which marked all the rest of her life.

1928

～～～～～～～～～～～～～～～～～～～～～～～～～～～

Versailles, May 4. I am here so that Gilles can breathe a fresher air than that of rue Saussure.

Gilles is deteriorating rapidly, worn-out, maniacal. I look after him as I love him, with the greatest tenderness. I too am deteriorating fast. I am failing under the weight of the burden, and if I didn't have the burden I would have nothing. Nothing worth taking trouble for, nothing capable of entering into me: an egotist's bliss.

By dint of sharing the pleasures of an hysteric who is not responsible for himself, I myself am becoming hysterical – and it is my misfortune to be responsible. I measure, I analyze, I accept. By doing so I have almost reached the cheerful resignation that I have so often asked Heaven to grant me.

Because of all this I have put aside my notebook. I take it up again rather like someone turning round for a last look when they reach a bend in the road, or like someone opening an old chest, going through old drawers.

Mother Marie-Madeleine of the Faithful Company of Jesus has just died. I loved seeing her and listening to her. She said 'My little one – ' and it was so sweet to my heart to listen to someone who could still call me her 'little one'. She said to me: 'My little one, your husband has done a great deal for you. Remind yourself how he found you in very dubious company and raised you to the altar. What would he do if you left him?' I answered truthfully: what he did when he left me, he'd smoke all the time, drink as much as possible, lead the basest and most riotous life, quite without control. 'So there you are,' she concluded. 'Your duty is clear, you must stay with your husband.' She also explained to me that giving up things and people is nothing because we will lose all that anyway; the vital thing is to give up self. 'So you see, my little one, in taking back your poor wretched husband you have renounced your self, because you had quite a good idea of what lay ahead for you. That is the greatest of all victories. It raises you and strengthens you, it is pleasing to God and He will help you.' Dear Mother Marie-Madeleine! She had known me since I was eight years old. She had a superior mind and great authority, and her piety was limitless and well-directed. Thanks to these gifts she became Reverend Mother and Assistant to the Superior General. It was she who took care of their relations with the outside world, and in effect ran the whole thing. She could get what she asked from everyone, she knew how to touch the soul and move the mind.

I saw her this winter, alert and very much alive, still supple as she knelt in the little chapel where she had taken me to pray with her. Now she is praying for me in heaven – the day I heard of her death I made her an inward promise to do my duty by Georges to the end, neither to leave him nor to send him away.

Mother Marie-Madeleine, I can feel you within me in the sweetness of my resignation and the firmness of my resolution. I am well aware that I do not live exactly as you would wish, but that will come. It is difficult to sort things out. I am so unworthy and so imperfect, still so closely connected with base considerations. I was unable to confess everything to you, I respected you too much. Now you know everything and you will rescue me from this sewer.

Uriage – September 23 to October 1

September 23. I have neglected my notebook again for quite a long time. The summer has gone by, a difficult one as far as I was concerned, atrocious on the one hand and very wonderful on the other.

In July various people urged us to come to a so-called 'convalescent' home situated on the hill which overlooks Grenoble. There we found no chance of convalescence, no peace, no care, dirt, discomfort – we had been completely had! Nothing but noise, day and night: trains whistling, slaughter-houses and factories, smell and smoke. Too exhausted for a long journey, we let ourself slide into this hotel at Uriage – to us it seems like Paradise – which is run by the widow of Serge Basset who lost his life as a war reporter for *le Figaro*.

One day when we were going past an old grey house buried in vines and fig trees, we decided on a whim to pull the bell beside the big door on which was written: Asylum of Saint Agnes. Perhaps the curiosity we felt, Gilles and I, was rather unhealthy. We knew that this roof sheltered children who were idiots from birth. The door opened and we found ourselves face to face with a woman of impressive calm and simplicity, clearly marked by nobility and dignity. We asked if we could visit the chapel, and innocently put ten francs into the box for the poor. We thought we might see some of the unhappy inmates. We saw none of them, but I at least left that place shaken to the quick, vanquished by the Mother Superior. She is one of those beings whose gaze could make water spring forth from rock. Georges was won over, too – in his way.

The next day I went back alone. I was welcomed by the Mother Superior as though she had been expecting me. She is so completely natural that when you are with her nothing seems surprising and she herself seems surprised by nothing. I gave her fifty francs, apologizing for having left so little the day before. I talked to her for a long, long time about myself. She listened to me with pious attention and told me to come back that afternoon, with my husband, so that she could show us 'her children.'

We were punctual. She took us to a playground . . . and there I saw sixty-seven unhappy creatures between eight and sixteen years old, scarred by the most inexorable suffering. I nearly fainted. Georges Ghika went green . . . Oh! Those cries, those contortions, those grimaces, that smell . . . once you have seen that, never never again can you complain of anything! I was ashamed of having talked so much about myself to Sister Marie-Xavier. I pressed the poor tremulous, rather dirty hands which reached out towards me. I searched those wandering, fixed or mad eyes for some glimmer of light. I laid my hand on those foreheads, tumultuous or stunned, feverish, so pale . . . To think that I had given them no more alms than a heedless passer-by might have done! I gave five hundred francs, Georges Ghika gave a hundred, and I knew that he was more disturbed than he liked to admit.

I have been going back there every day, and that is how I have given myself. I have come to know almost all of them, one by one. I have written a very good letter to all my friends explaining the nature of the work in a most moving way; up to now I've collected nearly five thousand francs including my own offering, and that is only the beginning. I will move heaven and earth to help them. I will go begging everywhere.

Sister Marie-Xavier is slender, tall, dark, clear-cut and direct, intelligent, active. She distils an atmosphere of peace and trust. I am hers. I have laid my burden at her feet. She has become my friend. She says: 'I forbid you to desert. You must stay where God has put you.' I said to her: 'Mother, when I look at these poor children and think of my devastated life, I could almost envy them for their inability to understand.' Promptly she answered: 'They are certainly to be envied for their inability to offend God.' I told her the story of my life because I did not want to gain her affectionate interest under false colours. She bent towards me and confided; 'I too had to struggle. It took me a long time to become accustomed to this hard task. I have been here for fourteen years; well, for the first five or six of them I often had to repress the idea of killing myself in order to have done with feeling disgust day after day, minute by minute. I conquered myself. I love my children. The more they are tested the better I love them. Now I don't ever want to leave them. I help them to suffer and I help them to die. And I love you, Princess, because you love them.'

They lack so many things! There are no baths or showers. They have got to have all that. They will have all that. What a long way I am now from Paris and its dissipations! Here is my wealth: the friendship of this saint and a little part in this work of abnegation and sacrifice. This is my road to Damascus! Oh! that my return to Paris does not make me forget this little corner! Please, God, do not let that happen! Never again would I be able to believe in myself. It seems to me that You put the Asylum of Saint Agnes and its inmates in my way on purpose, as though to tell me: 'Help them, and I will help you.'

September 24. We are packing to go down to Grenoble tomorrow. This hotel is shutting. It has started to be cold, white frost is making its appearance in the mornings. My heart is a sunless world, but when I think how cold my little patients will be it warms up at the touch of a charitable thought: go begging for them!

An amusing letter from Jacques Bonjean giving us news of Max Jacob, who is more faithful to Brittany than he is to his friendship with us. I love him at a distance. By that I mean: I wouldn't like him to be unhappy or ill, but I no longer have the courage or the wish to expose myself to his hypocrisy. They say that he has definitely left the monastery of Saint-Benoît, which was such a wonderfully peaceful and pious refuge for him. Max needs peace, he needs to accomplish his religious duties. Now he is unrestrained. He is living a life which wastes his energies, his money, his heart, his dignity as a man and an artist. He is surrounded by a crowd of second-rate young people who make fun of him. We are a long way from the fine meditations which Roscoff used to inspire in him every day.

September 25. I wrote to tell Sister Marie-Xavier that I wasn't well, and had the lovely surprise of a visit from her, in the company of the Reverend Mother General. Their visit made me better. I mean to improve conditions for their patients, carry a begging bowl round Paris on their behalf to all those people who don't know what to do with their wealth and are dying of a surfeit. I am haunted, gripped, vanquished, ready for anything.

. . . .

October 1. We will soon be leaving this sweet and charming place. Gilles is better physically, but his renewed strength simply serves to nourish the strength of his delusion, his dishonesty and his obscenity. He expresses himself only through that.

Yesterday evening he said to me – while his left hand never stopped plucking out hairs from above his left ear – 'I've thought of a very interesting film such as has never been seen, an obscene film – I mean one with absolutely nothing in it but obscenities . . .' Whereupon he began to describe for my benefit everything that his poor sick mind had been able to think up. He returned to the subject again this morning. I don't check him, it is better that it should come out. Being his confidant enables me to know where we are. He talks about it in pedantic detail, listening to himself, choosing his words, ponderously, his voice serious and sad. I play patience on my bed as I listen. I say 'Oh!' and 'Ah!' I try not to let my face show my disgust and sadness; I invent a nice affectionate little smile, the smile of a fond and indulgent comrade. And to think that for eighteen years we were such an amorously united pair!

We are leaving. We are going to Grenoble. We are thinking of going on to Aix-en-Provence and elsewhere, elsewhere. As far as I'm concerned, whether it's here or there it will be nothing but sorrow and desolation.

Aix-en-Provence, October 20. This morning I wrote to the Maharajah of Kapurthala on behalf of my work. Kapurthala is my friend. When I was twenty he wanted to number me among his wives and he's grateful that I became a princess, kept my beauty and my fame and a certain amount of money, and never made any appeal to his generosity. I knock at this door in the hope that it will open! I no longer use the words 'idiots from birth'. I say 'chronically ill, and poor – so poor!'

Return to Paris caused another interruption to the notebooks. Liane remained silent for almost three years, and says little to explain the fact. From then on she wrote chiefly when she was alone, during her husband's visits to Roumania to be with his mother who had suffered a stroke.

1931

~~~~~~

Cap-Brun – August 14 to August 30

August 14. I have opened this notebook and reread the sheets tucked into it from time to time over the last four and a half years. I was rather ashamed of them. I would like to tear them up. That packet of love letters from Mimy Franchetti – I would like to burn them. I shall not do so. I am so remote from all that, purified by pain.

I have now spent five years with this unhappy Georges Ghika, irresponsible and debauched, suppressing actions but overflowing with evil words. He has been drinking, smoking endlessly, reading atrocious books, blaspheming against everything which contributes to a sweet and serious life: against love; against marriage, the blessed union of two people who love each other; against order; against punctuality, regularity, good manners; against religion, beliefs of whatever kind; against divine law as well as against human laws; against everything. Poor discontented, bestial being, with his great ability to illuminate directed towards the most hellish landscapes. I have suffered in my mind and in my body. I used to go out to take my mind off it and to stoke up some courage; what met my eyes was as bad, or worse, but it did not belong to me. Intrigues, lies, dirtiness, hypocrisy: I fled my house to find it all elsewhere, but there I was not closely connected with it. I was there as a spectator of these dreary comedies. I would get home exhausted. There I would find Georges Ghika, high on alcohol, damaged by tobacco, drunk on his reading. His hair was greying and falling out, he was losing his teeth. He had lost his virility – he was lashed by the desire to rediscover it. So at night he would direct all his evil ardour onto me, would try and fail and begin again, all to no avail. To him that, and nothing else, is what is meant by love . . . He would fall asleep and snore while I, in despair, would pray . . . I pray with all my distress and with all the pain of a crushed and imprisoned woman who can see no way out but death. It's at these times that I say: 'God, let me die, let me die tonight, now. I am in an abyss of desolation. I no longer recognize my husband, my lover, my friend, my Georges. He has become my torturer. Of course he is not responsible for what he does, I know that I must not accuse him, condemn him, hold it against him! He is my punishment, my atonement, my salvation. May Your will, o God, be done.'

On the 13th of March in this year 1931 my horror broke all bounds. I could stand no more. I cried to God with all the power of my suffering: 'God, it is too much, too much. I can bear no more. Deliver me!' And behold a miracle! On the morning of the 13th my mother-in-law had a stroke followed by irreversible paralysis of the left side. On the 16th, when I was out, my husband received a telegram giving him news of this disaster. On the 17th, he left with his brother! They were pitiful, both of them; they were afraid they would find their mother dead.

He writes to me all the time, vague, hollow letters empty of what I long to find in them. He tries to inject them with love. Mariette's agony is long and terrible. I pray for her and for Georges: I ask for courage on their behalf. I give them to God – that God denied by both of them – and I ask that I may never see them again.

Tomorrow it's August 15, the feast of the Mother of God, my saint's day in the midst of flowers and a splendid decor under a burning sun. Georges Ghika has sent me his wishes and a cheque for two thousand francs. He does not know where I am. My good and charming notary, Maître Collet, has agreed to receive all my correspondence, so my husband writes to me care of him. I want to put him off the scent, introduce a bit of vagueness and mystery, avoid direct contact, escape the possibility of being taken by surprise.

August 20. Everything has gone well for Saint Agnes. I found donors. The old grey house, that sacred shelter for the worst of suffering, has been repaired and improved. They have magnificent central heating even in the chapel, running water, lovely shiny brass taps flowing with hot and cold. Gabrielle Chanel was spontaneously and splendidly generous. I collected nearly three hundred thousand francs. The repairs and improvements cost over two hundred and ten thousand; the rest provided linen, coal, comfort.

This work has become my reason for staying alive. Those unhappy ones and the admirable sisters are now my only family.

This corner where I am now is ideally pretty. By the sea, by the hills, there rises the blessed mount, the Mont du Soleil, with its unkempt gardens exhaling the intoxicating balsam of their sun-warmed perfumes. The doves start cooing early in the morning. I wake up to this soft sound, a gift from nature. You would think that all the peace on earth had collected here, making everything more beautiful. My heart, too, has found peace. Five years ago I suffered atrociously, suffered from being abandoned, from not being loved any more. I offered it all to God. And I want it to be like that for ever: a pious accomplishment of duty, a humble submission to the divine will. I am so deeply committed to this way that it is perfectly easy for me to avoid whatever might weaken my will and interrupt my progress.

The *Imitation* encourages, advises and guides me. I consult its magnificent words every day and they enlighten and console me. Every time I open this marvellous book I draw on resources of strength and enthusiasm. I read a chapter every evening.

August 28. Georges Ghika writes, writes, writes . . . A registered letter arrives from Roumania every day. I can foresee that he will come back to Paris at the end of the summer, that he is preparing to return to my house, to me, as though nothing had happened. His letters are affectionate, insinuating, full of detail. Anyone who didn't know might be taken in by them and feel very sorry for him, might accuse me of being hard and dry. No, really, I have forgiven; I have forgiven his mother, too; but with forgiveness there came a feeling of immense indifference.

August 30. Today I read my mass in my bedroom. I read it well and thoughtfully, responding with emotion to the sacred words on which my eyes used to rest every Sunday as I sat beside my mother in church. In those days I repeated these words like a little parrot while I looked at the people sitting round me, particularly the women. I remember Madame de Vogelsang. She would come to mass alone, or else with her mother, rather pink in the face, ploughing through the rows of people to get to her place, which was just in front of us. I would sniff at her; she smelt good. I would study her dresses; she was elegant and everything suited her. I wanted to get to know her, to kiss her. I was passionate and always drawn to women, nervous and disgusted in the presence of men. Their smell of tobacco made me wrinkle my nose. I loved the bishops and the officiating priests in their sacerdotal robes, the choir boys, the censors, the perfumes and the music of church, without bothering much about what my catechism taught me.

No doubt Freud could find plenty of clues to my character in all that – and a chance to prove himself wrong into the bargain. I went off the rails, but that was not my true direction, not my essence. My debauched husband was caught out when he married me. It was Reynaldo who understood me. I realized that one day when he was talking about my life. He looked deeply into my eyes; his own filled with a great tenderness and he quoted these words of Goethe's: 'Child! Even when you do wrong, you are never guilty.' How he touched me that day! Nevertheless I have been gravely guilty. I have offended my God and I have broken my parents' hearts.

My husband still doesn't know where I am. I tell him that I am moving about rather more than in fact I am. I answer his daily letters about once a week, according to what I have to say or what is passing through my mind.

Mourillon – Le Prieuré, September 2 to December 15

September 2. Here I am in Paradise, in an animated solitude. I have a room with bath in the Pavilion of the Romantics. The proprietor is very interesting: he has been abroad a lot and the seven or eight houses which comprise his little kingdom are full of amusing Chinese objects. We are 'paying guests'; it's the latest thing and very nice.

September 16. My peace here is rather threatened. Georges Ghika writes that his brother will be taking his place beside their mother and that he will be in Paris between the 23rd and 25th of this month. If he does not find me in the rue Saussure he says he intends to wait for me with the Brothers of Saint-Jean de Dieu.

One of Paris's 'lionesses', Fernande Cabanel, has turned up here quite by chance! The other day she appeared suddenly in a blaze of sunshine just as lunch was ending, wearing sumptuous pyjamas by Schiaparelli and followed by her companion, the young Greek

Xanaris. We exchanged lots of 'darlings!' and kisses and we see each other all the time.

Fernande is very beautiful in a sunlit garden, much more so than at the Ritz in Paris. Yesterday she was wearing adorable very wide pyjamas combining several shades of blue. I admired them, I do so love blue! When I got back from my walk this morning I found these ravishing trousers on my bed with a charming card. I am confused and pleased. I have thanked her. I sent her a box of red gladioli and I said: 'Fernande, I am going to send a hundred francs to my unhappy ones at Saint Agnes whom you have already helped – a hundred francs in your name, not more, because I want to be in your debt.'

September 19. I have been on the spree two days running.

On the 17th my dear old friend Mayol came to have lunch with me. We were once on the same bill at the Scala: he was singing his famous songs, I was dancing in sketches. I came downstairs on the stroke of twelve and saw my fat Mayol standing in front of the house in the sunlight with an enormous bunch of dahlias in his arms, dahlias like himself, splendid and colourful: champion dahlias! We fell into each others arms. Suzanne de Callias arrived. I introduced Mayol who said to her: 'I read a book of yours signed Menalkas and Willy, but I knew it was you . . .' – 'I'll sign a copy for you tomorrow,' she said. 'Done!' said Felix; then turned to me: 'Would you like to eat aioli at home?' 'Aioli with Mayol – Oh yes yes yes!' I replied. – 'I shall count on seeing both of you, I'll send my chauffeur to pick you up – he's my secretary too, a very nice boy.' – 'And your sweetie-pie as well?' – 'Yes, of course.'

By the time we reached dessert we had collected the whole of the Prieuré around us. Mayol was delighted – he has to have his little audience. We ran through the 'have-you-seens'. 'Do you remember, Félix?' – 'Do you remember, Liane?' 'And after the Sunday matinée, those dinners in my dressing-room with the artistes of our choice and Yvonne de Buffon. Our director used to contribute two bottles of champagne, one sweet for you, one dry for me! And then Good Friday, when everyone else closed but we didn't. The Scala was bursting. The packed house was resplendent with all the lady-butchers from les Halles – they crammed the boxes, attentive, merry, sumptuous in shiny satin and crackling silk, sparkling with heavy gold jewellery. Up went the curtain on Liane.

Cheers, applause. Encouraged, I gave of my best. I was much better than I usually was, I gave myself, I took off. I got an enormous bouquet on behalf of all the leading slaughter-house families. I blew kisses, I got them back – it would still be going on if the curtain hadn't been brought down.

'But now – now it's Mayol! How they clapped, how they clapped! The orchestra kept on having to stop and start again, Mayol opened his mouth, then shut it. Finally he pretended he was fed up and going off, then the "Shsh-shshes" began. Mayol sang. It was very moving, absolute silence. He bowed, he had finished, he disappeared. They called him back, thunderous applause, yells, stamping. Mayol came back. It started all over again. Usually he sang three songs and gave three encores. That evening he had to sing more than twenty. They simply wouldn't let him go. They pelted him with flowers. They weren't yelling any more, they were roaring: Mayol! Mayol! And he gave and gave until at last he simply couldn't utter another note.

'I was in the wings, hidden by a flat. "What a triumph, love! What a house" – "Sez you!" he spat as he scurried past. "I must fly – they are waiting for me across the road at the Eldorado, I've got to go through the whole thing again." And it was true. He hardly had time to gulp a soothing drink when he was back in the arms of his frenzied Good Friday admirers.'.........

September 20. Mayol lives on an estate surrounded by eight or ten pretty villas bought to mark the stages of his triumphal progress. As a whole it is called Clos Mayol, but he's given each of the villas the name of a music-hall where he used to sing: the Scala, the Ba-ta-clan, the Eldorado, the Moulin Rouge, etc. In spite of all this he has somehow managed to keep plenty of open, flowery space and a big open-air theatre where he gives benefits for this or that on every fine Sunday. Artistes from Marseilles, friends on the wing and people living near by all collaborate. It's very popular. In September they close down for the grape-harvest. He has a big vineyard which produces two thousand bottles of a light, heady, and treacherous red wine – as I learnt the other day to my cost and the household's delight.

There are two fountains in his courtyard made of multicoloured tiles. It is cool, sheltered from the hot sun by fine trees. He has had big fountains constructed all over the estate, all with basins of many-coloured tiles. It's pretty and unusual, very characteristic of the laughing Midi which makes the most of nothing and where everything grows easily thanks to the blue sky. It is the retreat of a great artiste.

So I had been invited to aioli. There were two kinds, one with lemon, the other without. In addition: a huge dish of cod, several dozen hard-boiled eggs, octopus stewed in wine, a multitude of snails, lots of bowls of fat winkles, a mountain of potatoes and carrots, beetroots, chick-peas, green beans, etc. More than a dozen dishes of aioli! A vast green melon as sweet as honey, an ice from Philippe, the best cake-shop, and champagne to follow the Clos Mayol wine and complete my tipsiness. The last beautiful grapes from the stripped vines, blue figs – their skin splitting as though wounded – peaches, pears, delicious coffee. 'A liqueur?' suggested Mayol. 'I have a little Marc which is not to be sniffed at.' – 'Stop, stop!' I cried. 'I couldn't manage another mouthful.' So he took us to visit his museum. Mayol everywhere – paintings, drawings, posters, photos. Portraits of all of us: I found three of myself, rather pretty, inscribed to my dear friend. There were also mementoes of the war, letters to Mayol from soldiers grateful for the gift of a song or a little money. Then he took his secateurs and cut us yet more great sheaves of his matchless dahlias.

September 23. Yesterday Fernande Cabanel and her companion Sacha Xanaris, took me into Toulon for the afternoon. On the way Fernande said to me: 'I have some very urgent shopping to do. I'm completely out of something which I have to have. It is making me ill. Yesterday I tried to use some of Sacha's drug but it's too heavy, too strong for me. It upset me dreadfully. Jean Cocteau is here, we'll look him up and he's sure to be able to give me an address.' – 'Fine,' I said. 'Jean is an old friend of mine and I'd like to see him again.' She took me down to the port, near the Arsenal, and led me along a horrible street with reeking gutters which ran parallel with the quay. It was lined on either side with the most frightful shady-looking hotels. She said: 'Oh God – Jean is living in one of these.' We went into a foul slum called Hôtel du Port et des Négociants. She asked for Jean; the proprietor was smiling and eager, all amiability and complicity. He sent for Liou, the Annamite boy – a prince's son, it seems – who serves Jean. Fernande scribbled a note. Liou took it away, then reappeared with three words of answer: 'In an hour.' We left the hotel by another door, through a fairly clean little bistro opening onto the quay. There was an antique shop next door. Sacha and I went in and began bargaining for all kinds of things. Fernande kept watch by the door. While we were looking at ornaments in the back of the shop Sacha told me: 'Two cops followed us down that street and saw us go in. They are over there now – look. This hotel is often raided because of drugs and pederasty. The proprietor procures little sailor-boys and it's not expensive.' Five minutes later we were sitting at table before some excellent coffee, croissants, butter and jam – four-o'clock tea is always when they eat their first meal. They sleep late in the mornings because they go to bed late. When they saw us sitting down the policemen came back to the hotel, suspecting something. Sacha was paler than usual, Fernande very nervy and agitated. We went back into the antique shop and Sacha gave me a Louis-Philippe glass, a blue one. We saw Liou go by, looking for us. He led us away along the quay and said: 'Jean is expecting the two ladies. Will Monsieur be kind enough to have a drink in the hotel restaurant. The ladies should follow me.' All this went on while the policemen were watching the house. On our way upstairs we passed two little sailor-boys running down very fast, their heads hanging. Liou opened the door of a sordid room, letting out a strong whiff of the drug. It was sinister – what an extraordinary pleasure it is! Jean was lying on the floor covered with a disgusting bedspread, behind a horribly filthy bed. His voice was deathly, dull, dry, hoarse. He said: 'What are you doing Liou? Shut the door. Don't let anyone in. I'm very ill.' I backed out onto the narrow landing, but Fernande went in: 'Jean, for pity's sake give me an address. Liane is here with me.' What can he have thought? That I too have started to smoke? He answered almost inaudibly: 'Liou, give her some of my special supply: three francs a gramme. Forgive me, if you knew how ill I am! Lock the door, Liou.'

I got a glimpse of Jean, thin, pale, drawn, a shadow of himself and he was already a shadow. He had a three-day beard and his clothes were in disorder, dirty and crumpled. We went into Liou's room, even more sordid. On the wall a drawing of Jean's, signed and inscribed 'To my dear Liou,' and a page of poetry in his handwriting: 'To my dear Liou.' 'How Jean squanders himself,' whispered Fernande while Liou opened a mould-smelling cupboard. Liou: 'Here are 700 grammes, Madame, that will be 2,100 francs.' Fernande: 'That's too much for me. I'm afraid of overdoing it if I have that big a supply.' He went back to the cupboard and took out a smaller pot. 'Here are 150 grammes for 450 francs.' – 'That will do,' said Fernande. 'That will keep me going for two months.' She paid and we left. Xanaris, very nervous, was waiting downstairs. 'The cops are still there, complete with their revolvers,' he said. 'Let's leave by the other door. Have you got it?' 'Yes,' said Fernande, happy and appeased. He took the box, looked at it. 'The princess had better look after it. She has a big handbag.' I understood that they were afraid of being picked up. Opium smokers are not brave. I didn't want to make a fuss because I'm fond of all of them, Jean and these two – I'm sorry for them, too – so I slid the drug into my bag as inconspicuously as possible. Whereupon they began to run – to run much more nimbly than I would ever have expected; I had a hard time keeping up. They hailed a taxi, plunged into it. I caught up, they pulled me in, the taxi drove off. 'Ouf!' went Fernande. 'Ouf!' went Sacha. We drove past the cops who didn't notice us. Perhaps they never had. 'Quick, Liane, hand over my box.' She snatched it, looked at it lovingly, squeezed it between her hands with a tender delight that I have sometimes seen in lovers. She explained: 'Jean's stuff is very good, light, quite old. The older the better, with opium. In China princes and emperors use an opium covered with mould that's hundreds of years old, and it's beyond compare.' – 'Oh poor Jean, poor Jean,' I said, obsessed by that painful image of decay and intoxication. Emaciated, tormented little Jean, whom I used to know when he was twenty. His talent, a gift from heaven; his poor mother, so beautiful with her white hair; he was trampling all that under foot, and for what! When Mayol spoke about him the other day he told me: 'Cocteau comes to my open-air theatre on Sunday evenings. *He wears badly.*' With those words he was trying to say it all.

This morning I was in the garden watching the household's children doing their gymnastics in the fresh air and sunlight, when I heard: 'Liane! Hey, Liane!' It was Fernande and Sacha. I went up to them. Fernande told me, 'We went back to Toulon yesterday evening. Coming out of the cinema we met a very pretty gentleman with big dreamy eyes, a little beard, a cane, spats, a dancing step – guess who!' – 'The cat has got my tongue.' – 'It was your beloved Reynaldo! He was coming out of a frightful bar called the Oasis, with a boy. They parted with a lot of simpering and just as the boy was leaving Reynaldo gave him an affectionate tap on the shoulder with his cane, then he started peering through the windows of the neighbouring cafés, looking for someone or something.' It really pained me . . . Jean, Reynaldo . . . 'And then,' said Sacha, 'a little further on we met Pierre Meyer with his coat-collar turned up and his hat pulled down over his nose, and an enormous flower in his buttonhole. He tried to avoid us. What he looks for is middle-aged men, rather pot-bellied.'

Jean, Reynaldo, Pierre! I left them with my hands over my ears, arguing with myself, clamping down on so many things to keep them from hurting me too much. To have adored Reynaldo for thirty-five years, perhaps more, only to hear this about him! Of course I told myself: but I knew that he was that way inclined. He works better after he has given way to animality, his music becomes more beautiful, he is purified. He is all ideals! But it hurt me, all the same. I overcame the pain, the disgust – I laughed a little: yes, I laughed, to drive away the tears.

September 24. Lunch with my dear good Mayol. Family, hospitality, exquisite food. A feast worthy of a bishop, and excellent coffee on the terrace. Mayol reminds me of Napoleon, surrounded as he is by his family who owe him everything. He has four engagements to sing, but he can't make up his mind to leave his beloved home, his people, his sun, his fruits and his flowers. I think I can understand. He retired on the crest of the wave. He didn't watch his star grow pale. He is still in a position to refuse to make a gift of his singing. In this way he will be spared the cruelties of dwindling fame. He lives among his own vines, in his own house, with his family, in his own country, on his well-earned gains. His green theatre is a plaything, echo-memory-habit. When he puts on a show it's for his good works. To the town of Toulon he has give a Rugby stadium; to his family he has given abundance. A happy man who bestows happiness: it is a comforting thing to see.

I shall preserve this memory carefully so that it can blot out a few others: the memory of a great artiste who has known how to run his life and remains happy with his lot until the end.

September 27. Cabanel, the lioness of Paris, fashion-setter, model and arbiter of elegance, the one they whisper about as she passes, the one they admire and copy; yesterday, as she was preparing her little pipe with graceful care, she said to me: 'Liane, I've got another year left, and if by then I haven't found my dream companion, husband or lover, I don't care about that – if I haven't found him I shall kill myself.' These demoralizing, though I suppose plucky, words made me feel terrible. I was sadly oppressed all the evening –

an evening dimmed by the eclipse of the moon which was almost entirely hidden by a brown mist except for a thumbnail segment which kept its brightness.

What poor things we women are, condemned to love! Cabanel is beautiful, strange, elegant, rare. Up till now she has been in control of events. She takes advantage of artificial paradises. As for me, I have a confused glimpse of a peace that may never come!

September 28. Telegram forwarded by Maître Collet's office: 'Will arrive Paris Sunday (that's yesterday) Love. Georges Ghika.' I am afraid the poor boy is deceiving himself. He thinks that I am in Paris and doesn't doubt for a moment that he is going to see me again, possess me again, that everything will go on as usual until the next escapade! I am not worrying, God, I put myself in Your hands, I submit in advance to Your decision whatever it may be. I am here, and here I shall stay quietly as long as You allow it. If You want my frightful misery to begin again – all right, Georges will turn up one day and I will welcome him. If not, he will become resigned to my absence, will make a corner for himself somewhere, will give himself over to his pleasures in his own way – and I shall continue to wander alone and abandoned to the very end.

. . . .

September 30. . . . . It has been announced in *le Figaro* that the great poet Jean Cocteau, who has been spending his holidays at Toulon for the last few years, has just been admitted to a nursing-home there, very ill with typhoid! . . .

. . . .

October 11. The director of Claridge's (in Paris) will let me have a room with a bathroom at a big reduction (for forty francs a day). He asks me to keep it a secret and he seems anxious to see me there. I am in no hurry to do anything. At the moment I'm trailing around in this beautiful weather with a monstrous depression. Letters keep on arriving from my husband, disconcerting, demoralizing, unworthy of me, unworthy of a man. Worthy of him. He is abject and irresponsible. Enough of that. I have still got some good friends in my twilight; but friends come and friends go. One ends up alone. I feel as though I were in a prison: grief and solitude. Oh to find God! My God, still beyond my reach, accept my piercing, deep and overwhelming sorrow.

I have just been with Cabanel and her little Xanaris. All they want is luxury and they smoke opium. At present they are out of money. Clothes, keeping up appearances, making a show – it's hard on their poor little incomes. She is looking for a rich man to dazzle; the boy will go back to his family in Greece. She's going to find herself penniless and without her companion. She is beautiful, her elegance is unusual and daring, hers and hers alone. Knowing how to dress like that is a sign of intelligence; it surpasses good taste and becomes art.

When I left them just now I said: 'Go on, find your little happiness. Enjoy yourselves for a while, put on your rose-coloured glasses! As for me, I am going to throw myself on my bed, bury my face in my hands and talk to God, no doubt it will do me good.' – 'To each his own drug,' murmured Xanaris as he kissed my hand.

I have made a feminine conquest this year. Women do usually like me and come after me. One can go on attracting them for a remarkably long time – I have often noticed that in others. In spite of their haggard faces and their puffy flesh, the old veterans of lesbian love go on inspiring real passions almost into their seventies! I suppose the enamoured young have times when they need a refuge from masculine brutality and inconstancy . . . They want to be liked by their elders, to attract them by the sweet tenderness of a loving friendship. There too, alas, one finds weeping and gnashing of teeth, betrayal and lies . . .

November 24. Things have been happening. I took to my bed with a slight pulmonary congestion. I had a high temperature and I spat blood – pretty pink, frothy blood. When I saw that I thought I had better call in a doctor. The Monets, our landlords, produced theirs: Doctor Jules Regnault, formerly of the navy, a crafty and rather bizarre Norman who has his fads and uses a lot of electricity, shocks and all kinds of little gadgets. His treatment exhausted me, laid me really and painfully low, and at the end of two weeks my congestion, which had been arrested too soon and too abruptly, came back in the form of a terribly violent bronchitis. This time I refused to cut it short. I let it develop and take its course, while I coughed and spat and sweated. Now I have been up for three days, feeling light and free and disintoxicated. In other words: never cut bronchitis short, the illness stays inside you, building up, and then explodes.

Meanwhile Georges Ghika arrived. On Sunday the 25th my door

opened and there was my husband, delighted to see me again, prancing about like a puppy, loaded with presents, as irresponsible as can be – and ill, too. What adventures and misadventures he'd been having! In June he developed a tumour under his upper lip. Because it might become awkward they lanced it, and since then it has spread. Georges doesn't appear to be worrying, except that he no longer dares to kiss me. So here I am at last, delivered from those desolating loveless embraces! I called in Doctor Regnault, who gave my husband a very thorough examination. The word 'syphilis' was uttered. Is that the truth? And is it to spare my sensibilities that the word 'hereditary' was added? It is always preferable to blame one's ancestors, less distressing and indecent. So the verdict has been pronounced: my husband becomes a syphilitic by inheritance. Nothing worries me, nothing upsets me. I am reassuringly here. He is not drinking any more, is smoking less and has not yet blasphemed. He looks dreadful. On my side the ordeal is lessened if I feel I can comfort and help him. I am not reproaching him; I am not questioning him; I repress. He admits nothing and confides nothing; he represses. He tells me about his stricken mother's terrible conditon of incurable infirmity.

November 25. .... The crisis! Nothing but the crisis! Lolo (Margot de La Bigne's lover) has lost half his fortune, perhaps more. Max is anxious. As for us, we remain calm. My sensations of distress have been focused on other causes, stirred up by other circumstances. To be short of money, to make do without a lot of things – I don't give a damn.

. . . .

December 7. This morning I went for a walk by myself in the grey, in the mist, in the warm wind which foretells a storm. I felt so good, alone in the universe, dreaming, cut loose. I no longer knew where I came from, I had no idea where I was going. Yesterday my chapter from the *Imitation* was about solitude and silence. I have just been granted an experience of it. I felt the sweetness of it. A great peace, a great calm and serenity flowed into me with the air I breathed.

December 15. Georges has jaundice! It declared itself unequivocally twenty-four hours ago. Doctor Regnault has been: he has ordered broth, Vichy water, orange juice and yoghurt. Georges looks frightful. He feels sick all the time. I am looking after him to the best of my ability. He is depressed, exhausted, aching, cross. All this makes it difficult for me. I daren't try to manage him too much; I have a hard time carrying out the doctor's orders because Georges jibs, Georges has his own theories, Georges belongs to Georges. Come what may, Georges alone is the master of Georges's destiny.

1932

Mourillon – Le Prieuré, January 1 to April 14

January 1. A door opening on the unknown prospect of a new road. This morning my husband came in to kiss me at about half-past one, then gave me a charming letter. Mayol sent me his brother and his secretary with two bottles of Cap Corse Muscadet, his kisses and his good wishes. I took my lunch in my husband's bedroom. I drank champagne and a cup of coffee too – complete orgy!

January 4. Gabrielle Chanel has sent five thousand francs to my little invalids at Saint Agnes'. So generous, particularly considering the general crisis. If it continues, how are we going to provide them with coal and warmth?

January 23. This might be entitled 'Confession'.

Yesterday evening I was feeling gay, light-hearted, friendly and affectionate towards all of poor humankind. I sang to myself: 'I am the happiest woman in the world.' I thanked God, I said some prayers, I thought about my parents.

Then, quite suddenly, I felt within me, against me, a flood of bitter reproach. The flood rose, submerged me, all of my life was hurled at me like stones, all of my sins like mud. It became a delirium, tears poured from my eyes, I accused myself, I asked pardon, I had become nothing but repentance and desolation. I said to myself: 'What have you done since your birth, and now that you are approaching death's door, what have you done with your life? Spoilt child, stupid egotist, indifferent pupil, you made a cold first communion without piety, faith or love. Your parents lived for you and you broke their hearts. Your brothers were brave and honourable officers and you brought shame on them. You dragged your family's name in the mud. You were a torment to your husband

and an overwhelmingly heavy moral burden to your son. You had mercy on no one! Not one of those who came near you found grace in your eyes. You never loved even the most magnificent of your lovers. Kings, great financiers, poets, children, old men, scholars – they all clustered round you and you deceived them all. You sold yourself – '

Then during the night I cried out: 'Yes, all that is true and still worse, still worse!' I admitted all my sins, my crimes against life . . . I said to myself: 'Is it possible that *that* was my role on this earth?' Then at last I stared at myself as though in a cruel and faithful mirror. I loved love, never a lover; I hunted for love down evil ways. I was a deranged little Messalina, cerebral, woefully vain. My suffering was true and immense. I want no excuses. I could have pleaded this or that reason – my youth, my foolishness, temptation, my poverty! I was a shameful creature, I had the face of a completely pure virgin and the banal, idiotic vanity of a simpering, talentless dancer prancing like a circus horse to the sound of the orchestra . . . 'And you will write this tomorrow,' I ordered myself. 'You will write down your brutal and abominable confession. Your memory will be accursed and you will be buried like a pauper in a common grave.' Oh! To submit entirely, to expiate – But Georges Ghika is my saviour! He redeems me! And I have dared to complain, to find ways of making people feel sorry for me! I am a monster of heartlessness and idiotic pride! How, how did it happen? Life is now starting up again. I have made great resolutions: no more self-pity, no more complaining, to do my duty at whatever cost, with Heaven's help to understand what it is and accomplish it. Not to think of myself any more, to give way, to bow down and to do so willingly, cheerfully, with enthusiasm even if my self feels pain and wants to rebel. In fact, to renounce myself completely, without making a show of it, for God – for forgiveness!

January 24. After yesterday's confession I felt completely broken. I slept well. This morning my exaltation had ebbed and I was able to think about it very coldly. I take back nothing. Yet I am what people call a charming woman.

February 7. Yesterday Reynaldo's surgeon came to examine Georges. 'At present you couldn't stand surgery,' he said after his questions and the examination. 'Your liver is enormous: hypertrophic cirrhosis of the liver. It's serious. You would be taking a great risk if you moved to Paris just now. A cold, influenza, over-fatigue – anything could make you turn up your toes.' He used that expression again as I was seeing him out, meaning 'to die'. Surgical jargon, no doubt!

February 8. Gilles is very ill. Tomorrow morning we are going to the radiographer. He has frequent sweats and faintness, and I'm none too solid myself. I'm sleeping badly, lying awake in spite of myself, out of worry.

February 9. My husband has jaundice: my niece is suffering from another stomach ulcer; Margot de La Bigne is fading away in nursing-homes after a series of operations; my mother-in-law has been dying for almost a year after a stroke which has paralysed the whole of one side. Help me, oh Lord, to accept, to serve, to love, to bear, to be pleasing in Your eyes through suffering. Increasingly I renounce self. I no longer love myself, I ask nothing for myself. I seek God. I may not have tried to find Him when I was surrounded by pathetic earthly joys, but I hope that I will do so in this distressful accumulation of sorrow.

I would like this notebook to contain no complaint of any kind. This is what I would like to promise God: no complaining, no lying, a plain account of facts, a complete submission to whatever may prove to be my lot. But I shall not be able to attain that kind of perfection without His help. I have already been tart and disagreeable this very morning at the radiographer's, because Georges was cold and so was I. Oh what a lot I have to do about myself before I can even begin to think of judging others!

February 17. Appalling news about my niece.

Several evenings running I have read the following words in my *Imitation*: 'You must separate yourself from your acquaintances and from your friends and wean your spirit from every kind of earthly consolation', and 'to become truly spiritual it is necessary to renounce those nearest to you as though they were strangers, and to beware of no one more than of oneself.' It seems to me that God is speaking to me and guiding me. I put myself in His hands.

February 19. .... I adore nougat, I have laid in a stock of it and I eat it every day. When I open my cupboard I am unable to restrain myself, I start chewing greedily. I will give up my nougat until Aimée's [her niece's] operation is over.

February 21. They operate on my child tomorrow. I am waiting in agony. She no longer seems to me to belong to this world – I may be wrong; they are keeping the truth from me. They are sparing me. I know that it is terribly serious.

My husband is confined to his bed. He is miserably weak physically. He is sharing my anxiety, he is trying to be less dry, less hard, less difficult. Dear God, sustain me through this ordeal. Help us, and help my child.

March 2. They are sending me telegrams saying that my little Aimée is going from strength to strength, that the doctor and the surgeon are very pleased . . . and I know the truth. There is no hope for her. Let us accept what we must accept, stiffen our resolution and do the best we can.

. . . .

March 16. My husband's doctor called this morning and found him much improved, but he didn't hide the fact that half the liver is ruined. I am very worried, so distressed for him and at the thought of what might happen to him, particularly if he leaves me. Villechaise made it clear: a cold, flu, exertion, over-tiredness, excess, one drop of alcohol . . .

March 23. Clouds hide the sun, wind drives the clouds away, there's a gleam of sunshine – and life is just like that. One must love the beautiful clouds and beautiful sorrows, make the best of little gleams of fugitive happiness.

Dear God, listen in this holy Passion week to the voice of the least of your servants, give her her daily bread, faith in You, hope in You, love of You. Accept and warm the numbness of your poor Marie Chassaigne, Marie-Anne who comes to you broken, worn out, footsore from the long road she has travelled, frantic with grief in the throes of remorse and despair of having too often offended against You.

April 1. I have been neglecting my notebook. The Easter holidays brought us visitors from Paris: my good old friend Lewis who brought me a magnificent basket; Madeleine Vionnet who came three days earlier with her handsome Russian husband Netchvolo-doff – a retired naval officer, tall, slim, elegant, with a stubborn, discontented, beaten look. He is hard on Madeleine, deceives her and spends all her money. As for her, it's quite simple: she loves him and finds it natural to put up with everything, forgive every-thing and work for him. She gave me five thousand francs for Saint Agnes. That was the pretext for her visit, but the real reason was to amuse Netch by showing him Liane and Prince Ghika. Madeleine is unhappy and she knows that I have been unhappy in the same way. Our sorrows make sisters of us. . . . .

Aimée has been at Roscoff for the last two days, lying in bed with her window open on the sea. She is full of plans. I say yes to everything.

April 5. The Prior of Saint Maximin came to see us. My husband asked him lots of questions in a gentle voice but with, perhaps, rather impertinent intentions. The Father sat beside the invalid's bed, answering him simply and seriously. He stayed for about an hour and I had a few moments with him in my room where he blessed me and we had quite an edifying little exchange. I made a small contribution.

April 9. We have decided to leave on the evening of the 18th. Georges's brother will meet him in Paris and take him straight to Cautru's nursing-home, the Villa Borghèse in Neuilly. He will be quieter and warmer there, the air will be fresher, the diet will be more varied. I shall stay in rue Saussure for three days to pick up threads again and put everything in order. . . . .

My god-daughter Margot de La Bigne spent Monday evening with me. She left on Tuesday morning to join a cruise on the *Paris*. She was so delighted to be going off like that, all on her own, to rest and breathe all that fresh and invigorating air. The poor girl spent eight months in bed after her operation. It was moving to meet again after all our disasters. She has written me a charming letter from Palma, Majorca: 'I thought you were looking well, God-mother, strong and decisive, and your face looked rested; but in spite of yourself your eyes, your beautiful face, were marked by distress and unhappiness.'

This morning I dropped my little pocket looking-glass when I was in the chemist's and it broke. I didn't care for that!

April 10. Spring is here, hot in the sun, cold at night and in the shade. Georges Ghika is braver about going out. He is preparing himself for the journey, a turning in the road, something new.

. . . .

Neuilly – Villa Borghèse, April 29 to June 7

. . . .

May 10. Aimée is here, shrunken, frail, delicate, but fresh and cheerful at having got rid of her aches and pains and believing herself to be well on the way to recovery. Aimée is here, weak and pretty and incredibly young – she hardly looks twenty-five and she is rising thirty-seven. Aimée is here, affectionate and happy. We meet again after so much sorrow, once again we have survived, and our time together is sweet. Thank You, God, and may Your will be fully and piously done since everything we have is lent to us by You.

Yesterday my friend and master Salomon Reinach sent his car for us. I saw him lying on a sofa, depressed, unhappy, his fine prophet's face scarred with pain. When I came into the room he could hardly restrain his tears. The room to which he is confined is handsome, spacious, tidy, fresh and sunny in spite of walls lined with books kept in the perfect order characteristic of a good library. His poor legs, covered with a woollen rug, refuse to work for him any more. Will his condition improve? One wants to believe it so much, one refuses to consider it hopeless. Salomon is following a frightfully strict regime. Professor Marcel Labbé is in charge of his treatment. He is in despair at being so inactive and can't resign himself to not writing and to reading much less than he used to. He could not prevent a few groans and complaints from escaping. We chatted. He told us about his condition in so far as he can judge of it, and we spoke about the President's death. Madame Reinach kindly came to join us. She is the affectionate companion who watches over everything and remains unmoved by outbursts of irritability. Being a doctor, she is valuable and beneficent at all times and in any circumstances. When I got back into the car she laid a beautiful sheaf of lilac and tulips in my lap.

Today the President of the Republic was elected. It is Albert Lebrun.

May 15. The other day I made my Easter devotions at six in the morning at a little wooden chapel in the rue de Chézy belonging to a clinic run by nuns. Georges Ghika waited for me outside in the street, in the rain, all through the service. The officiating priest was the one who confessed me. At the moment of communion I approached the holy table together with the sisters. They made a place for me by drawing aside their full skirts with such a charming movement of pious fraternity. And I was so far from feeling their fervour! Dear Lord, will you never grant me that grace?

I left the chapel very much moved, but upset. Meanwhile Georges Ghika had been alarming a lady who ran a bakery. He had been strolling up and down and she had been watching him. She opened her shutters and peered at him, whereupon she became so alarmed that she locked up her shop! If a crime had been committed in Neuilly that day, she would surely have reported my husband – 'He must be a Russian!' – and the police would have taken him in and interrogated him. I had a good laugh.

My Aimée left yesterday. The pretences and subterfuges held firm! I managed to seem credulous and stupid.

May 16. Max Jacob came to see us the other evening with a handsome set of false teeth 'which cost eleven thousand francs', said he with pride. They made him look younger, and also more diabolic than ever. He is busy trying to sell some paintings and place an article and some poems. He is very pleased with himself and is still living at the Hotel Nollet – on credit, so he says, while he waits for the result of the case he brought against the insurance company after his bad motor accident three years ago. The Nollet is expensive; they like artists there, and exploit them. Max paid for his teeth with seven thousand francs, one painting and two drawings. He is seeing a lot of Nathalie Barney and told us in a heavily meaningful way that she had forced 1,700 francs into his hands, saying: 'I have heard that you are in want, take this, you can pay me back later.' He had sent her a parcel of his manuscripts.

May 21. Yesterday evening my niece's surgeon, Doctor Bergeret, came to see me. He confirmed verbally that there is no hope. Judging by his experience, he gives her a year perhaps, or eighteen months.

May 30. .... A note from Salomon. I do so miss my drives with him! Paris, Saint-Germain, Paris, our talk, his generous affection, his lectures, our silly quarrels, the companionship . . . everything is disintegrating around me. He encouraged me to put up with things and do my duty. He made me write honestly in these notebooks – which he is sorry that he can no longer read.

June 7. We have been married twenty-two years! Gilles has written me two letters, one celebrating this anniversary, the other asking me to go with him to Roumania. I asked him for this second letter. Being face to face with me cramps his style, I thought that this way he would be more convincing. Well, he was not. I told him: 'Don't worry, I won't come with you. I have weighed the pros and cons. I ought to stay here so that is what I'll do.' He produced reasonable arguments. I shall not go. 'We will be so pleased to see each other again afterwards,' I told him. 'All I ask is that you don't do yourself too much harm.' If he had written: 'My wife, I love you, come with me, I shall be unhappy without you,' I might have been disarmed, or at any rate mollified. Nevertheless I think it was prudent from every point of view to decide not to go to Roumania in the midst of all those Ghikas and their satellites, knowing what it would be like.

While my husband is away I think I shall go to visit my dear asylum near Grenoble, then take a holiday with my old friend Lewis. He will soon be here to pick me up and take me to a charity tea at the George V, at which Yvette Guilbert will be singing. Old memories . . .

Paris – July 6 to December 29

July 6. We have been back in the flat for almost a month. A great deal of cleaning and tidying to be done, and one of my former maids, re-employed, to train. My husband leaves for Roumania tomorrow. He wants to see his mother before he and I set off on a seventy-day cruise on the *Washington* which will take us to Vancouver and back. I shall be getting ready for it. I lack the moral and physical strength to go to Roumania with him.

Because life has become so difficult Colette – whom I admire and like to see from time to time – has opened a shop selling beauty products in the rue Miromesnil. I went to the opening and she exclaimed: 'My fortune is made – here is Liane, beautiful Liane!', and she threw herself into my arms. I reeled – she is no mean weight – and let her sell me everything she wanted. A few friends approve of what she is doing, but most people blame her: 'With her talent, selling make-up!' No work is disreputable, and one thing will advance the other.

They have buried Gyp, Comtesse de Martel – eighty two years old, I believe. She once wrote to a friend: 'Dying is slow and difficult.' I already think the same.

July 12. Two notes and two telegrams from my husband. I feel more cheerful, more relaxed, full of self-confidence. Gilles is difficult in so many ways. The first time he left I thought I would die. The second time I was indignant, annoyed. This time it's all in the day's work. I have nothing left to regret, I have nothing more to expect, so let's adapt ourselves smoothly to this inevitable solitude.

Mother Marie-Xavier was here, upright and accessible, smiling with pleasure at seeing me again. Everything draws me towards her. I do so love that poor moving shelter-for-all-suffering. I foresee that it may become a refuge when I have truly succeeded in renouncing my self.

July 17. Alone . . . sad. Yes, it is sad to be alone towards the end of one's life, even though life with my husband has become a perpetual distress. I breathe more easily when we are apart, but still . . .

December 11. I am beginning this notebook on my return from a long sea voyage. I shall spread myself with pleasure on the details of this journey on board the steamer *Wisconsin*. It took us on board at Le Havre on September 12, carried us to Vancouver, and deposited us at Le Havre on November 27. I went on this cruise for the sake of my husband's health and to take his mind off his worries: his grief at seeing his mother so terribly crippled and at seeing me ageing so sadly because of his fault! Is it really because of his fault? And anyway, is it really so sad? As for him, he was anxious to give me the pleasure of this lovely cruise. But today I can only think of the great sorrow which greeted me when we got back; the death of my master and friend, Salomon Reinach. I can't bring myself to believe that I will never see him again. My friend, my matchless friend, I want to express here my inconsolable heart's emptiness and pain. I place the two last letters I had from him between these pages with pious emotion. The last of them reached me while I was on my first visit to San Francisco, then there was silence . . . he was no more. I no longer have the strength to go on, and tears are useless.

December 29. On the 24th we had a visit from Antoine Greffier, our Captain on the *Wisconsin*. We took him to a matinée at the Arts Theatre to see a play by Bernard Shaw, *Too True to be Good*. He was delighted and my husband was full of enthusiasm. I found it interesting but lacking in freshness and youth, dry and drying, the work of an old man; in short, very fine in its way, but demoralizing and conveying no impulse towards anything.

1933

∽∽∽∽∽∽∽∽∽∽∽∽∽∽∽∽∽∽∽∽∽∽∽∽∽

Paris – January 1 to April 14

January 1. I have known since yesterday that my little Aimée will soon be dead. The disease has recurred. It is implacably there and nothing more can be done. Her anguish is apparent in spite of all her efforts – she is very brave. My God, I offer You this year which will be a cruel one for me. Grant us all your blessing, help us to do our duty, give me strength, light and a greater faith.

January 4. When I got back from having lunch with my good Lewis, I saw in my *Figaro* that Georges Menier, husband of the most beautiful, the best, the most charming of wives, has died. On the same obituary page I found an announcement of the death of Manon Thiébaut, the woman who carried off my husband in 1926! She did us – particularly him – much harm. When I believe in God and have a heart full of that grace which is Heaven's best gift, I can bring myself to forgive her . . . During my bad times it is another matter! This evening I even tried to pray for her. . . . .

January 6. They are burying Manon Thiébaut this morning. I have not yet said anything to my husband. What point is there in stirring up those stupid abominations which laid our existence waste? Nothing can ever change what happened.

January 14. The other day we went to see Madame Salomon Reinach. Sad and pious pilgrimage. We found her shrunken and reduced, tears poured from her eyes. We wanted to see the lift which Salomon had longed for. He didn't have the time, alas, to use it much.

January 19. Madame Salomon Reinach died yesterday. I do not know the details. I am shattered. It seems to me that my pure, wise, matchless friend has now died twice over.

March 17. My little Aimée died at five in the morning on March 14. I have no child, no refuge left. I was able to help her and cherish her and surround her with affection for more than six weeks. The memory is simultaneously comforting and agonizing, because I watched her suffering, shrinking, changing. She was very brave, kept going and endured everything elegantly, even. She laughed, went out with me, seemed to enjoy her food while she could still eat. My husband was a great help and support; he was loving, generous and intelligent in what he did for Aimée.

She has been in her grave since yesterday, next to her father and her mother who were carried off by the same disease. Her death leaves me very much alone. Life passes . . . Aimée has gone and I – I! – am still here.

Good Friday, April 14. During this past week I have been rereading Perroy's beautiful book *la Montée au Calvaire.* In the two years since Mother Louise Tourbiez (one of my childhood friends) introduced me to this magnificent book I have followed our Saviour's passion in this way, page by page. As I read I experience inexpressible emotions.

It is a month today since my little Aimée died. That is a nail driven into my flesh that I can offer You, God the redeemer!

My husband and I went to spend two days at Bourges. I wanted to pray on the tomb which bears the names of my brother and his wife. That of Aimée is not yet there. I saw the two children; Christiane is not yet thirteen. Since her mother's death she has grown up a great deal. I have been appointed their deputy guardian. I accepted because I am the only one left of Aimée's father's family.

Good Friday: fast, prayers, retreat. A man appeared on earth two thousand years ago and that man was the son of God. Oh Jesus, my Jesus, You who are still concealed from me, I give You my torn, calloused heart, so cold and indifferent, do with it what You will. The example of Your passion and that of the admirable devotion of my beloved sisters at the Asylum of Saint Agnes inspires me with the courage to give up everything. I am ashamed of my frivolity and triviality. I feel low and ridiculous, humiliated at never having accomplished anything big, strong or beautiful.

How could I have done that when I have never been able to conquer myself even in little things!

Toulon – le Prieuré, August 7 to October 3

August 7. I return to this notebook which I abandoned several months ago. Shattered by my niece's death and suffering from colitis, I had to rest and follow a course of treatment. It was all very trying. My organism is too old to react properly. In the midst of all that my husband thought fit to announce one day that he was off to spend two months with his mother in Roumania. On July 30 he put me on the *Train Bleu* and that same night he took off for his native land in an aeroplane. I am a bit depressed, my last years really are being rather pathetic, but it is a relief to be alone.........

August 8. There was a splendid party on June 5th. I was dressed divinely for it by Lanvin. The preceding day I had a visit from my nephew, I began to tell him about this invitation, this little pleasure to come – and suddenly I stopped in the middle of a sentence, stabbed by our cruel grief, stammering: 'Oh Louis, how frightful! I ought not to have accepted, it's not three months since our Aimée was buried. I shan't go, I'll cancel the whole thing, forgive me!' Whereupon dear Louis began to urge me not to lose this chance to escape from the sadness of my fireside and my everyday life. He went further; 'I'll take you there myself!' he said, and he did. He took me to Fouquet's where we were all to meet and form a procession of period vehicles in which we drove to la Cascade. On arrival I made a sensation. Gaby Morlay, Trébor, Madeleine Carlier, Parysis all greeted me with cheers. Someone cried out: 'Oh how beautiful Princess Ghika is, she looks just like Liane de Pougy!' Laughter. An unknown lady looked me over, shrugged and said: 'She's a very good-looking woman, but how can you compare her with Liane de Pougy!' – 'But it *is* Liane,' someone explained. 'Oh go on with you!' said the lady. 'Liane de Pougy must be as old as the hills.'

My husband writes that his mother is worse, he found her much changed. The poor woman speaks about me with affection. She admired my last photo and the one of me with him done by Piaz which she had framed and put where she can see it from her bed.

August 11. Cabanel arrived yesterday evening, thinner, pretty, glad to be back in her lovely room at the Prieuré and to see me again. The dream won't last long: her neighbours – a naval officer and his wife – have already complained about the smell coming from her room since she has been there, the smell of opium. I went in to say good morning to her. She was lying there smoking with her little incandescent stove beside her, beautiful, calm and smiling.

The Sacha Guitrys have broken up. Yvonne Printemps has run off with Fresnay, rather a pretty little actor who is married to Berthe Bovy of the Comédie-Française. Sacha has been dreadfully unhappy; Bovy has made several suicide attempts. Yvonne says that she is happy. Can one be happy when others are in despair? . . . .

August 14. My saint's day tomorrow. I am alone, no family near me, no intimate friends, just my memories. Memories of vanished people and silenced voices. My husband sent me a telegram and a registered letter with his wishes . . . .

Cabanel went through a bad time yesterday: out of opium. Frantic to the point of loss of control. She was told of a couple who smoke so much that they have had to be put up somewhere else because of the smell. Cabanel spent a marvellous evening with them, her nerves were calmed. Today my Fernande is gay, energetic, taking things easily. Why are people so very hard on this vice when they say nothing against alcoholics who fritter away their wits, their teeth, their hair, their wisdom, their happiness and their family's happiness – and bring damaged children into the world? My poor Gilles with his dentures, his irresponsibility, his sparse grey hairs, his madman's maunderings; I saw the effects of alcohol on him when he came back from his flight with that girl seven years ago, and again two years ago when he got back from Roumania: three attacks of jaundice, incurable cirrhosis of the liver, and the existence we are condemned to lead at each other's sides.

August 16. My saint's day went off rather well: letters, chocolates from my nephew, telegrams. My own present to myself was Mayol's concert. There I found my dear old pal who sang me everything I asked for, rather naughty in the way he pointed me out to the public. Two ravishing little girls of twelve and thirteen did an exquisite dance. When it was over Mayol came on stage to sing. He laughed and said: 'My two little girls are a bit of all right, aren't they?

They're my daughters. I had them with Liane de Pougy!' And everyone laughed and looked at me.

August 22. Georges writes that malaria is rampant on the maternal estates. Now that my mother-in-law has had it herself she admits its presence in the neighbourhood, but she insists that it's only since the floods. In addition there is a plague of snakes, a collapsing house with no one to repair it, an unsaleable harvest. What a holiday! I believe my charming husband is bored to death, is seeing only the dreary side of life, is missing me and would like my state of health to provide him with an excuse for coming back sooner. I shall say nothing. He has almost no money. His journey cost eight thousand francs, kindly supplied by Aunt Jeanne.

August 24. The mistral has been blowing for two days without a break. It makes one tired and irritable, but there really is something magnificent simply in the privilege of feeling the wind and watching the raging sea. The prior of Saint Maximin has moved to Toulouse. The new prior has asked me if he can take his place. I am going to thank him and tell him to pray for me because my spiritual life is difficult.

. . . .

September 6. Henri de Rothschild has just published a book describing his youth before he got married. He refers to me in rather insulting terms that I might well have deserved but it happens not to be the truth. I met him at Angèle de Varenne's house. I can still hear Angèle saying: 'I like Liane, she's so straight that she doesn't even flutter an eyelash at our little Rothschild.' That wasn't always the case between friends. I never liked to be treacherous; I can't remember a time when I did that – flirted with a friend's lover or husband. I always waited for people to come to me, to love me, to tell me so, to prove it. Sometimes I let myself be won. And often – very often – I couldn't make up my mind: there were many occasions when I refused to give myself. They reproached me for being cold, they said I was made of ice. There were some men – and some women too, yes – who were never able to melt that ice. What I really did was love Love for Love's sake; and once my head had been won over, my body took great delight in giving itself. There were also a good many times when I was a little intoxicated animal with irresistible appetites . . . Then Georges Ghika came by, what a benefactor he was! He took me and placed me where, at my age, I ought to be.

Henri has been definitely unfair to Liane de Pougy and more than caddish to Princess Ghika. I sent him a letter, reproachful but in as nice a way as possible, ending like this: 'I forgive you, it was a mistake, wasn't it? But it was a mistake which wounded me, Henri, so for that you must send me a contribution towards buying coal for the patients in the Asylum of Saint Agnes, which you have already helped.' The cad hasn't even answered.

September 12. .... There was a picture in the paper of Célimène, Sacha and – I think – Gillaume de Ségur ('When Célimène rehearsed music-hall . . . with Sacha Guitry'). Sacha was the only one I could recognize. Sorel has had her nose done and her face lifted so often that she has ended with a different face. She is still pretty through it all, but one wonders who it is. I wrote to ask if she – she who is favoured so highly, so publicly, so universally – would make a little contribution to my asylum of Saint Agnes, and she never answered. She has no time, she forgot, perhaps she didn't even get my letter. What I expected from my long-ago comrade Célimène was some gesture as light and graceful as the flirting of a fan, something in the nature of a friendly and charming smile. Silence has reigned and I dare not disturb it.

....

September 19. Read a rather nice article about Lucie Delarue-formerly-Mardrus. She is adorable, childlike, yes – she gazes at you with ardour and amazement out of huge, wide-open eyes. She is not designed to cope with the practical side of life, but still she manages very well thanks to the talent which makes her independent, and her love of work. She is human in the best sense of the word, has been able to surround herself with a good deal of devotion and has the gift of making those who are dedicated and devoted to her perfectly happy. She publishes three novels a year, first in serial form, then as books. You think that she's off giving lectures some-where in central Europe and then you learn that she's been having a great success in Barcelona. She sculpts, rides horses, loves first one woman, then another, then yet another. Luckily she was able to escape from her husband, and since that experience she has never thought of marrying again, nor of winning the heart of any other man.

I was given a very affectionate welcome by her after my husband had left me. She played the violin for me and read me beautiful passages from her poems to distract me from my grief. At that time she was often close to me – very close, within touching distance – gazing at me with meaningful looks, gentle and silent. She seemed to be waiting for me to make some move, to give way to some impetuous impulse. There is still something charming about the thought of that time.

September 21. Found an article in the *Mercure de France* about the great Sappho, high priestess of lesbian love. It summed up pretty well all that can be said about that legendary and fabulous woman. Miss Barney – the Flossie of my *Idylle saphique* – loved to tell me about her in her own, idealizing way. We began a one-act play in blank verse about Sappho on her island, a happy, flowery island where all the women loved each other like very tender sisters served by almost invisible slaves, nimble, quick and devoted . . . sisters with a natural disposition to every kind of caress. I do not want to expand here on lesbianism, having already said all that I think about it in that same *Idylle saphique* – all, and more. Yes, having been witness to some distressing sights, some sinister results of the practice of that vice, I wanted to drive home my opinion rather fiercely. And anyway it was necessary to do so in those days, in order to find a publisher who would consent to bring out a book on the subject. I made it lyrical and sometimes slightly realistic. That was in the days of the Amazon's youth, and of my own. We were passionate, rebels against a woman's lot, voluptuous and cerebral little apostles, rather poetical, full of illusions and dreams. We loved long hair, pretty breasts, pouts, simpers, charm, grace; not boyishness. 'Why try to resemble our enemies?' Nathalie-Flossie used to murmur in her little nasal voice.

September 25. Yesterday evening Georges Ghika arrived from Marseilles, where an aeroplane had deposited him after a trip to Athens and Corfu. He comes to me in fairly good condition except for the tip of his nose which is deformed by two boils. He has brought me some charming presents: exquisite Roumanian choco-late, excellent cigarettes, and a magnificent bright blue silk dress embroidered with gold and silver which he bought in Corfu – a traditional dress opening like a coat – picture post cards of the Acropolis, toilet water. All this is very nice, but his nose – oh his nose! . . . and in addition to that he has skinned the knuckles of his left hand. 'Clumsiness – stumbled on a tramline in Athens,' he tells me. What a fine husband to get back!

The sea is rough. If it is still rough on Friday I shan't go. I shall send them off, Netch (Madeleine Vionnet's husband) and Georges to spend four days in the Balearics, and wait their return in peace and quiet. The Mediterranean has always been particularly unkind to me. I remember with horror those crossings from Marseilles to Algiers. They were one long agony and used to send me to bed for a whole week afterwards, my liver totally capsized.

September 26. I see in *Figaro* that the Germans are getting ready to attack us. They will invade through Switzerland by way of Geneva, there will be 'The Battle of Lyon'. So much for disarmament, our victory, all that spilt blood and the work of the League of Nations!

I am packing this journal; I will get it out again in the Balearics. Grant us your protection, dear God, on this little journey which will give so much pleasure to my old bad hat.

Paris – October 12 to 15

October 12. As it turned out, God did not want us to have the Balearics and everything conspired against us getting there. Being French I didn't need a visa; being Roumanian, my husband did – very complicated, with guarantees from two Spaniards who must be resident in Spain. The Spanish consul wanted nothing to do with the matter. In vain did Georges Ghika show his papers and declare himself to be the son of the diplomat Grégoire Ghika, the cousin of the minister Demetrius Ghika, the nephew of Queen Natalie of Serbia – nothing doing. We betook ourselves to the Roumanian consul in Marseilles, one Jean Fraissinet, a rich ship-owner. There our defeat was total: he didn't even see us, made us appear before an old grey-beard who drove us mad by gabbling endless arguments . . . imagine it! The boat just about to leave, our cabin booked, and this unscalable wall! Since no one could be better equipped than I am to do it, I have just written him four pages of fury from Paris. It has made me feel a little better.

October 15. When we got to Marseilles I went down with flu. While

I was in bed I had the joy of seeing my beloved Reynaldo's triumph reported in the papers. He wrote the music for an operetta, *O mon bel inconnu*, for which Sacha wrote the book. I was not able to go to the opening which took place just when I was feeling at my worst. Reynaldo gave me a little occupation. I piled up glowing articles about his music and his rare and precious gifts, I took up my pen with heartfelt joy, I congratulated him.........

Great agitation in Europe since yesterday. Germany has withdrawn from the League of Nations and refused control of armaments. What comment can one make on this crushing news? Thanks to Hitler, that is that: nothing for it but to wait for the war and prepare on our side.

1934

∾∾∾∾∾∾∾∾∾∾∾∾∾∾∾∾∾∾∾∾∾∾∾∾∾∾∾∾∾∾

Toulon – le Prieuré, August 7 to October 3

August 7. We complain, we rail, we rage, we swear that never again
. . . and here we all are, back at the Prieuré with its ideal position,
whimsical ways and almost perfect comfort. I have been back here
since July 30 when my husband put me onto the *Train Bleu.* I have
come back as I do each summer to live my little calvary of solitude.

Georges Ghika has gone to Roumania: he wants to see his poor
mother, who is still crippled: he also wants – I think – to be
away from me; he wants a change and some amusement; he wants
to assert his independence. I have become a little old thing, a very
charming little old thing, I must say. I am amazed at the extent to
which I can still be charming in my face, figure, style and character.
My walk has become rather heavier, that I do notice. My husband
has grown older, too, in the eyes of other people. For my part I
don't really notice it; I still see the rather ponderous and profound
adolescent in his beautiful eyes.

August 8. We have had the revolution, the beginning! Rioting and
massacres on the evening of February 6. They brought back
Doumergue, the dear old boy smiled at his good Parisians who had
been clamouring for a king and wanting to hang corrupt politicans,
whereupon they accepted the latter just as Doumergue wished. The
Stravisky affair, the death of Counsellor Prince, etc, all forgotten.
They made a start, they attempted a protest, but they fell back in
the same place, submitted to the same manipulation. On February 7
I went to tea at the Ritz. My husband insisted on coming to fetch
me. The two of us were in the Boulevard des Capucines at about
6.30 when an army of demonstrators went by, a long procession of
men walking at least ten abreast. They were grave, orderly, heads
up, eyes fixed on the horizon. They were singing. One felt that

they were ready to endure anything, and also to do anything. They were marching straight towards their goal, invincible. I turned to Georges Ghika and murmured: 'How beautiful they are, how I love them!' Impelled by I know not what, I moved in amongst them without fear, with sympathy and confidence. They didn't even see us, so intent were they on their goal and all the risks it involved. I shall never forget that sensation. A newspaper-seller was shutting up her kiosk as fast as she could. She said: 'Yesterday they were burning kiosks.' Yes, but it was not these men; it is the mob which follows in their wake which does the looting and stealing. Oh no, it was not *these* men!

Soon after that I went to Bandol, empty this year. The few people on the beach looked sad. The whole of France is experiencing a profound uneasiness. Everyone is wondering what is going to happen: war? revolution? perhaps both, the one bringing on the other.

Yesterday they showed Lyautey's funeral at the cinema, then that of Dollfuss. Hitler is going to be appointed supreme commander. What will he do? They say he is a visionary. Oh my God, grant us a being who is pure and strong, powerful like Mussolini. He one can only admire; everyone likes him.

August 9. I simply must make a mention here of the most fabulous, the most marvellous theatrical event of the year, unexampled, unique, incredible! The descent on the music hall of Cécile Sorel of the Comédie-Française. I saw Cécile close up at Armenonville in July. She was presiding over the competition for the prettiest hands in Paris, I was on the jury. She is fairly frightening, her body delicate, supple, quite fashionable, her face tortured, the eyes sunken and too wide open. They say that she has had her eyelids lifted and that now it's impossible for her to shut them completely. The day I saw her she had just come from the prison in which her husband, Comte Guillaume de Ségur, has been shut up for killing a woman in the street. He took fright and drove on, leaving his victim there, tried to snub the police, denied everything – succeeded in complicating his case which started out simply as that of a drunk who had been unlucky. Now he is locked up. He is not a bad fellow – a man about town without much to keep him busy, who lost his head. Naturally they asked me to perform; Varna, the director of the Palace, was very insistent. I refused. I no longer expect anything from life; I seek God with all the strength which remains to me.

August 18. Something extraordinary happened today. I had gone to Toulon to buy some silk thread. As I came out of the shop a silhouette very familiar to me was coming in, I glimpsed a half-ironic, half-amused smile: Nathalie! As soon as our eyes met I began almost to run away, making for the Café de la Rade. There I felt safe, lost in the crowd, alone at my table. I was beautiful: white pyjamas, long white crêpe de chine jacket with a navy blue belt. I haven't set eyes on Nathalie for eight years. Will that really turn out to be the last look?

August 20. Mussolini has won all hearts, including mine. His standard is that of order and peace, for the good of beautiful Italy. That corner of Europe has stopped suffering and bleeding, its wounds are healing. Let us hope that the Führer – now a dictator – will do the same thing. Let us hope that France too will find a man strong enough, steadfast enough, wise and pure enough to bring her back into the light and rediscover the strength and grandeur she has lost.

. . . .

September 11. I have just written a long letter to Max Jacob. I tell him that the only real earthly happiness I can now envisage is doing the washing-up for my invalid children, escaping from the ignoble sewer in which I have lived and in which my old age is bogged down. I tell Max: 'I know that you will understand and that you will love my wish to do their washing-up. Would I be worthy of the task? Would it not be too good for me? *Without rubber gloves!* And doing it cheerfully, singing old songs even if only "The atmospheric lobster" ' (which Max's mother used to sing him to sleep with when he was a baby – and which Max taught us at Roscoff, with roars of laughter). Max is predestined. If Jesus remains on His cross till the end of the world, Max will be there beside him, insulted, crucified, whipped, tortured, carrying his heavy cross with a bleeding heart. He does, of course, have instincts which are hard to overcome, his share of human baseness, but what grandeur and nobility there is in his incessant poverty, in the persistence of his efforts, in his impulses of love, in his inexhaustible and always alert charity!

October 3. Georges Ghika is with me again. He doesn't look too bad. He arrived with his trunks full of presents, an affectionate smile on his face, full of solicitude and all the details of his journey. He wanted to find out about Mussolini's work, so he visited Sabaudia and Littoria. He broke his journey at Rome and made an excursion as far as Ostia, to see the *autostrada*. He found everything magnificent. The Pontine marshes drained, two comfortable and charming townships built for ex-service men. Land has been allotted, farms built. Everything is governed and directed by a spirit of openness, clarity, precision and practicality. Georges was filled with admiration. Bravo! That is what patriotism ought to mean! At present Mussolini is my idol.

Arcachon – November 14 to November 19

November 14. Big hotel, half shut, half heated. Good food, and the people are charming and attentive, glad to have us here to provide them with something to do. We have covered the neighbourhood in every direction in spite of rain, thunder, wind, hail and cold. I put on my big rubber boots and my raincoat and off we go along the jetties, the beaches, the streets, window-shopping, buying warm underclothes and woollies, equipping ourselves for the weather.

November 17. Doumergue is now back at Tournefeuille. Why is France governed by old fogeys, so unlike the leaders of the other Powers? How envious I am of Italy with her Mussolini! Our leaders are old, white-haired, flabby, sly, selfish. They intrigue, they talk drivel. Yet France is so beautiful, so majestic, so magnificent. We ought to have a young King, a dictator, a president, a man of energy, open in his dealings, a saviour, a child of France entirely dedicated to reviving and renewing the sickening, stagnant, crumbling government which is at present preparing the darkest pages in our history!

. . . .

1935

∽∽∽∽∽∽∽∽∽∽∽∽∽∽∽∽∽∽∽∽∽∽∽∽∽∽∽∽

Le Havre – July 8 to August 20

July 8. My husband left me here a week ago – it is pure luck that the hotel people happen to be charming – and has gone off as he does every summer to play the naughty boy and the infamous husband. His excuse, as usual, is his mother's continuing illness. Who could argue with such an excuse?

I return to my blue notebook yet again, and start with some very sad news. The day I left Paris, skimming my *Figaro*, I saw that Frédéric de Madrazzo, perhaps my most intimate and dearest friend, was dead. His health was always very delicate in all kinds of way. He lost his mother when he was very small. While he was still a little boy his father's imperious love for Mademoiselle Hahn (Reynaldo's sister) gave him an amiably indifferent step-mother.

Today he is the only thing I want to talk about. I am unhappy – unhappy for my own sake, not his. Frédéric was extremely musical – but he was brought up very close to Reynaldo and Reynaldo wanted to be a musician, so Jou-jou made way for him, remembered that his father was a painter and turned his energies in that direction. He always obliterated himself before the friend of his infancy whom he loved wildly and completely until the end – Reynaldo hardly let himself love – Frédéric so ugly, Reynaldo so beautiful, prodigiously beautiful, a dream of beauty, beautiful with so many beauties, beauty of mind, of mystery, of the finest culture, of sensibility.

One day when I was about twenty-four I fell ill, became anaemic, every day that spring I was made to drink the sharp green juice of three bunches of cress. This cure restored me, but it gave me a crop of big red pimples which completely disfigured me. Frédéric came to see me. I didn't mind showing myself to him. He thought that I was ruined for ever and he found words, gestures . . . how well I remember. He knelt down beside my bed, kissed my hands and said: 'Look after yourself, I will go to work, I will give you all the money you need. I, at any rate, will always be here, whatever the others do. You mustn't be unhappy, you mustn't worry. Have courage!' He came to lull me to sleep every evening, lying at the end of my bed. He played with my feet, my lovely feet (size 37 – that's small considering that I am tall: one metre 68) with their long toes which the pedicurists used to say were beyond compare and which now hurt me so much! So Frédéric played with my feet, his nervous, sensitive hands started to roam higher. I laughed, he told me stories, then became strange, incoherent. How could this emotion be concealed from our gay, quick youth? I could not hold out against it. He gazed at me with wild eyes, paused, then blankets flew in every direction and he fell on me, crazy, quite out of control, sobbing and weeping. Alas – he was too nervous, too excited, all he could do was devour me so passionately that I almost fainted and he spent himself. He was soaking, my sheets were wringing wet. We never tried again, we hardly even referred to it. He was more or less an invert, his love of beauty led him towards handsome men. Reynaldo represented his first meeting with beauty. Freud could explain it better than I can.

July 9. My husband wrote to me on June 8th, the day of our jubilee – our silver wedding. And I had a nice poem in English from the dear boy, as well. Distance is already having its effect. I get a fond and charming letter every day – the little holiday (!) task. He is at Florence staying with his Aunt Jeanne and sends me magnificent postcards of the Duce, who fascinates me. Pleasant habits which have survived catastrophe.

July 11. When my god-daughter Margot lost her mother she came on a bundle of letters addressed to her grandmother, Valtesse de La Bigne; twenty-four of them were from me. She put them in an auction! My twenty-four letters fetched sixty francs. Indecent treachery! Nothing on earth would surprise me now.

July 12. Mother Saint-Anselme writes to give me news of Mother Marie-Xavier. Alas, I know that she is very ill, quite worn out and without strength, and that she cannot take the absolutely indispensable rest which she ought to take. I beg her, I advise her, I send her the means for it; for one reason or another all she will consent to are half-measures. I know, I can feel that quite soon this friend is going to leave me, leave me even more broken, even more desolate. God wants me to be alone – and it is moving and splendid to be able to hear those three words in my soul: God wants me!

July 14. A touching note from Yvonne de Bray. I haven't seen her: she lives most of the time in a Neuilly nursing-home the name of which is not divulged. She takes a cure, returns to life, relapses. Last spring she attempted to go on tour with a series of sketches; the first stop was Brussels; they had to bring down the curtain and return the money. She is an incurable dipsomaniac, drinking everything she can lay hands on, even her eau de cologne. She will never get another engagement and will lose all her friends. It is appallingly cruel to see that mind foundering in madness. Have pity on her God, You endowed her with such gifts.

July 15. Anniversary of the day on which I got married and on which, with one thrust which quite deprived me of breath, I lost my virginity.

July 17. Heaven has sent me a friend in my moral solitude: François Siraudrey who writes me beautiful pious letters, tells me what books to read, and at the end of the month sends me twenty-five francs for coal for Saint Agnes. He is punctual, he is good, his thought is elevated and he wants mine to be the same. I answer his letters and follow his advice to the best of my ability. He also sends me pictures with beautiful prayers printed on the back. It compensates a little for all the blasphemy I hear, all the irony heaped on me. I find it rather comforting to think that somewhere there is a good and pious man who is thinking of me, prays for me, takes the trouble to send me advice. He has given me a guardian angel, Pauline Leroy, a pious young woman who has just died of tuberculosis at the age of thirty-three. She suffered a great deal, and a few days before her death she promised him that she would be my good angel in heaven and would watch over me. I feel all this, I am moved by it, but I have not earned the marvellous boon of an absolute faith. Brother François is poor, he works and deprives himself for the sake of Saint Agnes and in order to write to me and make me read this or that. I am lukewarm, he wants to drive me on to apostleship! Alas, I am a very long way from that. He doesn't realize – can't even imagine – my conditon and my sad surroundings.

. . . .

August 12. Have been reading some odd little childish songs – our poets go in for them at times. There was this by Cocteau: 'Amstram-gram-bouret-bour-et-ratatam', and readers roared with delight. Between each couplet of one of his songs, Max Jacob had the line: 'I-want-to-make-pipi-and-I'm-going-to-make-it-here.' I don't really understand the artistic value of this kind of thing, or what is funny about it.

August 18. Benjy arrived at six o'clock in the morning and I had him without interruption until half-past nine in the evening. I was exhausted: talking English all day – an effort; talking loudly because of his deafness – an effort. What a dear thing he is! I am pretty sure that several times during the day he made little passes at me – little amorous wheedlings. He brought me some of what used to be my favourite scent, and he had ordered me a magnificent pot of hydrangeas – flowers that frighten me, but how could I tell him that? I accepted them – grinning like someone whose toes are being trampled!

August 19. Georges arrives the day after tomorrow: back to our accustomed ways, back to hearing cynicism and blasphemy, back to the pain which comes from lack of tenderness. My Benjy, on the other hand, heaps me with it, takes me in his arms, kisses me. But I cannot and will not surrender. He leaves this evening on the Southampton boat which sails at eleven o'clock. I am rather tired from talking so much English; but these signs of affection, this desire, these offered arms and lips have cheered me up. And he is eighty years old! Men, poor fellows, never give up. Alfred! Eternally loving, unable to see my wrinkles – or else liking them – melting with tenderness at the sight of me.

August 20. Alfred left yesterday evening. He was tender, cheerful, generous, he even managed to make a display of passion – in vain. My virtue triumphed over his pressing advances. At times I really had to put up quite a struggle. This surfacing of youthful love is beautiful. Soon I shall have nothing to envy Ninon de Lenclos. It has all been quite transfiguring – a woman needs to feel loved.

1936

〜〜〜〜〜〜〜〜〜〜〜〜〜〜〜〜〜〜〜〜〜〜〜〜〜

Le Havre – August 1 to December 26

August 1. I return to these notebooks after a year's interruption. In the last few months some serious things have happened. My mother-in-law died in Bucharest on December 19. When they received news of her attack, my husband and his brother left by train in order to pay her their last respects and be invested with their estates – big words for what in fact came to them.

France has had a decisive election and is now in the hands of Léon Blum and his set. I once had a slight acquaintance with Léon Blum, in Henry Bernstein's set. He is a cultivated man who carries weight, a thinker, a decent man. He seemed to me to be afraid of responsibilities – it is now his fate to have them forced on him by circumstances. There have been strikes, first one, then another, finally general: a sure and silent method without cruelty or bloodshed, but still implacable.

Cécile Sorel is singing and dancing at the Alcazar with her husband, Guillaume de Ségur, grandson of the famous countess. They need the money. That sort of thing proves how the times have changed. Mistinguett is making a film at the age of sixty-six, and she will be good in it. Her talent is human, comic, full of feeling. Child of the Paris streets that she is, she is so French! One feels rather sorry for Sorel, but one marvels at Mistinguett.

Colette is a commander [of the Legion of Honour]. She has had to shut up her beauty shop, but she keeps a little back-door ajar for favoured customers.

And now we come to the bloody days of the Spanish revolution, which takes precedence over everything else at the moment. Churches burnt down, streets turned into fields of battle. No more respect for anything, butchery. Those who can escape the flood of destruction by emigrating are lucky. They are pouring into the south of our own tormented country.

As for us, we are here in this dear, charming little hotel with its ravishing view of the harbour and its boats, surrounded by greenery, flowers and birdsong. Down there they are killing each other, lying in wait, burning; here we have the usual antiquated music of the merry-go-rounds and the coming and going of many coloured cars. Here we will wait for what is to come, for what they will tell us. Leaving my France in such a condition will make me unhappy; but at my age, at the end of my life, what else can I do? I will try to find some peace and quiet in England. I shall retire there, and then my God I shall pray to You every hour of every day to have pity on my country; yes, I shall spend my exile in prayer, and no sacrifice will seem too hard in my attempts to reach and move You, oh my Lord God, thou who are also our Father.

August 5. A Saint Anne's day letter from Max Jacob. He never forgets. These are hard days for the old poet, the great artist in his decline. I thanked him and he sent us a copy of the new edition of his *Saint-Matorel*, which can be considered as his masterpiece. He spoke of how much he missed our summers at Roscoff, saying: 'Roscoff, our Paradise lost.'

Rather worrying letter from our old friend Alfred Benjamin. He is over eighty. I am afraid he is ill. I want to see him again, to go to England, which may become our refuge one of these days whether we like it or not, as it did for our ancestors. And two days ago, as though destiny were bent on fulfilling my wish, I open a newspaper and see an advertisement for an excursion to England: August 21 to August 24, leaving on the *Ile-de-France* and returning on the *Normandie*. Once in London, of course, all we shall want to do is see Benjy, so we will dump the rest of the group. Georges went to see the Company; we were enrolled; they even told him that because we had been the Company's clients and spoilt children in the past, they would put a very good cabin at my disposal – the members of this little cruise are only allowed to use one particular deck.

. . . .

August 27. Here we are, back again, tired, dazzled, enchanted. It all went off quite beautifully.

We set off – rather moved – on the *Ile-de-France* at three o'clock on the 21st. The ship stopped off Southampton and we left her hospitable decks for an ugly little tender. Then nearly two hours crossing the wide, calm bay, the night air brisk, stars, lights. We saw the Isle of Wight and great luminous ships gliding past, unreal and silent. The special train was waiting for us when we disembarked and we reached Waterloo at 1.20 in the morning, two hours late. I was sure my dear Benjy would have gone away, but no sooner had I set foot on the platform than I saw him romping towards us, laughing and waving. We went off in a magnificent Daimler, as fine in its way as the *Ile-de-France*. A room was waiting for us at the Grosvenor Hotel, a big bunch of lilies of the valley on the table between our beds, my favourite English scent on the dressing-table, pink crystals for my bath, chocolates, excellent cigarettes – every kind of spoiling, in fact. We gazed at each other fondly over supper. It was a lovely, friendly, joyful occasion, our confident and tender youth was there within us and around us.

August 28. All of Saturday was devoted to Alfred. He gave me a magnificent red and white scarf to wear over my head when on deck, which is the fashion at the moment. This beautiful scarf was signed 'Rodier' – long live French taste and those who appreciate it! We lunched at the Savoy, still quite elegant for the summer, cosmopolitan, the food exquisite. After lunch a little walk and a good siesta, then we dressed for dinner and a cabaret – at the Savoy again. I wore a pretty dinner suit of black satin with a big white flower on the lapel and another magnificent new scarf made of black cashmere round my neck. Good dinner, elegant, quiet people, dancing, cabaret acts. I was tired to death but felt happy and spoilt, plunged back into the atmosphere of my youth when I was pleased with myself and people loved me.

August 30. On the Sunday I told Alfred to order the Grosvenor's famous 'grilled bones'. They were exquisite. We went to rest, I packed my case, and after tea Alfred took us to catch the train at Waterloo. The suburbs, then a little of that radiant English country-side, meadows, trees, heather – carpets of mauve heather sur-rounded by the world's most beautiful greenery. On board the *Normandie* the purser had us conducted to 'Mont Saint Michel', a ravishing suite: luxurious and pretty dinging-room, bedroom decorated in pale lemon yellow, the beds covered in pink satin, bathroom, showers, a vestibule with closets. At one-thirty they came to lay a lovely table for our lunch. It didn't last long, but it was a fairy tale!

The other day Georges bought a copy of the Popular Front newspaper from a young red who brandished it under our noses. He was enchanted when the young man said 'Thanks, comrade'. He's such a child – hard to put up with – laying down the law about everything, sarcastic, unsociable, looking down his nose at poor human nature and reacting against anything that's established. At his best he is not a bad little chap. My pity for him is so affectionate that I can no longer get angry.

. . . .

September 4. Letter from dear Benjy. As he says so nicely, how pleasant for me that my last days are brightened by such a solid and loving affection!

Georges enjoys the news from Spain as though he were watching some horrible ballet. He is going on about how sorry he is that we didn't go to Pau instead of coming here, because on the frontier he could have had a near view of the disaster, been able to hear the sound of battle, machine-guns, aeroplanes, bombs. I said to him: 'How bored you would be in Heaven.'

. . . .

November 16. 'What does he know, who has never been tested?' I read that fine line in yesterday's chapter of the *Imitation of Jesus Christ.* It is true that a satisfied, full-fed person who has been successful almost without a struggle is never sensitive or interesting. 'Who knows himself who has not suffered?' said the poet. Suffering is good, it purifies, sanctifies, enlarges, elevates. We must tell ourselves all that in order to comfort ourselves and make it more bearable. Joy is only for little children – yet how well they know how to cry from their earliest days! . . . .

November 18. And now there has been a strike at my Ritz! To think that an institution of the Ritz's elegance should be touched by such a manifestation of modernity! Some guests have left, others haven't come. I am going to send my condolences to our charming and faithful Olivier, so sincere and devoted, his affection mingled with his strict sense of etiquette; Olivier, friend and confidant of Marcel Proust whose invalid's existence made him depend greatly on gossip and tittle-tattle.

. . . .

December 4. The papers are full of the adventures of King Edward VIII who is madly in love with a charming American and wants to marry her. The clergy, severe and cold, have expressed their displeasure. They allege that coronation is a sacrament, that a king's wife must be a queen, and that because Mrs Simpson has been divorced she can't possibly fulfil the conditions. Give way, or abdicate. The King does not want to give way; the Duke of York is getting ready to take his place. What a beautiful love story! The people of England are quite crestfallen. They seem to be very fond of their king, who on his side has lent himself to the job's innumerable demands with great good will and much style.

December 5. More articles about Edward VIII and Mrs Simpson. Everyone is thrilled: a king carried away by love, ready to renounce his throne! Young English people have been demonstrating in his favour outside Buckingham Palace. It really is the apotheosis of love. Imagine Georges Ghika renouncing his Liane, twenty-eight years ago!

December 9. My old Benjy thinks the King is wrong. He himself has always put snobbery and material success before love, so he has no experience of the great disturbances which make life worth living.

December 11. Edward VIII has just abdicated. He has sacrificed his crown for love of a woman. He did not give way; that is royal. He has left everything for the one he loves: he is a marvellous and courageous lover. The story is a larger version of my own. I was rather younger than Mrs Simpson at the time of my marriage to Georges Ghika who was many years younger than I was but who was very serious, basically very serious and didn't often laugh.

December 26. A mildly happy Christmas; spoiling by Georges, traditional lunch.

Charming, affectionate, optimistic letter from Max Jacob. A pity we are so far apart! He wishes us a share of his peace – that day's peace, or that hour's, or even that moment's, given how unstable, tumultuous and capricious he is, as changeable as the sea or the wind! He veers between genius and absurdity, love and hate, gentleness and rage, kindness and cruelty, but he is not able to be ungenerous. Dear Max, dear Max, my new-year's heart wishes him so much good!

1937

〜〜〜〜〜〜〜〜〜〜〜〜〜〜〜〜〜〜〜〜〜〜〜〜

Le Havre – January 3 to March 10

January 3. Farewell to a tragic year, and may 1937 prove to be assuagement, balm, convalescence, renewal! The war in Spain continues, it is no longer a civil or guerrilla war but a European war, a war between the parties. Reds of every nationality are taking part and coming to the rescue. Europe is a chess-board, whites against reds. Alas, when all are brothers . . .

January 9. The year began in an almost symbolic fog; there is no brightness in sad European life.

We are getting ready to spend a few days in Paris during the coming week. It is an event, and I realize sadly that my strength is failing and the least thing exhausts me.

I saw something at the cinema which broke my heart. The film described a day in the hard life of the miners of Charleroi. We were spared nothing, not even the sight of unhappy children of fourteen or fifteen with blackened faces. How can we go on laughing, amusing ourselves, breathing fresh air, gorging ourselves, when our brothers are bent under the weight of their work in a hell such as that! How those people must hate us! I understand, yes I understand the hate in the air these days. It is only a few people, and always the same ones, who enjoy the blessings of civilization. We ourselves are the real barbarians, the real tyrants. I don't know; I no longer know what is good and what is bad. You have made the earth so beautiful, God, and this is how we use it. From now on I understand revolt and protest, I understand why brothers kill each other.

January 11. I have calmed down. That is the trouble: we calm down, we accept, and everything goes on as before. I am packing bit by bit, a woman fussing over herself and avoiding fatigue – and those other people down there in the depths of the mines, continue as before. I try not to forget anything which might contribute to our comfort – and those people down there . . . Yes, I do work for Saint Agnes – that has fallen to my lot – I do what I can for it. In spite of all the difficulties and worries, in spite of people's becoming poorer, we do still manage to find charitable and generous benefactors.

January 27. We are back in Paris where we spent ten days at the Hôtel de Castille . . . where Jean Cocteau has been staying. So Jean was a neighbour, still bouncy, sparkling, dazzling, smoking his opium at fixed times.

February 8. . . . . Are we going to South America or to Switzerland? Nothing has been decided yet. To be undecided is to dream a little.

My husband has just gone out: a little shopping, a letter to post. I often stand by the window to watch him leaving. He always looks up, we smile and throw kisses. The people going by and the taxidrivers on the rank watch us and must say to themselves: 'How those two do love each other.' At bottom they are right. I would detest him so much if I were not fond of him!

February 16. Georges was quite determined to persuade me into a wonderful cruise to Buenos Aires, Rio, Montevideo, etc, and had found a ship which met all our conditions: date of departure, price, comfort. And now we read in this morning's *le Petit Havre* that there have been outbreaks of trouble on board, scenes at the various ports, and that it would not be possible to disembark and see all those lovely unknown countries, which would be the purpose of the voyage. It would be pointless to go in those conditions. We agree about this and have told Aunt Jeanne and our close friends, and now we are looking for some other dream. It will probably be Switzerland, beautiful, stodgy, grand, slow. Perhaps it will win me over by being peaceful and welcoming? I like obeying fate's mysterious decrees. Heaven no longer wants to grant me another lovely cruise.

Mother Marie-Xavier has written me a letter which ends like this: 'We have lost Nathalie, the dwarf who used to hit herself when she was happy. Her death was holy. Ten minutes before her last breath, having received extreme unction, she said to me: "I give my life to dear God so that he will let you keep yours a very long time.* Thank you, Mother, and all the sisters." ' I was moved to tears. How beautiful and peaceful it is, that little nook of suffering so remote from wars, slaughter, lies – that little dream-nook.

Articles on 'The Beauties of the Past'. I am in good company (Cavalieri, Cléo de Mérode), but how ugly the photos are, and the style of the captions is as out of date as we are!

March 1. The first day of the month in which we will leave Le Havre. Yet another stage finished. We were here waiting to go on a cruise. Cruises seem to be done with. It will be Paris – transit – then Grenoble, that corner of Heaven, and finally Switzerland. We have a 'pretext' – I can't say a 'reason' – which is to take Georges to his Aunt Jeanne. And I feel within me a strong desire to live in peace, quietly, in that beautiful landscape where the air is freshened by snow. It is an egotistical desire, but my strength has run out: it is a rather mad desire. How can it be anything but mad, to long for peace in any place where there are men? It is at Grenoble that I want to end my days. Will that be given me? Will I be allowed one day to wash dishes for my invalids and the holy sisters, their poor dishes of chipped enamel? To obey the rule, within hearing of the convent bell; to play a part in that shelter of suffering – of suffering, yes, but also of devotion, piety, goodness, renunciation? There I could have opened my hands and let everything go. Am I capable of that? To be capable of it would be to be worthy of it. Lord, speak just one word . . .

. . . .

Paris – Hôtel de Castille, March 18 to April 10

March 18. We have been here since yesterday evening, with an enormous amount of luggage.

We left the Grand Hotel, or rather its proprietors, without much regret, their helpfulness and friendliness faded out in the course of our long stay. Nevertheless, sickly and unbalanced Madame cried when the time came to say goodbye, and gave me two roses to pin to my mink. May Heaven bless them.

* Mother Marie-Xavier died in 1956 at the age of ninety.

March 19. Cécile Sorel has tried to poison herself. Her husband Guillaume de Ségur had left her; he has gone off with quite a young girl. Jean Cocteau, who came by yesterday, told us all about it. I suddenly noticed a shadow of embarrassment in his look, a hesitation in his voice. He was remembering that I had been abandoned, and how distressed I was. He exclaimed: 'I've simply got to have an hour's sleep, I'm absolutely exhausted!' and disappeared.

March 22. . . . . We went for a drive round the lakes in the Bois, to Neuilly and to Boulogne. There I saw a brand new plaque bearing the name of Salomon Reinach. I shut my eyes, I saw the master's dear handsome face, the indulgent, reflective look he kept specially for me, his rather reserved smile, the characteristic serenity of his expression, even at the very end. So then I wanted to go slowly past his house. I saw the shady enclosure which used to protect him, the wide bay-window behind which stood his big desk; behind the desk was the chaise-longue on which he lay for several months, his whole body in pain, his mind so alive. We went to see him there. I took him flowers, and when I was leaving, just as I was disappearing through the door, he very quickly blew me a pert little kiss off the tips of his fingers, with a delightful smile. Salomon . . . I feel brimming with tenderness and dreams, I loved him so much. I often used to disturb him. I knew that, I rather made a game of it for my own amusement. I used to tease him, I often made him cross. I abused the deep and affectionate interest he took in me. How badly I needed his purity, his friendship, the support he gave me, and his knowledge too.

April 10. We leave tomorrow. I have had a great deal to do. I went to rue Saussure to collect the last of the things we will need. I shut it all up, said farewell to my dear family portraits and my family mementos. Will I ever see them again? Since then I have had an aching heart and the sorrowful and tormented feelings of an emigré. There are a lot of rumours, one meets a great many anxious people. Now the forty-hour week is a fact the big stores all shut on Mondays. They say the Exhibition will open on May 3rd and that nothing is ready. The building sites are often deserted. Foreigners are doubtful about coming – announce that they will, then postpone or cancel. I am leaving my Paris with a heavy heart.

My friends have been exquisitely attentive, competing with each other to spoil me.

I have seen a friend of Max's, Sauguet the musician, who had
been staying at Saint-Benoît. He says Max is well, and working,
that he dresses like a peasant, that he gets physical strength from
the fresh calm air of the Loire valley and moral strength from his
solitude.

Vevey – April 22 and 23

April 22. We have been in this magical, peaceful place since yesterday, in a quiet, comfortable hotel on the lake-shore. Our ground-
floor room is huge and blue, with a pretty bathroom. There is a
stream of cars going past the hotel, which is on a street corner, but
no hooting to be heard: the cars pass silently, slow up at the cross-
roads, glide furtively away. An impression of gentleness and peace
struck me the moment I got out of the train at Geneva yesterday.
I shall describe my ten days at Grenoble and my agonizing visits to
the asylum tomorrow. Mother Marie-Xavier's affection gave me
plenty of moral courage, but I was very weak physically, panting
for the calm restfulness of a lakeside resort, for the cleanliness,
neatness and delicious slowness which Switzerland provides.

The sky is grey, the clouds are low, the mountain is shrouded,
the sea-gulls have disappeared, it's the time of day for melancholy
thoughts . . . I want to turn mine to my marvellous saint, to her
life of sacrifice, to that illumination which radiates from her, throwing light and warmth. Oh how badly my emigré's soul needs her,
and how I bless You, dear God, for giving her to me.

April 23. To go back to Grenoble. Having arrived very early in the
morning, I did not send a message to Mother Marie-Xavier because
I knew she was not well and the last thing I wanted to do was tire
her. We booked the best room in the Hôtel de l'Europe – oh dear,
poor France! Forty-five francs a day, beds which didn't match (one
of them simply a frame and a mattress on the floor), two windows
opening onto an incessantly noisy street, trams, hysterical hooting,
bells, the lot. No curtains in the windows, just thin blinds with
makeshift cords which wouldn't work . . . every morning the night's
dirty linen piled in the hall. We were as good as gold and didn't
murmur. After all, we had before us the most marvellous example
of sacrifice and renunciation: Mother Marie-Xavier. As soon as I
had unpacked and rested a little, I could wait no longer; towards

the end of the first day I sent her a message by telephone saying that I was there – at last! – and had come in order to see her. The next day my holy Mother came to the hotel, together with the little Polish sister, Sister Saint Augustine. We were much moved, very happy. Mother Marie-Xavier looked well, better than I had expected after three years of bad health. Oh how sweet and good it was to see her and listen to her. She wanted to have us to lunch the next day, and the day after that as well. I accepted. The sister had prepared us a delicious feast, and sat down with us although she didn't eat – that is the rule. I gave her a small sum of money from us both, necessary for the purchase of some water rights which she wanted badly and for which she was being charged far too much. We had bought sweets and apple turnovers for the children and gave them a party: sausages and brioches for the little ones, cheese for the big ones. Oh how appalling it was when we went in to see this agonizing spectacle. We had forgotten. There were a hundred and ten of them, and worse – yes, worse. Faces tortured and convulsed, eyes anguished, hunted, crazy or blank. Surrounded by these poor creatures, I thought I would fail, I wanted to push my way to the door, to flee. I looked at my holy Mother and I held firm, I made the rounds, I saw everything, I talked to them in so far as I could, stomach quaking, nostrils pinched, sustained by her splendid example. There is one child which has lived in a wicker cradle for six years without stirring, horrifying, the hands of a new-born infant, a long serious face, heavy eyebrows, a woman's eyes, an atrophied body. She was surrounded by the howling, twitching crowd. Some of them wept, some jigged, they slobbered, wrung their hands, threw themselves on the floor. Some of them came up to us and touched us, babbling incomprehensibly, their wet mouths grinning from ear to ear. All of them gave off a frightful smell in spite of the incessant care which Gabrielle Chanel's generosity has made possible.

Afterwards we were horrified, broken. For the first time I said to myself: 'They ought to be put to sleep for ever.' When I accused myself of this rebellion to Mother Marie-Xavier she said: 'They are being cared for; that is enough, our task is not useless.' It is all immense, magnificent, sublime. Faced with such sanctity, it is I, I who am and who feel myself to be the poorest creature on earth. Sanctity of the stricken, of pitiless suffering; sanctity of devotion. I tell myself: these are the Lord's beloved. What, on either hand, are they expiating?

We went back the next day; then a third time, when they sang me two songs. One of the least afflicted read us a little speech with great emotion. We pressed a great many poor little damp, misshapen hands. We promised that we would come back . . .

I am too much moved to be able to express myself properly. You who are reading what I say – go to see them, spend just five minutes with them and you will never again be able to complain of anything.

1940

〜〜〜〜〜〜〜〜〜〜〜〜〜〜〜〜〜〜〜〜〜〜〜〜

Lausanne – Clinique de Bois-Cerf, October 15 to October 21

October 15, the Feast of Saint Teresa of Avila. Praise the Lord, o my soul; inspire me, o Holy Spirit, to express God's goodness towards His poor, misguided, sinful creature. Great Saint Teresa who burnt with love of Him, awaken my poor heart which would be broken, bruised, bleeding if it had not been – by God's marvellous grace – recovered.

It is on my knees that I ought to be writing these lines; it is on my knees that I think, that I prepare them, that I attempt to co-ordinate my thoughts. I never succeed. Cries break out, outbursts of feeling throw my whole being into such a turmoil that I am quite unable to write methodically about the extraordinary events which brought me here to the dear Trinitarian Ladies of Bois-Cerf, to their example, their faith and their devotion.

It was God who willed it, God who guided me. The sinner has disappeared, Liane de Pougy of the forty blue notebooks full of iniquity and scandal, lightness, frivolity, intrigue and lies – Liane de Pougy is no more. 'My God, my suffering at having offended You is extreme.'

October 16. 'The sight of the Lord is beyond compare.'

First movement of divine grace towards me, June 8, 1910, my marriage with Prince Georges Ghika, ending my dizzy descent into disorder and sin. After my little Georges's act of – say it! – so much courage as well as of love, I completely changed my life. Wedding at the town hall, wedding according to my religion, after obtaining dispensation, at Saint-Philippe-de-Roule. Confession, which I thought of as a necessary formality and dispatched quite lightly. Not wanting to hide anything or to lie, but being unable all the same to give the details of my interminable list of sins, I settled for saying: 'Father, I have lived a very free life. Apart from killing and stealing I have done everything.' I came away with a load off my mind, believing that I had amply fulfilled my duty and thinking that I could put myself right with God like that. I went on living the life of an elegant woman, pagan, free in language even if careful in behaviour, frivolous, egoistical, whimsical. All my whims were highly approved of by Georges, Georges the atheist, the free-thinker who believed in nothing – which never ceases to stab me.

October 17. .... My dream would be to shut myself away and see no one but our dear Trinitarian Ladies who have really become everything to me now, family and friends. Their example is beautiful: it has won me over and carried me along with it. I hope I can stay here, can die here. I am not free of fear; events follow each other violently, explode, scatter us, as God wills.

To go back to my story . . . After my marriage my conduct improved, but no faith, no prayer; absolute aridity: a more or less graceful, more or less charming animal drawn back into the herd by adequate emotions.

The war of 1914: our house in Saint-Germain turned into a dressing-station, devotion to the motherland, yes, but it was an unthinking sort of excitement; Marco's departure when he volunteered with Gilbert Garros; his death . . . I fell victim to an indescribable despair, a grief made far worse by remorse at not having been a good mother, at not having loved that child enough, at having preferred Georges – that is to say myself – to my son. I became very ill, a nervous disease, food and space phobia. I learnt the cruelties of nursing-homes. During this physical collapse I came to perceive the fact that I had a soul which had woken up under the pressure of suffering, a soul which was looking for the light, which was looking for something which cannot be found on earth. I began to pray to my good and powerful patron Saint Anne, mother of Mary – Mary who was so pure that my unworthiness dared not turn towards her. I could no longer remember my prayers very well; I dug down into my memory; it was painful and difficult. I spoke to Saint Anne often, asking for forgiveness and help. In that way, bit by bit, I contrived a sort of fervent piety, a religion all my own, still very remote from the true way, but taking me – with God's help – in the right direction. Some undesirable friendships were not able to hold me back; gradually I was able to sacrifice them. Some of them chose to leave me. I began to resist my own inclinations and their passions. I began to go into churches. Not daring to go in further than the holy-water stoup, I stammered prayers, was present during parts of masses, spoke to God, glimpsed Jesus on His cross, and at last I made my confession to good Abbé Duchemin at Saint-Germain. I told him everything that came into my mind and I made my act of contrition with all my heart, but I was still very far from the 'extreme suffering' which I feel today when the weight of my sins crushes me to the point of feeling dizzy as I ask how could I, how could I, when I didn't even have the excuse of liking that frivolous life of so-called pleasure.

The Jesuit Father Pierre Charles tells us that while we must certainly repent of our sins and rid ourselves of them, we should at the same time see them as a means of proving God's loving-kindness and the miraculous forgiveness he grants us. I was advised to read his book last spring, by Father Sanson who stayed a short while at Bois-Cerf, and my dear Sister Marguerite who runs the clinic and looks after all bodily matters as well as those of the soul, when the need arises. This book made me better able to trust in God, to give myself over to His will, and to conduct my life in such a way as to be close to God every hour of the day. I had made a beginning – very imperfectly – when an old Superior of the Faithful Company of Jesus (the convent of my childhood) – who is still at their house in Amiens and who had maintained a pious correspondence with me – advised me to read *The Road to Calvary* during Lent. It overwhelmed me. That book awoke the love for Jesus that had been sleeping in my heart.

Sister Marguerite also gave me several pamphlets, one of them about the Mass. I had remained impervious to these rites and our beliefs. I was ignorant, I didn't understand or want to understand. I rejected whatever might have shown me the way.

October 18. There was the death of my son . . .

There was my husband's flight one July morning in 1926. That quite crushed me. That violent blow changed me completely, stripped me. Then, when my husband came back, cynical and dissolute, a wild horse trampling everything underfoot, sickly and ill – that was cruel. I took him back, I love him.

I try to set him a good example, I pray for him. There is no visible sign yet, except perhaps for a change in his language. Blasphemy, obscene words and sacrilegious irony have gradually disappeared. He is fond of the sisters and they are fond of him. He is charming to them, gentle, friendly, doing whatever he can to please them and doing it willingly. He enjoys arranging the flowers in their pretty chapel, takes me there twice a day and waits for me near the door, in the garden. Grant me, o God, the conversion of my husband Georges, my friend, my devoted companion, my unhappy child.

And then there was the appearance in our life of the reverend Father Rzewuski.

October 19. We had met him in Paris, remarkably handsome, young, attractive, full of the joy of life, much in demand, much liked. We had lunch with him in the rue de Lubeck at the house of Madame Mac Cormick, whose portrait he was painting. Impossible to forget him.

Last December 24 Georges and I were waiting for Sister Marguerite in the hall at Bois-Cerf when we beheld a most striking apparition in the person of a Dominican father in his white habit, with his black cape slung over his shoulder. He was going up the main staircase, upright, erect, illuminated as though he were going up to heaven itself. His eyes swept over us. I was disturbed, and said to Georges: 'Don't you think he's very like that young Polish artist we met at Madame Mac Cormick's?' A few weeks later, when we were installed here, we were lunching in the dining-room when Georges said to me: 'Look, there's the Dominican father.' He was dressed soberly in black, and to his natural elegance and innate charm there was added a sort of extra grace. At about five o'clock that evening Georges came in and said: 'Guess who spoke to me – the Dominican father! I met him in the garden on my way back from Aunt Jeanne.' And it was indeed him! And Father Rzewuski came . . . and he became our friend, my counsellor and my support. In him I confide the inevitable scruples which sometimes nag me, my fears, my ordeals. For instance, during one of our first meetings I said to him: 'Oh Father, how I envy you for not having been, as I am, a last-minute recruit.' – 'Alas,' he said, 'but neither was I one of the early ones. It is only twelve years since I took refuge in Saint-Maximin, leaving everything in order to find everything!' – 'Who or what pushed you towards God? What event brought about this vocation, your conversion? Some great sorrow, some insurmountable disgust?' He looked at me gravely: 'Neither sorrow nor disgust, but an immense inner emptiness which only the love of God and of my neighbour could fill.' How happy I was to hear those words addressed to myself, so simply. Since then our friendship in Jesus has become closer. Father Rzewuski's visits are one of my holy pleasures. I have talked to him about my remorse, about my often despairing repentance. He has always restored my courage; he has always found the right words. I have told him how much I envy him for having had so many beautiful things to sacrifice to God: he was handsome, young, intelligent, clever, well-born and he had his art. He laid everything at the feet of God; he became, as he says, a beggar. Magnificent beggar who always gives a thousand times more than he receives! And what have I to offer to my God? I no longer have youth, beauty or strength.

October 21. We were staying in a nearby hotel and both of us were suffering physically as well as morally. Occasionally I came to Bois-Cerf to confess and take communion – perhaps three times a year. One day I met a severe little almoner who told me: 'But Madame, you have to go to mass every Sunday, on pain of mortal sin.' I made excuses, pleading my age and my unbelieving husband, who made everything difficult. He was insistent. I almost lost my temper and we were very cross with each other. But his words tormented me. With God's grace they worked in me and brought about a change in me. Now I go to the six-forty-five mass every Sunday; I pray with all my heart, I take communion and I would not miss it for anything in the world.

So then I began to want very much to move to the Bois-Cerf clinic. There were difficulties which Sister Marguerite smoothed out to the best of her ability, but there was still the problem of leaving the Carlton, the hotel chosen for us by Aunt Jeanne where we had been staying for eighteen months. Moving was quite a problem with all that baggage. Family pictures, rugs, little pieces of furniture – we had brought with us everything we most loved. The proprietors thought we were installed there for ever. I prayed to God, begging Him with all my heart to lead us to Bois-Cerf. One morning I woke up (here comes the miracle!) covered all over with red blotches. I thought of measles, of scarletina. I sent for the doctor who pronounced firmly: food poisoning. The proprietor, very vexed, said I should consult a specialist. I saw Professor Ramel: 'Food poisoning'. They made a great fuss but I remained unmoved and three weeks later we arrived at Bois-Cerf! It was at least two months before I got rid of those blotches; I almost loved them.